RETHINKING DECENTRALIZATION

MCGILL-QUEEN'S/BRIAN MULRONEY INSTITUTE OF GOVERNMENT STUDIES IN LEADERSHIP, PUBLIC POLICY, AND GOVERNANCE

Series editor: Donald E. Abelson

Titles in this series address critical issues facing Canada at home and abroad and the efforts policymakers at all levels of government have made to address a host of complex and multifaceted policy concerns. Books in this series receive financial support from the Brian Mulroney Institute of Government at St Francis Xavier University; in keeping with the institute's mandate, these studies explore how leaders involved in key policy initiatives arrived at their decisions and what lessons can be learned. Combining rigorous academic analysis with thoughtful recommendations, this series compels readers to think more critically about how and why elected officials make certain policy choices, and how, in concert with other stakeholders, they can better navigate an increasingly complicated and crowded marketplace of ideas.

4 The Age of Consequence
The Ordeals of Public Policy in Canada
Charles McMillan

5 Government
Have Presidents and Prime Ministers Misdiagnosed the Patient?
Donald J. Savoie

6 Cyber-Threats to Canadian Democracy
Edited by Holly Ann Garnett and Michael Pal

7 The Canadian Federal Election of 2021
Edited by Jon H. Pammett and Christopher Dornan

8 CETA Implementation and Implications
Unravelling the Puzzle
Edited by Robert G. Finbow

9 Multilateral Sanctions Revisited
Lessons Learned from Margaret Doxey
Edited by Andrea Charron and Clara Portela

10 Booze, Cigarettes, and Constitutional Dust-Ups
Canada's Quest for Interprovincial Free Trade
Ryan Manucha

11 NORAD
In Perpetuity and Beyond
Andrea Charron and James Fergusson

12 Under the Weather
Reimagining Mobility in the Climate Crisis
Stephanie Sodero

13 Rethinking Decentralization
Mapping the Meaning of Subsidiarity in Federal Political Culture
Jacob Deem

Rethinking Decentralization

Mapping the Meaning of Subsidiarity in Federal Political Culture

JACOB DEEM

McGill-Queen's University Press
Montreal & Kingston • London • Chicago

ISBN 978-0-2280-1735-6 (cloth)
ISBN 978-0-2280-1736-3 (paper)
ISBN 978-0-2280-1840-7 (ePDF)

Legal deposit third quarter 2023
Bibliothèque nationale du Québec

Funded by the Government of Canada | Financé par le gouvernement du Canada | Canada | Canada Council for the Arts | Conseil des arts du Canada

We acknowledge the support of the Canada Council for the Arts.

Nous remercions le Conseil des arts du Canada de son soutien.

Library and Archives Canada Cataloguing in Publication

Title: Rethinking decentralization : mapping the meaning of subsidiarity in federal political culture / Jacob Deem.
Names: Deem, Jacob, author.
Series: McGill-Queen's/Brian Mulroney Institute of Government studies in leadership, public policy, and governance ; 13.
Description: Series statement: McGill-Queen's/Brian Mulroney Institute of Government studies in leadership, public policy, and governance ; 13 | Includes bibliographical references and index.
Identifiers: Canadiana (print) 20230136087 | Canadiana (ebook) 20230136125 | ISBN 9780228017363 (paper) | ISBN 9780228017356 (cloth) | ISBN 9780228018407 (ePDF)
Subjects: LCSH: Federal government. | LCSH: Subsidiarity. | LCSH: Decentralization in government. | LCSH: Political participation. | LCSH: Political culture.
Classification: LCC JC355 .D44 2023 | DDC 321.02/3—dc23

This book was typeset by True to Type in 10.5/13 Sabon

This book is dedicated to my wife and greatest inspiration,
Rachel

Like captains of old, we seem to have a map of federalism that has several areas relatively well charted ... but that contains some quite unexplored areas, including a blank that we have tentatively called federal political culture.

Ivo D. Duchacek, *Comparative Federalism: The Territorial Dimension of Politics*

For years Brussels has talked about this idea that the power should be flowing from Brussels back to the member states ... They have a fancy word for it, it's called "subsidiarity." Nobody knows what it means and I promise not to use it again.

Former UK prime minister, David Cameron, speech delivered at Siemens Headquarters, 2 February 2016

Contents

Tables and Figures

TABLES

FIGURES

Acknowledgments

The subtitle of this book – mapping the meaning of subsidiarity in federal political culture – captures the transition subsidiarity has undergone as a principle of governance. A particular theme is subsidiarity's meaning of support, help, and assistance. It is therefore especially appropriate to acknowledge the support I have received in writing this book.

I am very grateful to the Australian Research Council (ARC) for funding the research for this book, and to my colleagues on the ARC Discovery Project, "Confronting the Devolution Paradox." Of those involved in the project, two in particular deserve a special mention: Professor A.J. Brown and Associate Professor Robyn Hollander. This book also significantly benefited from the feedback, advice, support, and enthusiasm of Professor John Kincaid, Dr Paolo Dardanelli, Professor Ailsa Henderson, Professor Nicholas Aroney, Dr Sean Mueller, Professor John Parkinson, Dr Annika Werner, Jennifer Menzies, and all the wonderful scholars in the International Political Science Association Research Committee 28.

Outside the academic circle, I am extremely fortunate to be surrounded by a truly amazing family. This book simply would not have been possible without the support of my wife Rachel; my parents Úna and Philip; my brother Ciaran; my mother-in-law Chris; and my siblings-in-law Melissa, Tim, and Amy. Each of you contributed to this book in more ways than you know, and I am grateful for each of you.

RETHINKING DECENTRALIZATION

I

Introduction

What makes a federation successful? In the "age of federalism,"[1] where about forty per cent of the world's population lives in federal countries,[2] we have a lot riding on the answer to this question. Despite the widespread adoption of federalism as a system of government, cracks are showing in the federal model. Many scholars and practitioners are concerned that federal countries are not living up to their potential, are far removed from their foundations, or are struggling to adapt to new challenges in the twenty-first century. For example, in the US, political polarization is heavily reshaping ideas about the vertical allocation of power, and a rise in administrative presidency has seen the states increasingly rely on litigation and judicial review over Congressional protections of federalism;[3] Canada faces ongoing challenges in accommodating multiple national identities within in its federation;[4] Australia is said to no longer be an authentic federation at all;[5] and Belgium continues to grapple with debates about whether federalism is a suitable model of government.[6] The impacts of the coronavirus pandemic have also highlighted the importance of questions about how key policy responsibilities such as health are allocated between levels of government, and have presented fresh economic hurdles for federations to overcome. Against the backdrop of these challenges, the question of what makes a federation successful takes on renewed significance, as federal countries look to reform and strengthen their institutions and practices.

The question of what makes a federation successful is the subject of extensive scholarship and analysis.[7] However, that literature tends to focus on the threshold features to the successful formation of a federation such as a written constitution, democratic governance and a viable fiscal system.[8] While these factors are certainly important, they have limited power explaining success or thriving in established federations. Accordingly, this book focuses on two related and potentially overlapping drivers of successful federalism: decentralization and citizens' values. These factors are more variable over time and between federations and as such offer better practical lessons and insights for improving how federations work. This introductory section therefore elaborates on these two core ideas.

Experts and policymakers hoping to answer the question of how to strengthen federalism often look to decentralization, arguing that a federation's success hinges on its ability to devolve power to subnational governments. Take, for example, Livingston's description of the demand for recognition of subnational diversities as being directly related to the "strength" of the federal system as a whole,[9] while Saunders goes further, considering decentralization as *the* defining feature of federalism: "Federalism ... is understood as a system of government in which power constitutionally is decentralized, as an alternative to unitary government."[10] Federalism has always involved a delicate balancing act between centralizing and decentralizing forces – promoting national cohesion but celebrating local diversity; achieving economies of scale but allocating resources efficiently; and facilitating equality for all citizens but encouraging innovative solutions to local problems. Proponents of the view that successful federalism is predicated on decentralization argue that when the balancing act is skewed too far in favour of centralization and national power, federalism will not reach its full potential and may even fail.

The key issue is that over time, we have seen most federations evolve to become more centralized than decentralized. For example, an international project by Dardanelli and colleagues tracked dynamic de/centralization (shifts in the vertical distribution of power over time) in six federations and found that in all except one (Canada), legislative, administrative, and fiscal responsibility had generally become more centralized than decentralized over the life of the federation.[11] Does this mean that these federations are becoming less successful? Perhaps. But we must be cautious about charging headlong into an argument for greater decentralization as a cure-all for the ailments of modern federations. While centralization can sometimes be viewed cynically as a power-grab by the centre, at other times centralization is a valid and even necessary response to new challenges or global developments. A more nuanced view is therefore to regard the vertical allocation of power and relationships between levels of government as important to federal success, with the degree of decentralization as being one part of a larger picture.

Such nuance raises its own questions, however. If decentralization is only one part of the picture, what are the other parts? When should decentralization be foregrounded, and when is it less important? Who should decide when and how to de/centralize, and how should they decide?

This book answers those questions by examining the role of the "subsidiarity principle" in guiding successful federal governance. Subsidiarity is typically defined in a decentralist way as the view that decisions should be made as close to the people as possible,[12] but in fact has a much richer and broader meaning. This book reviews the history and scholarship of subsidiarity to present a fresh understanding of the principle as being made up of three complementary elements:

1 *decentralism*: the typical view just presented – notably, throughout this book I will use "decentralism" to refer to the specific element of subsidiarity, and "decentralization" to describe the wider process or push to allocate power at a local level;
2 *nonabsorption*: the view that one level of government should not absorb the functions of another; and
3 *support*: a call for higher levels of government to support and empower lower levels.

These elements are detailed more fully in chapter 3. A key aim of this book is to demonstrate how this broader understanding of the principle can help deliver a more holistic approach to allocating power within a federation. Subsidiarity has long been thought to have a special association or importance to the federal doctrine;[13] Bednar even claimed that "subsidiarity is the soul of federalism."[14] But scholars invoking the connection between subsidiarity and federalism tend to focus on the narrow, decentralist interpretation of the principle. In doing so, are we missing out on a richer and more useful role for subsidiarity in federal governance? In this book, I suggest that we are, and provide the means for overcoming this gap.

The second line of inquiry for this book is to examine the role citizens play in building and maintaining federal structures and contributing to federal success. Have citizens acquiesced to or even welcomed the centralization observed in many federations? And if so, will they resist decentralizing reform efforts? Concepts of federal political culture loom large in this space. Specifically, scholars have long theorized that federal institutions are animated and maintained by "a tradition of specific values, attitudes, beliefs and interests that, though often only dimly perceived, are closely intertwined with established federal principles."[15] Arguably, the strength and success of a federation is tied to the political predisposition of its citizens: according to Elazar, "there is no federal system that is commonly viewed as successful by the standards of federalism whose people do not think federal, that does not have a federal political culture and a strong will to use federal principles and arrangements."[16] This book follows Michael Burgess's observation that the phrase "federal spirit" is as ambiguous as it is seductive – identifying the way in which federal values, attitudes and beliefs create and sustain a successful federation is a difficult undertaking, but the difficulty of the task reinforces rather than diminishes its importance. Federal political culture, as a subset of a nation's political culture, potentially captures a broad array of values, beliefs, traditions, and practices, and can even include art, music, and literature – these are discussed further in chapter 2. While this book draws on a wide variety of indicators of federal political culture, its main focus is the direct attitudes citizens have about federal institutions and design principles, which Brown and others term "federal constitutional values."[17] This narrower focus, supported by references to broader social factors, offers the most powerful means of assessing how citizens' views contribute to successful federalism.

This book makes use of public attitude data collected as part of a broader comparative study of citizens' values and attitudes toward a range of federal and constitutional issues in eight countries – six federations (Australia, Belgium, Canada, Germany, Switzerland, and the United States of America) and two nonfederal nations (France and the United Kingdom).[18] Together, the eight cases offer an excellent mix of established Western democracies within and outside of Europe from which to study the relationship between subsidiarity and federalism. The case selection spans some of the oldest federations in the world (US, Canada, Switzerland) and a more recently established one (Belgium), and compares highly decentralized federations (Germany, Switzerland) with a more centralized one (Australia). Additionally, to test how entangled subsidiarity and federal values really are, two nonfederal countries were included: the UK and France. While both countries have a multilevel system of government (especially the UK, with devolutions to Scottish, Welsh, and Northern Irish parliaments), both are steadfastly and constitutionally nonfederal. This allows us to test whether the federal spirit (which may be present even in the absence of formal federal structures[19]) is consistent with or essential to subsidiarity values outside of traditional federal arrangements.

The two lines of inquiry for this book coalesce when we consider how public value for subsidiarity might relate to federal constitutional values and contribute to successful federal governance. Such a potential interaction has never been considered or investigated in an empirical sense, with the limited exception that some scholars have focused on the way decentralist values align with or support a federal spirit.[20] In his treatment of federal political culture, Duchacek suggested that: "the tendency or habit of thinking primarily in terms of local (territorial) initiative and responsibility ... may perhaps present *prima facie* evidence of a 'federal political culture.'"[21] In other words, a successful federation is one whose people think in local or decentralized terms. Naturally, there is some overlap between Duchacek's view and the argument that subsidiarity (as a principle of decentralization) is key to federalism. We might even rework Duchacek's statement to say, "thinking primarily in terms of *subsidiarity* may present evidence of a federal political culture." However, invoking subsidiarity in this way raises the same issues described above – subsidiarity is about more than just decentralization. Accordingly, in developing an account of subsidiarity's role in federal political culture, we must be careful to consider the principle's full meaning.

This train of thought leads us to a useful question: does a *subsidiarity* political culture exist, and how might it function in relation to or even as a subcomponent of federal political culture? In terms of identifying the factors that make a federation successful, is a strong civic value for subsidiarity as a principle of decentralism, nonabsorption and support a core ingredient in federalism's success – i.e., there is no federation viewed as successful whose people do not "think subsidiarity." When Duchacek posed the existence of a federal political culture, he observed that: "Like captains of old, we seem to have a map of federalism that has several areas relatively well charted ... but that contains some quite unexplored areas, including a blank that we have tentatively called federal political culture."[22] Years and many studies into federal values later, we might consider the map a little more complete, but another blank space stands clear: how do citizens' attitudes toward decentralization and subsidiarity relate to or even drive success in federations? This book charts a new course: it is the first study of its kind to measure and compare public attitudes toward subsidiarity in the broad meaning of the principle. In doing so, the book represents a significant step in the study of public attitudes in federations and provides new insights into successful federal governance.

UNDERSTANDING "SUCCESS" IN A FEDERATION

Underpinning this book's examination of whether decentralization and subsidiarity are essential to a successful federation is the question: what does "success" look like? Conversely, how would we know if a federation has failed? In the context of the cases studied in this book, the finality of the terms "success" and "failure" is itself problematic – it is more accurate to think of federations as succeed*ing* or fail*ing* because where they are currently experiencing success, failure still looms as a threat, while conversely there is always hope that any shortcomings in a federation can be overcome. Further, because federalism is multifaceted, a federation might simultaneously be succeeding in some areas and falling short in others.[23] Accordingly, the core goal in this book is to point to factors and areas of strength in each federation that can be built upon, and areas in need of reform that can lead to greater success. In that regard, "success" is meant an aspirational term, guiding improvement, rather than a hard criterion. Nevertheless, before we can pursue questions about the role decentralization and subsidiarity play in federal success, we must clarify how to judge what success looks like.

Such a task is easier identified than completed. The factors that make a nation successful (e.g., a thriving population and/or economic prosperity) do not necessarily point to success of the federal model – a country might do well economically *despite* a failing federal model, for instance. Additionally, when we think of success in aspirational terms, we would expect success to be a form of thriving rather than mere survival.[24] Accordingly, in identifying successful federalism we must be careful to focus on aspects specific or unique to federalism.

In a broad sense, we can understand a successful federation as one that delivers the core benefits of federalism; namely, dividing power between centralized and decentralized levels of government, bringing together different regional, cultural or linguistic groups in a stable country while respecting their uniqueness, balancing local understandings of a problem and its solution with economies of scale at a central level, and encouraging civic participation. While it is unlikely a federation would ever achieve perfection across all these benefits, a federation that comes close to the mark can rightly be regarded as succeeding.

Drawing on Eckstein's congruence theory, another indicator of success would be the alignment between the structures and institutions of a country and its societal norms and values.[25] Erk applied congruence theory in a federal setting, observing that that "political institutions change in order to be congruent with the society"[26] – when this occurs, we might regard the federation as succeeding. Invoking a value for federalism here introduces an unavoidable degree of circular reasoning – federal values are both part of the evidence of success and the reason for the success. However, as Burgess identifies, public commitment to federalism as an idea "must be construed in itself as a public good. It is both the means and the end to be attained."[27] This tension is explored further in chapter 2, but for now we can identify that public attitudes are relevant to successful federalism, potentially as both evidence of the success and a contributor.

Examining both the delivery of core federal benefits and the congruence between institutional and societal factors as a holistic approach offers a compelling means of understanding how federations succeed. Helpfully, Burgess offers four criteria by which we might understand federal success, bringing together the perspectives outlined above:[28]

1 The *primary goals* upon which the federation was founded (e.g., Canada's goal in creating a bicultural society, or Belgium's aim in keeping the country from breaking apart);
2 The *subjective views* of its citizens (do citizens believe their federal system is working well?);
3 The *values, interests, and identities* underpinning the federation; and
4 The federation's ability *to adapt, adjust, and innovate* to respond to new challenges.[29]

Crucially, these criteria allow plenty of flexibility and nuance in considering each country. The primary goals for federation differ between countries: in broad terms we can distinguish between "coming together" federations such as the US and Australia, where several autonomous governments or regions join together to form a nation, and "holding together" federations such as Belgium, where a previously unitary country devolves power and autonomy to subnational regions in order to prevent secession. Naturally, the subjective views of citizens will differ between nations, and this book unpacks and analyzes the different values, interests, and identities underpinning each federation. Acknowledging the federation's capacity for adaptation is also important, although it potentially stands in conflict to the first criterion – too much adjustment over time may see the federation abandon the primary goals on which it was founded. Conversely, rigid adherence to the historical context on which the federation was founded may see it neglect the challenges of the present. Accordingly, these criteria are taken as general guides for distinguishing between *more* and *less* successful elements of the federations examined in this book, rather than as hard benchmarks against which a federation is graded.

The four criteria also match the two lines of inquiry pursued in this book. Specifically, in examining the role subsidiarity might play in helping a federation succeed, we can look for evidence of the principle in the primary goals of the federation and in efforts to adapt and innovate (criteria 1 and 4), while on the issue of federal political culture, the subjective views of citizens and the values underpinning the federation have clear relevance to criteria 2 and 3. The next two sections of this chapter elaborate on how each line of inquiry contributes to understanding success in federations, contextualizing the key challenges this book seeks to address.

SUBSIDIARITY IN SUCCESSFUL FEDERATIONS: A QUEST FOR MEANING

Subsidiarity is increasingly prominent in discussions and debates about how power should be allocated within society. Its adoption as a core principle within the European Union accelerated its popularity, leading to a resurgence in efforts to explore how it operates in federal systems.[30] Advocates of the subsidiarity principle's importance to successful federalism tend to look for evidence of the principle in the constitutional foundations of a federation (criterion 1),[31] or seek to hold up the principle as guiding federal reform or policymaking in response to novel challenges (criterion 4).[32] For example, Halberstam observes that "federal systems across the world are generally designed according to the principle of subsidiarity."[33] Scholars of long-standing federations have gone to great lengths to demonstrate subsidiarity's impact and use in constitutional drafting, even when those documents long predate the common usage of the word "subsidiarity." For instance, Calabresi and Bickford provide a comprehensive challenge to Bermann's earlier claim that there is little evidence of subsidiarity in US constitutional practice;[34] they argue that the US Supreme Court has repeatedly used subsidiarity as a constitutional principle in key federalism cases.[35] Similarly, in Australia some scholars suggest that the principle is implicit in the constitution – for instance, Evans argues that: "the framers [of the Constitution] would not have been expressly aware of the principle of subsidiarity ... However, they certainly embraced the principle's sentiment in the Australian *Constitution*."[36]

The principle's use is more keenly apparent in more recently drafted constitutions. For example, subsidiarity is most clearly operationalized through Article 72(2) of the German Basic Law, which states that the federal government's ability to legislate in relation to concurrent powers is limited to situations where national legislation is in the national interest and necessary to establish "equivalent living conditions." This is a clear realization of both the decentralist and nonabsorptionist dimensions of subsidiarity. Specifically, the limitation on national control protects the Länder (German regional governments, akin to American states or Canadian provinces) from central interference (nonabsorption) and codifies a preference for decentralized jurisdiction (decentralism). The third dimension (support) is also evident in the form of power-sharing and fiscal equalization that *supports* poorer Länder.

On Burgess's fourth criteria (adaptation and innovation), subsidiarity has strong utility in helping guide decision-making with policy fields, in turn assisting federations to develop solutions to challenges. For example, Hinz's study of schooling in Victoria (Australia) noted that adopting subsidiarity and empowering school principals to make more decisions resulted in more positive educational outcomes for students.[37] Of course, subsidiarity's utility in this space is not limited to federations – see, for example, case studies of subsidiarity's use in school, housing, and health policy in Lombardy (Italy).[38] But given federalism aims to balance localized decision-making with economies of scale, the question of where policy decisions are made is even more crucial, and subsidiarity's potential to assist increases in proportion.

Subsidiarity's surge in popularity has simultaneously highlighted several challenges to realizing its full potential, however. "Subsidiarity" as a term rarely enters public discourse, and in policy and academic circles, even when it is "well-known, most respected, carefully studied," it is "almost entirely ignored in practice."[39] Accordingly, while its value as a high-level principle seems well-established, as soon as it comes to more concrete questions of institutional or policy design, subsidiarity appears to suffer an ongoing quest for meaning. This quest can be understood in two ways. First, the principle suffers from definitional problems, making subsidiarity difficult to conceptualize. In other words, what *does* "subsidiarity" mean? We have touched on this issue already in observing that subsidarity's typical definition as a principle of decentralization fails to capture the full extent of its history and potential meaning. However, the problem runs more deeply and with more insidious consequences – not only is subsidiarity sometimes misinterpreted or narrowly defined, it has gained a negative reputation as the "epitome of confusion,"[40] or simply as "gobbledygook."[41] Føllesdal observes that "alas, the popularity of subsidiarity stems from its obfuscation of the central issues."[42] This quote captures a fundamental problem – subsidiarity is poorly understood, but its ill-defined meaning might actually be the source of some of its popularity, thereby discouraging efforts to reach a clearer conceptualization of the principle.

The second problem, usually stemming from the first, is that subsidiarity is often regarded as a principle of little substance when it comes to concrete applications, raising concern that it may be meaningless for governance purposes. For instance, in their consideration of subsidiarity in the European Court of Justice, Moens and Trone argue that "the Treaty provisions [relating to subsidiarity] have been rendered essentially meaningless platitudes so far as judicial enforcement is concerned."[43] McDonagh raised similar questions about whether subsidiarity was a principle of "sop or substance" in the Union, and concluded that "subsidiarity has largely remained conceptual rather than operational,"[44] while Ritzer and colleagues described subsidiarity as a "dull sword."[45] The problem extends beyond subsidiarity's impact (or perceived lack thereof) in Europe and its enforcement by the European Court of Justice. In the context of federalism, in 1994 Bermann urged US and European policymakers to take subsidiarity seriously, but acknowledged that adopting the principle as a meaningful political instrument would "not be an easy task."[46] Evans's claim that Australia can no longer be viewed as an authentic federation was based on her view that subsidiarity had been "disregarded" as a constitutional principle.[47] In the German context, Taylor suggested that subsidiarity might be "dying a slow death,"[48] because of reforms to the Basic Law giving the federal government more power, while Brouillet questioned whether it was appropriate for the Canadian Supreme Court to "open Pandora's Box" by considering subsidiarity as a constitutional principle.[49] The common thread linking these critiques is the perception that subsidiarity is falling short as a genuinely helpful and meaningful principle within a federation. Bermann put it neatly when he argued that "subsidiarity, in other words, must not only mean something; it must matter."[50]

Thus, the subsidiarity literature is plagued by questions over what "subsidiarity" means, and whether it is a meaningful principle. Until these questions are resolved, there is a risk that policymakers will avoid it, thereby denying citizens a more informed debate about measures that could potentially restore their faith in public institutions by bringing government closer to them. Further, even when subsidiarity is invoked, if its meaning is applied too narrowly, then the principle may fail to make a meaningful contribution to the success of a federation.

The quest for subsidiarity's meaning is therefore not just an academic indulgence – when properly operationalized, the principle has strong potential to achieve good outcomes for citizens, but equally, where the principle is not fully realized, citizens might be missing out. A good example is the contrasting uses of the principle to guide federal reform in Switzerland from 2008, and Australia (2014–16).[51] In both countries, policymakers adopted subsidiarity as a core principle to help disentangle national and subnational responsibilities, but the Swiss engagement with the principle stands out as being deeper and more genuine than the Australian effort. The reform process in Switzerland is widely regarded as having been a success,[52] with significant policy responsibilities rebalanced between the national and cantonal governments. Conversely, the Australian attempt failed, and was unceremoniously abandoned halfway through the process.[53] It would be disingenuous to attribute the difference in outcome completely to Switzerland's adoption of the subsidiarity principle and Australia's failure to do the same. Procedurally, the Swiss reforms were helped by a strong consensus between the federal and canton governments, especially their finance departments,[54] while the Australian effort was hampered by the political churn of a change in prime minister, as well as a lack of incentive on the federal government's part to relinquish power. But equally, we cannot discount the possibility that these divergences were underpinned by differences in the way subsidiarity was adopted and understood in Switzerland and Australia, which led to, or were perhaps driven by, varying levels of commitment to the subsidiarity principle. Further, and drawing on the importance of public values, are there differing federal and subsidiarity values at play that influenced the different outcomes? Was there something more than financial pragmatism that helped Swiss reformers find the common ground needed to achieve change? And could the Australian process have survived a change in prime minister if attachment to subsidiarity values was more widely held? We can only answer these questions by undertaking a deeper exploration of subsidiarity's meaning and its relationship to federalism, in turn clarifying subsidiarity's role in shaping successful federal practices.

SUBSIDIARITY AND FEDERAL VALUES: WHY STUDY PUBLIC ATTITUDES?

One could be forgiven for questioning the value of studying public attitudes toward deep and often complex governance principles such as subsidiarity and federalism. Many scholars and policymakers alike are skeptical of the average citizen's ability to engage with issues of federalism. Chief among these critics was the formidable Riker, whose theory of the federal bargain emphasized the role of political elites in the origin of a federation.[55] Additionally, Gray and Brown note (and challenge) that "many political leaders and commentators presume that if it exists at all, public awareness of federalism is unsophisticated."[56] Former Australian Prime Minister John Howard displayed such a view as he justified increasing centralization under his government by arguing that "the Australian people aren't especially concerned about theories of governance ... they want good outcomes and are not particularly fussed about which level of government delivers those outcomes."[57] Similarly, Jacobs suggested that US citizens are more concerned with whether a particular policy is favourable or unfavourable than which level of government should be responsible for it.[58] In Canada, Fafard and colleagues argue that Canadian citizens' perceptions and knowledge of the federal system is similarly lacking.[59]

There are several strong reasons to capture public sentiment, despite apparent skepticism of its value. Fundamentally, in a democratic society, we should want to hear the views of citizens. James Madison famously argued: "public opinion sets bounds to every government, and is the real sovereign in every free one."[60] Even if citizens' views display a limited understanding of the system, they should nevertheless be valued as an expression of a participatory system of government. More concretely, however, it is likely that citizens' views do add a useful perspective to federal debates. For example, elsewhere I have demonstrated that when asked which level(s) of government survey participants thought should be responsible for particular policy issues (and why), Australians gave logical and insightful justifications for their responses.[61] Similarly, Arceneaux found evidence in the US that "policymakers respond to changes in attitudes about how functional responsibilities should be distributed within the federal system."[62] Both Switzerland and Australia recognize the importance of citizens' voices in federal reform by requiring a referendum for constitutional change that would formally rebalance federal responsibilities.

Further, political developments around the world demonstrate that the age of public apathy to allocations of responsibility is well and truly over, if indeed it ever existed. In the US, strong political polarization has emboldened state governments to pursue a more combative (and litigious) stance in intergovernmental relations.[63] The Capitol Hill riots in January 2021, while not necessarily motivated by issues of federalism, nevertheless reinforce the importance of understanding the values and attitudes of citizens, as by paying attention to their beliefs we can be alert to potentially dangerous actions based on those beliefs. Protests in 2017 in Catalonia (Spain) demonstrated the enduring public interest in divisions of power and the strong views that citizens hold on such issues, while Scotland held a referendum on its independence from the United Kingdom in 2014. The Quiet Revolution in Canada and Flemish protests in Belgium in the 1960s and 1970s serve as further historical examples of the power of public mobilization on federal issues.

Taken together, these perspectives, arguments, and examples point to the importance of federal political culture. As Smith put it, "the political roles, processes and institutions of a country only make sense in the context of the political beliefs, attitudes and values of its citizens."[64] Even Riker conceded that civic attachment to the federal idea was necessary for its maintenance, and in his later works he engaged in comparing federal and nonfederal countries and noted that once a federation is established "what maintains or destroys local autonomy is not the more or less superficial feature of federalism but the more profound characteristics of the political culture."[65] While the "superficiality" of federalism may be contested, there is no doubt there is an important role for better understanding political culture. Studying public attitudes is the best way to uncover the values that make up a core component of federal political culture.

This book draws on a decades' research into public attitudes toward subsidiarity and federalism around the world. Specifically, the study draws on data from the International Constitutional Values Surveys 2016–18 (ICVS). The surveys are the most recent iterations of a longstanding project investigating public attitudes toward federalism and other constitutional features, initially in Australia (2008–16; the Australian Constitutional Values Surveys or ACVS) and then internationally from 2016.[66] The surveys were fielded in Australia, Canada, Germany, the UK, and the US in 2016; repeated in Australia in 2017; and in Belgium, Canada, France, Germany, Switzerland, the UK, and the US in 2018. The opportunity to study and compare public attitudes toward subsidiarity is a rare and important one, although it must be kept in mind that the investigation of federal and subsidiarity values was at times necessarily guided or limited (especially in terms of case selection and the amount of survey space that could be dedicated to relevant measures) by the needs of the wider project.

To highlight the value and insights studying public attitudes provides, figure 1.1 presents the results from a question from ICVS designed to address Burgess's second criterion of federal success (the subjective views of citizens). Respondents to the survey were presented with a brief description of their federal (or nonfederal as in the French and UK cases) system of government – e.g., US respondents were informed that their system has three levels – federal, state, and local. Participants were then asked how well they thought such a system was working. Responses varied considerably, with less than 40 per cent of Belgians expressing satisfaction with the current operation of their system, compared to over 80 per cent of Swiss respondents who thought their system was working well. On this one result alone, we can already see a case for regarding the Swiss federation as being more successful than the Belgian model, although there is of course far more of the story to uncover. Subsequent chapters explore these results in detail, examining *why* there are such extreme differences in overall satisfaction with federalism's operation, and how these might contribute to better understanding the factors that drive successful federalism.

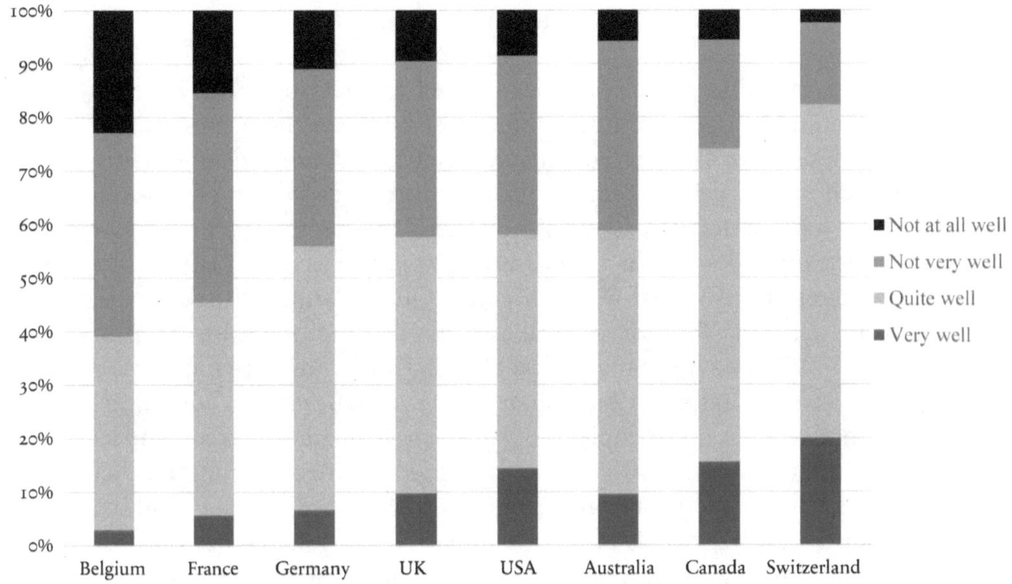

Figure 1.1 "How well do you think this kind of [federal system] works in [country]?" (ICVS 2017–18)

Public values, ideas, and beliefs about federalism (criterion 3) stand out as being key to better understanding why citizens have such divergent perceptions of how well federalism is working in their country. Where citizens, either individually or as a collective, do not feel the current system is working well, is it because they have a strong attachment to the federal model but feel that the current system does not deliver? Or are they skeptical of federalism's worth, and therefore resist a governing structure that is federated? Equally, where citizens are pleased with the current system, is it because the institutional elements of federal governance align with and deliver on values they hold dear? Bringing subsidiarity values into the mix, does attachment to notions of decentralism, nonabsorption, and support correlate with endorsement of federalism design principles? Are the values so intertwined that we might say they come from the same foundation? Or is the relationship between subsidiarity and federal values more nuanced, such that the exact interplay is unique to each country? These questions are explored further in chapter 4, which describes the survey items used to measure subsidiarity and federal values.

OVERVIEW OF THE EIGHT CASES

Having introduced the countries studied in this book, and encountered some initial significant differences between them, this section provides an overview of federalism, decentralization, and subsidiarity in each case. A brief summary of the history of each country is given here – a more detailed analysis is provided in chapters 5–7.

Australia federated in 1901, drawing together the six British colonial states of New South Wales, Victoria, Queensland, South Australia, Tasmania, and Western Australia as the Commonwealth of Australia.[67] Williams notes that unlike the US Constitution (which served as an inspiration for the Australian effort), "the *Australian Constitution* was not written as a people's constitution. Instead, it was a compact between the Australian colonies designed to meet, amongst other things, the needs of trade and commerce."[68] Accordingly, in thinking about the primary goals of the Australian federation, the key purpose in federating was to harness the economic and defensive benefits of a unified government on the Australian continent, while preserving the governments of the six colonies. The Australian Constitution divides power between the Commonwealth and state governments,[69] ostensibly preferring decentralization by leaving residual powers in the hands of the states, but resolving conflict between federal and state laws in the Commonwealth's favour.[70]

Over time, however, the Australian federation has become increasingly centralized. Movement began in 1920 with the key *Engineers Case*, where the High Court rejected the doctrine of reserve state powers and took a limited approach to the federalist notion of intergovernmental immunity.[71] The centralization process accelerated during and after World War II, as the Commonwealth took control of most major taxation sources,[72] and, in the decades that followed, used its superior fiscal position to influence and even take over areas that constitutionally were decentralized to the states. Accordingly, Australia now finds itself with a highly centralized federation – while the states formally retain significant responsibilities, in practice their reliance on federal funding limits their autonomy in key policy areas.

Belgium federated in 1993 and is unique amongst the federations studied in this book in that it can be regarded as a "holding together" federation – that is, the country was previously a unitary state, but adopted a federal model to satisfy divisions between the Dutch-

and French-speaking communities. Belgium's move to federate has been described as "paradoxical" because of fears that federating would strengthen local identities at the expense of national unity, in turn undermining the federation itself.[73] To an extent, those fears have proved well-founded, although Thijssen, Arras, and Sinardet have observed that these identifies have been stirred up by political parties for strategic gain, rather than necessarily being based on cultural factors.[74] Nevertheless, the internal divisions have led to enduring debates over the correct centre of gravity for the Belgium federation, and indeed whether federation is an appropriate fit for Belgium at all.[75]

In contrast to many established federations, Canada was founded as a highly centralized federation in 1867, drawing together British and French colonies in a tight compact designed to prevent the regional autonomy believed to have contributed to the US Civil War.[76] The British North America Act,[77] which forms the constitutional foundation of the Canadian system, provided many centralizing features.[78] Since federation, however, Canada has followed a path of decentralization, and "defies assumptions about the inevitability of centralization in modern federation."[79] Scholars have noted that, especially since the 1960s, Canada has become increasingly decentralized in both policy and fiscal arenas.[80] While there have been some notable exceptions in certain policy fields such as social welfare and language policy,[81] the overall trend is one of provinces taking on increased responsibility and fiscal capacity, a trend which is "exceptional" compared to the centralization of most modern federations.[82]

France is the first of two nonfederal countries in this study. As a unitary country, it does not constitutionally enshrine autonomy of its subnational units – instead, Alistair Cole and colleagues identify as many as six layers of public administration between the French citizen and Europe, all with shifting and ill-defined levels of responsibility, autonomy, and political control.[83] Nevertheless, the country did engage in significant decentralization processes in the 1980s, and again in 2016.[84] Including France in this study of federal nations will therefore yield important insights into the role of decentralization and subsidiarity values.

The Federal Republic of Germany federated in 1949, bringing together the Western Länder following World War II. After Reunification in 1989, the Eastern Länder were added to the federation. However, Germany's history of federalism and decentralization is far older than the twentieth century, dating as far back as the Middle Ages and the Holy Roman Empire. The Holy Roman Empire was a loose federation of principalities held together under the emperor, but which was in practice heavily decentralized.[85] Decentralization therefore clearly runs deep, and the modern German federation remains highly decentralized. Despite some centralization, especially following a round of reforms in 2006, the sixteen Länder still enjoy significant legislative, administrative, and fiscal autonomy,[86] as well as a say in national politics through the Bundesrat, the upper chamber of the federal parliament.

Switzerland has a reputation as being one of the most decentralized federations in the world. Its history of confederalism though the Middle Ages (and retention of the confederal label *Confoederatio Helvitica*) inform the division of powers between the national government and twenty-six cantons, heavily favouring decentralization to the latter. The Swiss federation features three major linguistic groups (German, French, and Italian), as well as clear regional differences in religious beliefs (Protestant and Catholic). Since its federation in 1848, Switzerland has become more centralized (almost inevitably so, given how decentralized it was at the outset), although most movement has occurred in the legislative (rather than the administrative) sphere.[87] Unlike other federations, many of the centralizing changes have been approved by the Swiss people at referenda, leading Dardanelli and Mueller to observe that "collective attitudes have become more favourable to central vs cantonal policy-making over time," and while political actors have sometimes been frustrated by the requirement of obtaining citizen approval, "they have generally managed to secure it."[88]

The United Kingdom is the second nonfederal country examined in this book. Formally a unitary nation, the UK has nevertheless devolved some authority over local matters to Scottish, Welsh, and Northern Irish parliaments. Additionally, while international relations will generally be outside the scope of this book, the UK's relationship with the European Union and the subsequent Brexit are relevant because of the strong decentralist rhetoric expounded by "leave" campaigners. Relatedly, subsidiarity, or at least the values underpinning the principle, featured in the debate.[89]

In addition to a tumultuous Brexit, the UK has also been through a referendum on Scottish independence in 2014 (which narrowly voted to remain in the UK) and seen a resurgence of "Englishness" or English identity. These factors have led to recent considerations of whether the UK would be well- or better served by a federal system, further heightening the value in studying public attitudes toward federal ideals.

The United States is the final case studied in this book. As the world's oldest federation, the US has experienced the full range of de/centralization of the years, from fractious civil war to strong centralization. In 1920, Paul H. Douglas (who later became a senator) wrote that "no question of government has been more vigorously debated than … centralization versus states' rights,"[90] and in the decades since the question has remained hotly contested. In recent years, heavily polarized politics have added a new dimension to US federalism. Specifically, where previously the Senate acted as a powerful forum for states to protect their interests in national decision-making, partisan politics have forced states to increasingly rely on litigation and judicial review. In terms of a potential federal political culture, removing federal debates from the democratic Congressional forum to the comparatively elite legal system may impact the way citizens engage with the federation. Additionally, the context of increased polarization might have temporary effects on federal views (e.g., responders may feel that "federalism/decentralization is bad when my preferred candidate is president, but it is good when the 'other side' is in office"). Over time, however, these temporary changes may have deeper impacts on attitudes toward decentralization, subsidiarity, and federalism.

BOOK OUTLINE

This book is divided into three parts. The first part (chapters 2–4) covers the background debates and contexts of understanding decentralization, subsidiarity, and federal political culture, and for measuring public values. The second part (chapters 5–7) examines the results of the public attitude surveys and their implications for subsidiarity and federalism in the eight case countries. The third part (chapters 8–9) considers the wider implications of this research for the role(s) decentralization and subsidiarity play in federal governance. Like many inquiries in this space, the book adopts the overarching theme of a journey to find subsidiarity's meaning in federal political culture (see *In Search of a Federal Spirit*,[91] *The Federal Principle: A Journey Through*

Time in Quest of Meaning,[92] and Duchacek's reference to the maps of "captains of old"[93]). The journey metaphor is appropriate because federations are not static – even if they change slowly, the degree of decentralization and extent to which subsidiarity is given effect is always in motion. Accordingly, while this book reveals fresh and compelling conclusions about federal governance, those conclusions are subject to the caveat that the public values and ideas, and the institutions themselves, will change in time. However, the process by which this study reaches those conclusions will endure to provide guidance to future federal scholars.

Chapter 2 takes a closer look at the concept of federal political culture, detailing efforts to understand the sociological elements of federalism. The chapter considers different approaches to understanding the relationship between federal institutions and federal society as the basis for federal political culture, and examines the appropriateness of measuring a national federal political culture in multinational federations. These are core theoretical issues that frame the empirical investigations presented in this book.

Chapter 3 examines how subsidiarity's meaning has been lost, and how it might be recovered. Specifically, chapter 3 traces the history of the key ideas underpinning subsidiarity to highlight how the principle has become fragmented and confused. It also showcases how those ideas have become interwoven with federalism – at times they are almost inseparable, while at other points in history they are quite distinct. The chapter then addresses the challenge of defining subsidiarity's meaning by presenting a new way of conceptualizing the principle as being made up of three elements: decentralism, non-absorption, and support.

Chapter 4 takes on an empirical lens, exploring previous efforts to understand and measure federal political culture. It applies those insights to a new area of investigation: public attitudes toward subsidiarity. The chapter explains the development of the measures and concludes with an initial comparison of federal and subsidiarity values in each country, revealing significant differences and patterns among them.

Chapters 5–7 analyze the results in greater detail. They group the selected countries thematically according to the pattern of subsidiarity values apparent in each country. This process alone reveals that there are important differences in attitudes toward subsidiarity between countries that align with the histories and federal structures of each country. Chapter 5 considers three classic federations: the US, Switzerland, and Germany. Public attitudes in these countries are characterized by strong attachment to all three elements of subsidiarity, although decentralist and nonabsorptionist aspects tend to be especially highly valued. These results seem to reflect deep histories of nonabsorption confederalism in each country and were likely the federations scholars such as Elazar had in mind when they claimed that a decentralist mindset is essential to successful federalism.

Chapter 6 examines Australia, Canada, and the UK. This grouping is interesting because it includes a highly decentralized federation (Canada), a fairly centralized one (Australia), and a devolved unity (the UK). Despite vastly different federal institutions, these countries share a history via British colonialism and the importation of a Westminster governance model (with variations) to Canada and Australia. Subsidiarity values in the three countries followed a similar pattern, where decentralist elements were the least strongly valued (albeit to different degrees across the three cases) and supportive subsidiarity was the most highly valued. The chapter explores the similarities and differences between the three nations to suggest that, despite their differing contexts and modern adaptations of Westminster governance, reforms in these countries that empower and support communities are more likely to be successful than further efforts to simply decentralize or devolve power.

Chapter 7 discusses the remaining two cases: Belgium and France. The two countries are very different in that Belgium is a federation and France is not; although as highlighted in figure 1.1, civic satisfaction with the current system is lowest in those two nations. These divergences permit further insights into subsidiarity values (which also differ significantly between the cases) and federal values because they demonstrate how federal structures are no guarantee of a corresponding attachment to decentralization (Belgium), and conversely a strong preference for decentralization can be found amongst citizens in a unitary nation (France). Accordingly, given the live debates about the adequacy of federalism in these countries – specifically, whether Belgium should retain its federal structure, and conversely whether France should adopt one – chapter 7 uses the insights gained from the analysis of public attitudes to draw out more generalizable lessons about when and how decentralization and subsidiarity values might support federation.

Chapter 8 draws together the analysis of the preceding chapters to offer some lessons about achieving and maintaining success in a federation. It focuses on trust and citizens' views about how the system should look in the future as key markers of federal success moving forward. Specifically, the analysis shows that subsidiarity values offer the best insights into the perceived trustworthiness of each level of government, and seem to play a moderating role between the deep, principled ideas that make up federal constitutional values and concrete evaluations of how the federal system might be reformed. Using these insights, the chapter comments on how subsidiarity can be used to overcome nationally significant challenges in each country studied.

Chapter 9 concludes by considering the wider implication arising from this study, emphasizing that researchers and policymakers must approach subsidiarity, decentralization, and their relationship with federalism in a way that is sensitive to and can account for variations in subsidiarity's meaning. It comments on the enduring appeal and importance of understanding federal political culture and the values that compose it, and concludes with the observation that subsidiarity's quest for meaning must now take a new direction, shifting from questions about whether the principle has meaning, to questions about how best to give effect to that meaning in federal settings.

PART ONE

Background and Context

2

Understanding Federal Political Culture

2 March 1982. US President Ronald Reagan addresses a rally in Cheyenne, Wyoming, pledging support for a local senator at the upcoming mid-term elections. Affectionately known as the "Cowboy President" by his supporters, Reagan draws on this carefully cultivated image as he addresses the crowd: "I've been looking forward to coming home to the Great American West. While Washington, as usual, seems paralyzed by handwringers, the people here are filled with … frontier spirit. … You and your forebears tamed a wild frontier … *So now load up the musket and help us conquer this wild growth and centralization of power which threatens all that we've created.*"[1]

Reagan's invocation of the frontier spirit and Western imagery was no accident. Indeed, historian David Smith argues that Reagan's use of the "Frontier Myth" was a key part of what made him so successful at the polls.[2] However, the excerpt above also highlights the importance of imagery and sociology in understanding federalism. Arguably, the combination of Reagan's cowboy persona and small-government policies was so electorally effective because it resonated with America's federal political culture. Elazar noted that "the American cowboy as the archetypal figure in American folklore is presented as the most prominent manifestation of federal political culture."[3] In particular, Elazar argued that the mythologized American cowboy could work for and with others toward a common goal "without surrendering one iota of his independence,"[4] and that the common greeting of "pardner" emphasized a sense of equality and comity between cowboys.[5] These features of the popular cowboy mythology were, according to Elazar, evidence of a deeper political culture that valued the core federal principles of independence and power-sharing that sustained American federalism.

Elazar's observations speak to a long-standing effort to better understand the sociological elements of federalism. More generally, the study of political culture is a well-established but often underestimated component of understanding political systems, and exploring the ways in which citizens' attitudes, beliefs, and values maintain, challenge, or transform political systems has powerful explanatory value. In the subfield of federal political culture, Kincaid and Cole noted arguments that "public opinion influences the distribution of powers as well as the legitimacy of the various orders of government."[6] As highlighted in chapter 1, scholarly awareness of federal political culture as a driver of federal success is several decades old, but efforts to empirically measure federal political culture are much more recent. This chapter examines the theoretical foundations of federal political culture research, and empirical matters are covered in chapter 4. This chapter pursues three core questions: (1) how do scholars conceptualize federal political culture and its importance, (2) how does understanding federal political culture contribute to successful federalism, and (3) what role does decentralization play in federal political culture? On the first question, the chapter pays special attention to the ways in which federal political culture handles the relationship between institutional and social factors.[7] Also of interest are concepts of "nationhood" and nationality which exist in many federations. The second question is addressed with reference to Burgess's criteria for successful federations, but also examines advantages of studying success in nonfederations as well. The final section addresses the importance many theorists place on decentralization as a key component of federal political culture. This paves the way for chapter 3, which discusses subsidiarity and challenges the conventional approach of treating subsidiarity and decentralization as almost synonymous.

CONCEPTUALIZING FEDERAL POLITICAL CULTURE

Societal values play an important role in the maintenance and success of political systems and institutions. For instance, in their seminal study of public attitudes, *The Civic Culture*, Almond and Verba argued that a political culture of democracy explains the persistence of a democratic regime: democracy thrives where citizens value it and are committed to protecting and maintaining its key features.[8] Similarly, as has already been discussed, scholars have long argued that a strong federal political culture is essential to successful federalism.[9]

However, while invoking political culture as an explanation is alluring, we must be careful not to overextend it and risk using "political culture" as a fuzzy catch-all. For instance, Hague, Harrop, and McCormick highlight that "there is a danger of invoking cultural factors when we can think of nothing else."[10] It may be tempting to use political culture as a stopgap explanation for political phenomena that are difficult to explain.[11]

Accordingly, it is critical that research invoking political culture provides a clear account of its underlying premises and assumptions. Federal political culture, as a subpolitical culture, must address two core dilemmas. First, how should we conceptualize the social and institutional elements of federalism into an integrated model of successful federalism? And second, at what level of nationhood should federal political culture be measured? This section examines how these questions have been addressed in the federalism literature, while chapter 4 revisits them from a methodological perspective.

Society and Institutions in Federal Political Culture

Studies of political institutions increasingly acknowledge the importance of wider factors beyond formal institutions such as courts, and aim to account for norms, social rules, and culture.[12] Naturally, such a perspective invokes the broader theoretical debate about the tension between agents and structures, or as Hay prefers, between the conduct of political actors and the context in which such actions occur.[13] This tension is one of the fundamental controversies of political science, and while it is not necessary for this book to pursue the deeper ontological aspects of the dispute,[14] it is important to address the core issue of how to understand the relationship between formal federal institutions, and the societal elements of federalism (the "federal society"). In particular, two core ideas emerge: treating formal institutions and the federal society as related but separate, as in congruence theory, or integrating the social and institutional variables by focusing on public attitudes toward federal institutions. While these two approaches have many commonalities, highlighting the distinction in their understanding of the relationship between social and institutional factors clarifies the approach taken in this book.

THE FEDERAL SOCIETY

Any discussion of the social aspects of federalism must begin with William Livingston. In his early works, Livingston was convinced that "the essential nature of federalism is to be sought for, not in the shadings of legal and constitutional terminology, but in the forces – economic, social, political, cultural – that have made the outward forms of federalism necessary."[15] This perspective offered a fresh insight into understanding federalism, although it was a controversial one.[16] Much of the critique of Livingston's approach can be summarized by Stein's question: "what utility is there in identifying a federal society, assuming that some consensus can be reached on what is meant by the term?."[17] Much of the sociological research on federalism since then has been dedicated to answering that question.

One such answer relies on congruence theory, which claims that political institutions gravitate toward congruence with societal values. As Eckstein described it, the core of congruence theory is the view that "governments perform well to the extent that their authority patterns are congruent with the authority patterns of other units of society."[18] Similarly, Erk states that "the basic argument is that political institutions change in order to be congruent with the society."[19] In the context of identifying a federal society, the utility is therefore predictive – where institutions are not aligned with the society, we would expect institutional reform to move closer to the underlying society, and where there is congruence, we can predict stability and longevity of the federal institutions. This argument aligns well with the claims of political culture theorists. Indeed, Almond and Verba observed that "political cultures may or may not be congruent with the structures of the political system."[20] The same is true of federal political culture as a subcategory of political culture: Erk's aim to demonstrate that "the political institutions of federalism adapt to achieve congruence with the underlying societal structure"[21] fits perfectly with Elazar's claim that there is no successful federation that does not have a federal political culture.[22] It is for this reason that Livingston's approach resonates with congruence theorists: "Institutional devices, both in form and function, are only the surface manifestations of the deeper federal quality of the society that lies beneath the surface. The essence of federalism lies not in the institutional or constitutional structure but in the society itself."[23]

The focus on society means that congruence theory tends to emphasize the social aspects of federalism, while the formal institutional elements of federalism, such as the constitutional allocation of responsibility, fiscal powers, and electoral processes, are treated as a separate variable. Indeed, the core premise of congruence theory is that the federal institutions change over time to align with federal society. For instance, Erk's study of the federal society in Austria, Belgium, Canada, Germany, and Switzerland was targeted at linguistic markers of diversity, and social policy areas such as media regulation and education, observing how the latter changed over time to align with the former. In that regard, the primacy given to social elements is therefore quite explicit – Erk explained of her book: "*Explaining Federalism* puts society before the state."[24]

Recognizing the pathways by which federal institutions change to align with societal values is a valuable insight. However, giving primacy to social over institutional factors risks missing part of the story. Specifically, this approach is limited in its ability to account for the possibility that citizens' views and societal values are shaped by institutions. Citizens are socialized not only in a federal society, but in the context of a particular set of federal institutions. Further, changes to those institutions might over time change the values held within the federal society. This is not to say that institutions always shape society – rather, the relationship is more circular and mutually influential than the approach proposed under congruence theory. Of course, this can lead to a chicken-and-egg dilemma where it is difficult to separate when society changes the institution, and when institutions change societal values. Livingston himself struggled with this issue, noting the difficulty in distinguishing between "society and the instrumentalities it employs."[25] Burgess observes that "Livingston's concluding remarks left these questions unanswered. Indeed, it is tempting to suggest that ultimately he was confounded by his own analysis ... His final sentence took the form of a plea: it was to 'the pattern of these diversities that we must go if we would assess the federal qualities of the society.'"[26]

FEDERAL CONSTITUTIONAL VALUES

Accordingly, it might be preferable to choose a more agnostic approach and measure societal values in their institutional context without making claims about the primacy of one over the other. From that foundation, one can then look to other factors to theorize about directions of influence. In its most obvious form, this involves looking at citizens' perceptions and attitudes toward federal structures, such as Duchacek's reference to thinking in terms of local initiative.[27] Here, we are interested in citizens' values, but in the targeted sense of how these values are applied to federal institutions. Brown, Deem, and Kincaid refer to these as "federal constitutional values" – "citizen attachment to *governmental arrangements* or *decision-making processes* which are definitional of federal systems, where embedded in constitutional practices, with this attachment recognized as central to a federal political culture, even if not its entirety."[28] Similarly, McGrane and Berdhal's study of Canadian federal political culture emphasized a values-based approach,[29] citing Preston King's earlier distinction between "federalism" as a normative concept involving federal principles, and "federation" as the institutional arrangements of a federal country.[30] Fafard and colleagues took a slightly different approach in their focus on citizens' knowledge and awareness of federal structures as markers of federal political culture.[31] The logic behind this approach is that if citizens do not understand the federal system, they cannot be said to be "thinking federal." While civic awareness of federalism is certainly important, especially in terms of accountability for violations of the federal bargain, this approach is open to the critique that citizens can hold federal values without knowing a great deal about their system of government. For example, someone might appreciate a "two heads are better than one" approach to policymaking without understanding collaborative federalism, or see value in dividing responsibility among different governments without knowing who is responsible for what.[32] Conversely, citizens' views can also be influenced by responses to particular policies and crises – assessments which might be arrived at with little or no awareness of federal principles.[33] Therefore, this book studies citizens' attitudes rather than knowledge as the foundation for assessing public value of federal principles.

Broader sociological elements such as language, art, and acceptance of diversity are also included in federal political culture, though their influence is harder to capture. Elazar suggested that we might find federal political culture reflected in the music, art, and literature of a nation.[34] To support his point, Elazar highlighted how the archetypal cowboy of American folklore embodies a spirit of federalism, as described at the beginning of this chapter.[35] We can add similar examples from just about any federation. In Australia, "State of Origin" rugby league games, pitting players from Queensland and New South Wales against one another under the slogan "mate against mate, state against state," also seem to capture a federalist balance between national and state loyalties.[36] In Switzerland, polyphonic music, which is notable for bringing together two independent melodies, "has long been regarded as a sign of high culture and civilization."[37] However, while this broad approach adds flavour and richness to the concept of federal political culture, it is necessarily abstract. It is difficult to tell where to draw the line between culture and federal political culture: when is an appreciation of a particular form of music a reflection of federal values, and when is it just art? When is a game of football evidence of deep political views, and when is it just a game? Accordingly, this book follows previous efforts to empirically measure federal political culture (discussed further in chapter 4) by focusing on federal constitutional values,[38] relegating the wider social and cultural examples to supporting points rather than as the core analysis.

Nationhood and Federal Political Culture

A further challenge for federal political culture research is to consider whether country-wide political cultures are an appropriate unit of study. Political culture can in one direction transcend borders (as in Huntington's famous *Clash of Civilizations*),[39] and in the other direction break down into smaller regional subcultures.[40] For instance, Wiseman lamented that Canadian political culture was too often viewed as a nationally cohesive outlook, when he argued that it should in fact be more regionally sensitive.[41] This is especially relevant to the study of public attitudes toward federalism and subsidiarity, because these doctrines are designed to accommodate and even promote subnational variation.

When it comes to measuring political culture in a federation, the challenges are therefore especially great. In addition to finding a way to capture aggregate values at the country level, researchers must be able to detect subnational variations, which may be formally reflected in the federal structure (e.g., Quebec within the Canadian federation) or not (e.g., East and West Germany). These subnations may be territorial, linguistic, ethnic, or religious, or even some combination of them (e.g., Switzerland).

When considering subnational political cultures, recognizing that the concept of "nationality" and "national identity" might be contested is especially important in countries such as Belgium, Canada, and the UK. The connection between national identity and political culture is the subject of a small but important literature.[42] For instance, Verba concluded that nations are the "foci of identification and loyalty,"[43] while, Deutsch considered national integration as the way of overcoming attachment to or identification with smaller ethnic, cultural, or linguistic groups.[44] Henderson's *Hierarchy of Belonging* stands out as an especially important investigation of national identity and political culture. Henderson focused on national identities in Quebec and Scotland, and argued that the various ways in which one identifies as Quebecois or Scottish impact on the way an individual relates to the state and with others. Such inquiries touch on the question here: how does identification with a nation influence one's relationship with the state in terms of the value placed on federal principles?

According to Henderson, "nation"[45] can refer to two ideas: one objective and one subjective. Objectively, a nation can be defined by signifiers such as its geopolitical borders and shared language.[46] Subjectively, a nation can be a matter of perception and a sense of sharedness or connectedness that groups of people feel toward one another. In reality, Henderson argues, the true concept of "nation" is probably a combination of the two, where the perception of connectedness people share is influenced by concrete characteristics such as language and tradition.

National identity can also be conceptualized in more objective or more subjective ways. Objectively, citizenship, demographic markers, or linguistic ties can determine identification with a nation.[47] Subjectively, national identity can be seen (and measured) as a sense of belonging to a particular group, and as an exercise in self-labelling.

Accounts of federal political culture must be sensitive to these different concepts of nationhood and national identity. While federalism, as a system that celebrates and protects diversity, can accommodate different national identities in the same country, we must be careful to avoid making generalizations about the federal political culture of a country where the concept of nationhood might be contested. Accordingly, the surveys used in this study made use of interlocking representative samples, designed to provide a sample that is not only representative of the country as a whole, but that can also detect significant subnational groups. The close attention given to each country in the following chapters explores the intricacies of aggregating public attitudes according to the unique circumstances of each case.

SUCCESS AND FEDERAL POLITICAL CULTURE

Despite conceptual differences in understanding the social and institutional elements of federalism, theories of federal political culture are united in their argument that successful federal governance is predicated on the alignment of societal values and federal institutions. The argument has strong intuitive resonance. The foundational principles of federalism exist in delicate balance; as Fafard and colleagues put it, "federalism has the task of reconciling principles that are, *prima facie* contradictory."[48] Federalism must balance autonomy with unity, decentralization with centralization, and local and national identities. Any political system built on such fragile foundations will therefore only survive if its people commit, as a society, to maintaining the federal structures. Nevertheless, we must do more than just rely on intuition to truly understand the key to successful federalism. Accordingly, this book's core aim is to locate the role of political culture in successful federations, and within that to understand the importance of decentralization and subsidiarity as potential core elements of federal political culture.

Again, properly conceptualizing the relationship between social and institutional elements is critical here. Burgess's criteria laid out in chapter 1 offer a good example, featuring two broadly institutional factors (criteria 1 [original purpose] and 4 [adaptation and innovation]) and two social factors (criteria 2 [citizens' perceptions] and 3 [values and principles]). By placing institutional and social factors alongside one another, Burgess's criteria emphasize the importance of acknowledging and including sociological factors in understanding federal success. A further theme, which is revisited in chapter 4, is that a focus on federal constitutional values is best placed to detect these social elements.

Within the social elements of federal success, it is also important to recognize the nuances and complexities associated with sociological research. As one example, Elazar's reference to the American cowboy as a feature of federal political culture in the US is an inherently masculine image, raising important questions about femininity in federalism and federal political culture. The value citizens place on diversity and tolerance of others raises similar tensions.[49] For example, Livingston argued that a value for diversity in society would carry through to a desire for diverse institutions, which a federal system delivers.[50] The difficulty of this approach is that it relies on contested and conflicting views of diversity. Take, for instance, the metaphor of the "Canadian mosaic," where Canadian (political) culture is the product of many individual ethnicities and cultures.[51] According to Bell and Tepperman, "to become a Canadian has never meant giving up another culture, nor adopting a code, credo or way of life."[52] The Canadian mosaic is often contrasted with the American "melting pot" metaphor, where ethnic groups and migrants are expected to assimilate and "Americanize."[53] In their own way, both metaphors place an emphasis on diversity: the mosaic is beautiful because of its individual, distinct pieces, while the richness of the melting pot is enhanced by each new culture added to the mix. But the different approaches to diversity do not appear to be reflected in sociological measures of federal political culture in Canada and the US. For instance, Kincaid and Cole assessed value for diversity in North American federations by measuring disagreement with the statement "a country in which everyone speaks the same language is preferable."[54] More importantly, in both cases, "diversity" is itself very narrowly applied. Both countries have documented histories of racial intolerance. The treatment of various ethnic groups and migrants to Canada have led some to argue that "the faces in Gibbon's mosaic are white – never red, yellow, brown, or black,"[55] while Kymlicka notes that despite Canada's successful multicultural policies and integration of immigrants, second-generation "visible migrants" (that is, migrants who do not fit Gibbon's white mosaic) report on average a lower sense of belonging to Canada than white migrants or their parents, even though they also have a strong sense of pride in Canada.[56] Equally, America's record of racial intolerance toward ethnic minorities undermines claims that its value for diversity contributes to a strong federal political culture.

The nuances of such questions are important, but necessarily vary from country to country. Accordingly, while important to note from a broad perspective in this theory-driven chapter, they are best addressed in the individual case studies set out in chapters 5–7.

Success in Nonfederations

An often-overlooked extension of federal political culture's utility is that it can also extend to nonfederations, which would be expected to be similarly successful if their institutions align with nonfederal values. For example, in stable unitary states, such as New Zealand, where debates about federating are rare,[57] we would expect an absence of a federal society, or a federal political culture that devalues core federal principles. Acknowledging unitary countries is important because it also highlights the fact that countries can fall under reform pressure if their unitary institutions do not match vibrant federal political cultures. The late-twentieth century Belgium is a good example here, as its unitary structure did not match the underlying federal society, resulting in a series of devolutionary reforms culminating in federalism in 1993 (the nuances of these ideas are explored further in chapter 7). Further, Livingston noted that despite being formally unitary, both France and the UK had elements of a federal society.[58] Accordingly, this book includes the UK and France as case studies to further test the role and importance of federal political culture in nonfederal states.

FEDERAL POLITICAL CULTURE AND DECENTRALIZATION

As a final point of discussion, this chapter considers why it is important to review the role of decentralization in federal political culture. All federal constitutional values put reform pressure on a system that is perceived to be falling short in its delivery of those values. A system seen as failing to recognize the diversity within the federation will be pressured to do more to accommodate its different peoples (e.g., the recognition of French as an official language in Canada). A federation that does not demonstrate enough cooperation between jurisdictions will be pressured to be more collaborative (e.g., federal reforms in Switzerland in the 2000s). De/centralist values are potentially more relevant, however, because where de/centralization is an issue, the reform options available to policymakers are both fewer in number and more drastic. Where diversity or collaboration might be manifested in any number of ways, de/centralizing pressures can only be satisfied through structural reform.

For this reason, explanations of the social element of federalism (and federal success) commonly place a value of decentralization at their core. As highlighted in chapter 1, early ideas about federal political culture centred on the extent to which people think in local terms.[59] Investigations of federal political culture also often look at attitudes and other indicia of a preference for decentralization as evidence of a societal value for federal principles. For example, Cole, Kincaid, and Rodriguez's pioneering efforts to study public attitudes toward federal principles asked respondents whether they agreed with the statement that "a federal form of government in which power is divided between a national government and state/provincial and local governments, is preferable to any other kind of government."[60] Similarly, Erk's characterization of the federal societies in Austria, Belgium, Canada, Germany and Switzerland hinges on her assessment of their decentralist values.[61] Specifically, her focus on public education and media regulation as policy domains most likely to test the existence of a federal society was based on her assessment that "the pressures towards congruence – both the centralist and decentralist variants – are most pronounced in cultural policy areas."[62]

Citizens' ideas about the degree to which responsibility should be de/centralized are intimately tied to their perceptions of the performance of each level of government.[63] And while these perceptions might have inherent contradictions based on specific policy areas (a "devolution paradox"),[64] the extent to which citizens' views are generalizable across policy domains is essential to maintaining trust and confidence in the federation as a whole and in each constituent unit.

Accordingly, it is critical that we better understand the role of decentralization in federal constitutional values (and broader federal political cultures). Is decentralization, as early theorists suggested, fundamental to the values that maintain the federation? Or is it more peripheral – nevertheless important, but not as critical to federalism as is often assumed? To put it another way, how much centralization in public attitudes can a federation tolerate before it stops succeeding?

Here, the theorized role for subsidiarity comes to the fore. Specifically, as a principle with at least some degree of value for decentralization, subsidiarity might provide the driving force for encouraging decentralization in a federation. For this reason, Weinstock suggested that subsidiarity is a "rule rather than a principle," as it "tells us how power should be organized within a federal arrangement."[65] From this perspective, decentralization is critical to federal success and subsidiarity is the foundation for that decentralization. Extending this argument to federal political culture, we might therefore expect that a value for subsidiarity (as decentralism) is essential to federal political culture.

However, there are two issues with that approach. First, subsidiarity's status as a rule is uncertain, especially from a legal perspective. With the exception of Canada's Supreme Court,[66] few courts from federal countries have been willing to enforce subsidiarity;[67] the German Federal Constitutional Court has even explicitly shied away from subsidiarity, which it views as a political principle and not a legal principle.[68] Second, as discussed in chapter 1, subsidiarity is more than just a principle of decentralization, despite that being its common modern usage. If subsidiarity has a broader meaning, what are its implications for decentralization and its role in federal political culture? Certainly, there is a risk that acknowledging a wider meaning for subsidiarity could dilute its importance to federalism, as it would move away from the direct relationship laid out above (federalism needs decentralization, subsidiarity *is* decentralization, therefore federalism needs subsidiarity). However, this book argues the opposite, and that better understanding subsidiarity (and public value for the principle) in more holistic terms increases its importance to federal success. Specifically, taking a broader view reveals that subsidiarity can enhance federalism in more ways than just providing a rule for the vertical distribution of power, and that public attitudes toward the different elements of subsidiarity can similarly support federalism in a variety of ways.

To substantiate this claim, the next chapter details the difficulties of locating subsidiarity's meaning in the current literature and modern policymaking. It focuses on how the narrowing of subsidiarity's definition to a principle of decentralization has caused the principle to lose much of its value, and proposes a new solution for how we might find its meaning once more.

3

How Subsidiarity Lost Its Meaning

2 February 2016. On this cold and cloudy Tuesday, UK Prime Minister David Cameron addresses the media and workers at a factory in Manchester. He is under growing pressure about the UK's place in the European Union – two opinion polls from the previous week alone show that public opinion about leaving or remaining in Europe is on a knife-edge. Cameron has just returned from a round of negotiations aimed at giving the UK greater freedom while still remaining part of the Union. He hopes this renegotiated platform will serve as the basis for citizens to happily vote to remain in the EU at the promised referendum on the issue. One key feature of the renegotiated package, he proclaims, is a review of the EU powers that could be handed back to the British Parliament. In describing the basis for the review, he tries to highlight how the EU is steeped in archaic and obscuring terminology: "For years Brussels has talked about this idea that the power should be flowing from Brussels back to the member states ... They have a fancy word for it, it's called 'subsidiarity.' *Nobody knows what it means* and I promise not to use it again."[1]

How did we get here – to the point that "nobody" knows what subsidiarity means? When did we know what it meant? Did we ever know? And if we have lost subsidiarity's meaning, how do we find it again?

Answering these questions is the crucial first step in uncovering how we can use subsidiarity to better understand success in federations. This chapter takes as its touchstone Føllesdal's observation that "different historical and theoretical traditions of subsidiarity yield strikingly different and sometimes incompatible implications for the allocation and use of authority within a multilevel social, legal, or political order."[2] The chapter traces subsidiarity's development through history, with the aim of showing how different values and ideas have waxed and waned to contribute to subsidiarity's meaning. The goal here is to highlight pivotal developments in subsidiarity thought, rather than providing a comprehensive account of subsidiarity's usage through the centuries. This examination will highlight how themes of decentralization have always been present in subsidiarity's history, but they have varied in emphasis over time. Further, tracing subsidiarity's history also reveals how subsidiarity and federalism have converged and diverged over time.

Having shown how subsidiarity's meaning has evolved and fractured, the chapter then explains how it might be rediscovered. The chapter draws together the differing perspectives and meanings attributed to subsidiarity over the years into a new model for understanding subsidiarity, conceptualizing the principle as a value for decentralism, nonabsorption, and support. It describes each of the three elements before demonstrating how they fit together to form the subsidiarity principle. The aim here is to present a more holistic approach to the principle that offers a better way of exploring subsidiarity and its relationship with decentralization and federalism.

A HISTORY OF SUBSIDIARITY

The term "subsidiarity" first emerged in the nineteenth century.[3] However, to truly understand subsidiarity's meaning, we must first look at the ideas and values that underpin the principle, some of which date back to ancient Greece and Rome. This section's discussion of the history of subsidiarity therefore begins with these ancient civilizations, before turning its attention to the evolution of the principle in Europe in the Middle Ages and nineteenth century, and then finally considers subsidiarity in modern times. The purpose of this section is to highlight key milestones and changes in how subsidiarity has been conceptualized and used, rather than to chart the entire history of the principle. Accordingly, developments such as the principle's (implicit[4]) inclusion in the drafting of constitutions in the nineteenth and twentieth centuries are left to later chapters discussing each of the eight countries analyzed in this book.

Ancient Greece

Some scholars trace subsidiarity as far back as ancient Greece, and particularly to the writings of Aristotle.[5] Aroney notes Aristotle's insistence that, although the *polis* ("city" or "community") was constituted for the common good, it should not replace or supplant the smaller groups and households of which it was composed.[6] In particular, Aristotle emphasized self-sufficiency; specifically, the various spheres (households, villages, the polis) enjoyed different degrees of self-sufficiency.[7] Thus, there were some things that the household could do for itself, while there were other things that needed to be provided by higher orders, and the fact that this support was needed did not render the household inferior or less important.

Such a dynamic also played out, albeit on a much larger scale, in the Greek leagues. While the various leagues had greater or lesser degrees of incorporation, they can be broadly characterized as the Greek city-states uniting, largely for defence and trade, but determined to retain as much individual autonomy as possible.[8] The rationale behind this form of union[9] was a recognition that some responsibilities were better handled above the city-state, while others were best left at a more local level. This created a hierarchy of competency, where responsibility only moved to a higher level if that level could do a better job or would be more competent than the lower one. Notably, the clear delineation of responsibilities was also an important early development in federal thinking and led prominent federal scholar Edward Augustus Freeman to describe the Achaian (Aegean) League as one of "the most perfect developments of the Federal principle which the world has ever seen."[10]

Similarly, Solomon Rufus Davis saw the Aegean League as a forerunner to today's federalism. In particular, Davis noted the word "*foedus*," or covenant, as being especially relevant. The "federal contract" that brought the Greek city-states together relied on mutual recognition and respect and marked out clear lines of responsibility.[11] This was crucial, as it allowed the various spheres to interact with one another, if not quite as equals, certainly as two bargaining parties (as opposed to a higher order directing the lower orders).

In summary, Aristotle's main contribution to subsidiarity was his exploration of the role of the household vis-à-vis the polis. This discussion laid the foundation for later debates about the role of the state in relation to the individual. In Aristotle's writings, we see a clear preference for decentralization, but the more important value is in establishing a firm boundary to protect against unnecessary interference in the functions of the individual or household. On a broader scale, the Greek leagues also provided a model for subsidiarity, where responsibilities were decentralized where possible, and kept clearly separate.

Ancient Rome

The word "subsidiarity" has its roots in Latin, although there is some debate as to its precise lineage. Some scholars claim "subsidiarity" is derived from *subsidium*, which means "to help or aid."[12] Others credit the coining of "subsidiarity" to nineteenth century scholar Luigi Taparelli, who derived it from *sub sedo*,[13] which refers to subordinate clauses in a sentence.[14]

Regardless of the etymological concerns, it is clear that the idea underpinning this Latin usage is one of aid and support. A subordinate clause in a sentence provides additional information, detail, or colour to the independent clause, but cannot stand alone as its own sentence. The subordinate clause supports the independent clause by enriching its meaning, while the independent clause supports the subordinate by providing a platform or foundation for its message.

This notion of support is furthered another meaning of sub sedo: in addition to referring to subordinate clauses in a sentence, it also described auxiliary troops in the ancient Roman legions.[15] The Roman auxiliaries were separate to, but not entirely independent from, the legion proper.[16] They provided specialized troops to supplement the Roman army and compensate for the legion's weaknesses (usually through providing cavalry and archers).[17] But while the auxiliaries were a crucial component to Roman military success, they in turn relied on the might of the legion; auxiliary troops alone could not have hoped to stand against Rome's enemies. Thus, as with sentence clauses, sub sedo in the military sense implied support and the coming together of constituent elements to achieve a greater outcome.

However, even this view is contested. Specifically, John F. Cox argues that "subsidiarity" derives from *subsidiaries*, meaning "of or belonging to the reserves."[18] According to Cox, the term referred to troops in the Roman legion stationed in the third line of battle, who were held in reserve, only intervening if they were absolutely required.[19] While they still played a supporting role, the emphasis here is clearly on non-intervention unless necessary, and in this light can be viewed as an extension of the ancient Greek idea that the various spheres (polis, league, etc.) should not intervene or interfere with one another's affairs.

Objectively, it is unlikely that we will ever determine which picture of the role of auxiliary and reserve troops is more accurate. Nor is it strictly necessary to do so. Instead, it is useful to consider that these divergent interpretations of the auxiliary functions arise as reflections of the differences in understandings of subsidiarity. It is entirely possible that the respective proponents' own perspectives and ideas about the principle colour their interpretation of the role of subsidium, sub sedo, or subsidiares, and their utility in making sense of subsidiarity.

The two approaches to subsidiarity's connection to the Roman military are united in their lack of an emphasis on decentralism. In a military setting, a rigid, centralized decision-making process is clearly desirable, but the lack of decentralization extended to wider Roman governance. Indeed, when defined in modern terms, the subsidiarity principle was largely rejected. While the empire did make use of regional government, this was a strategy of centralizing the power, rather than decentralizing it.[20] By dividing power among provincial governors, the emperor ensured that each was reliant on the centre for stable government, and none could amass enough power to challenge his rule.[21] In particular, Edwards cites the example of how Roman Emperor Diocletian increased the number of provinces to dilute the authority of regional governors, thus strengthening the power of the central emperor.[22] This consolidation of power in Rome's hands was in many respects the antithesis of common modern accounts of the principle. Nevertheless, the connection between subsidiarity and the Roman legions (either as sub sedo supporting auxiliaries, or subsidiaries reserve troops) provides a clear lesson that subsidiarity can be meaningful beyond or even without explicit decentralization. Further, the Latin roots of "subsidiarity" embed these ideas of non-absorption and support into the principle itself.

Aquinas

St Thomas Aquinas's contribution to subsidiarity was an extension of Aristotle's writings.[23] For instance, where Aristotle spoke of the self-sufficiency of the household, neighbourhood, and the city, Aquinas added the province above the city, proclaiming its self-sufficiency in matters of defence.[24] Aquinas also made important, usually theologically based, qualifications to some of Aristotle's ideas. One important example is the way that Aquinas insisted that, while Aristotle was correct in asserting that man is a political animal, the fulfillment one received from participating in the (political) affairs of the polis was to be understood only in terms of human or natural goods; sacred fulfillment could only come from God.[25] Thus, Aquinas preferred to describe humans as "social" or "political and social" animals.[26] According to Aroney, this language reflected Aquinas's recognition of the many "non-political" forms of association of his time, namely "families, fraternities, religious orders, guilds, and universities."[27] This recognition led to Aquinas developing a typology of societies, distinguishing between public societies (cities, provinces, and kingdoms), and private societies (households, business partnerships, craft guilds, and religious associations).[28] Importantly, Aquinas "understood these various forms of society to possess both a degree of separateness and independence from one another and a degree of integration and interdependence."[29]

By extending Aristotle's work, Aquinas opened the principle up for the Catholic Church to incorporate subsidiarity into its social doctrine (discussed ahead). More importantly, however, we can see how Aquinas's use of the Aristotelian/Greek notions of independence and non-interference combine with the Roman notion of support, whereby private associations allow individuals to come together to assist one another but are in turn protected from undue interference by the state. This marked a beginning-point for the merging and intertwining of these core themes of subsidiarity.

Holy Roman Empire

The Holy Roman Empire, which covered much of Western and central Europe throughout the Middle Ages, was a hotbed of religious, political, and social reform and provided much of the foundation for modern thinking about subsidiarity and federalism. Unlike many of its feudal counterparts in Europe, the Holy Roman Empire was characterized by exceptionally strong provinces. Ludolph Hugo (1630–1704), official historian of the Duchy of Hannover and later vice-chancellor of Hannover,[30] observed that "any prince has in his territory as much power as the Emperor has in the whole Empire."[31]

Føllesdal echoes that assessment, pointing out that the Holy Roman Empire was very atypical, historically speaking, in terms of the substantial power wielded by the territories within the Empire.[32] Indeed, the power wielded by the territorial governments was so strong that Freeman, who saw federalism as a balance between "national" and "subnational" power,[33] considered the Holy Roman Empire "so widely removed from the perfection of the Federal idea."[34] Equally, Samuel von Pufendorf (1632–1694), who lived in the empire, described it as a "monstrous creature," and a "bastard mutant."[35]

Atypical as it was, the extreme decentralization of the Holy Roman Empire provided fertile ground for the values that underpin subsidiarity. The works of philosopher Johannes Althusius (c. 1557–1638) have been especially influential in the development of the principle of subsidiarity,[36] and, for many scholars, cemented the link between subsidiarity and federalism. Known as the "father of federalism,"[37] Althusius wrote his seminal work *Politica* at a time of particularly tumultuous religious and social upheaval. Published in 1603, *Politica* was written shortly after the Dutch revolt and Cologne War and shortly before the beginning of the Thirty Years' War.

After publishing *Politica*, Althusius became the syndic (governor) of Emden, a key city on the border of what is now Germany and the Netherlands.[38] As syndic, Althusius was deeply concerned with maintaining the city's autonomy and religious freedom (predominantly Calvinist) against its Lutheran provincial lord and Catholic Holy Roman Emperor.[39] In doing so, Althusius merged the federalist ideas of territorial divisions of power, with subsidiarity's preference for decentralism and community support. His writing therefore echoes Aristotle's ideas about spheres of excusive competence. Like Aristotle, Althusius also followed a hierarchy or progression, from the individual, to the family, to civil associations ("collegium"), and then the state (itself structured from city, to province, to supreme magistrate).[40] Indeed, Althusius opened *Politica* with the statement "politics is the art of associating men,"[41] a line reminiscent of Aristotle's famous comment that man is naturally a political animal.[42] However, Althusius departed from Aristotle by prosecuting a more forceful decentralist argument. While revising the second edition of *Politica*, Althusius (who had by then been the syndic of Emden for six years) added a chapter titled "Tyranny and Its Remedies," and described tyranny as "the contrary of just and upright administration," where a higher order of government "cruelly overthrows and destroys the most important goods of the commonwealth."[43] These goods included "the functions of the associated body ... or of the rights of private person,"[44] and thus Althusius saw interference with associations or individuals as an affront to good governance.

The historical context in which Althusius wrote is a key element in understanding his contribution to the development of the subsidiarity principle and his firm emphasis on decentralism. Føllesdal argues that the Althusian "conception of subsidiarity yields a weak centre. The subunits enjoy a privileged position in this conception, with veto rights ... [and] few if any restrictions on their internal powers."[45] Althusius's position is firmly grounded in Emden's own independence, following its revolt into city-statehood in 1595. Accordingly, the Althusian conceptions of decentralization, subsidiarity, and federalism are heavily contextual, and where later political orders have given such prominence to subunits, they "tend to be weak and oligarchic confederal arrangements."[46] Nevertheless, Althusius's strong arguments for decentralization have endured in modern approaches to subsidiarity and federalism.

However, Althusius did also recognize that provinces and the "supreme magistrate" have a place in good administration. Just as "no man is self-sufficient" and must therefore rely on and associate with others, the province and supreme magistrate provide functions which cannot be achieved by civil associations or cities alone. Thus, while Althusius resisted intrusions on the rights of lower orders wherever possible, he acknowledged that there were times when the centre was necessary to facilitate a "good life." Føllesdal argues that this conception is proscriptive (rather than prescriptive), because it protects the autonomy of lower orders, but provides few if any "obligations of central units to assist subunits or require central units to act."[47] Of course, that is not to say that Althusius saw no role for the centre. Rather, Althusius's approach meant that there was no positive duty imposed on the centre to act or support lower levels; there are simply responsibilities that are better handled at a higher level. In that regard, Althusian conceptions of subsidiarity can be seen as a step away from the themes of aid and assistance developed in ancient Rome.

Confederalism

Føllesdal draws out a particular "confederalist" conceptualization of subsidiarity, which takes design cues from early thinking about the relationship between the thirteen original American states under the

Articles of Confederation (1781–89).[48] In particular, this conceptualization is characterized by an emphasis on decentralized government as the best guarantee for liberty and protection against tyranny. Like Althusian subsidiarity, it is proscriptive, fiercely arguing against undue interference from the centre and placing few if any obligations on higher orders. Where the two approaches differ is their view of the individual. Under the Althusian conception, communities and associations are justified (required, even) in order to fulfill the needs of individuals. The legitimacy and autonomy of these associations therefore derives from individuals, but after that point the individual is of little concern to the concept. By contrast, confederalism according to Føllesdal takes the individual as its main focus: "the principle of subsidiarity is, on this confederal account, thought to offer the best protection of individual liberty against tyranny."[49] Under this conception, subsidiarity is thus justified as a protection of individual freedom, and draws heavily on nonabsorptionist ideas.

Catholic Social Doctrine

Subsidiarity's most significant development was its adoption and incorporation into Catholic social doctrine. Indeed, the Catholic Church's use of the principle often eclipses all that came before, such that some scholars attribute the creation of the principle to the church.[50] While Aquinas' works were an important first step in the principle's use by the church, the formal adoption of subsidiarity in Catholicism begins with Pope Leo XIII's 1891 encyclical *Rerum Novarum*.[51] In that encyclical, Leo XIII stated:

> Here we are reminded of confraternities, societies and religious orders … The annals of every nation down to our own days bear witness to what they have accomplished for the human race. It is indisputable that on grounds of reason alone such associations, being perfectly blameless in their objects, possess the sanction of the law of nature … The rulers of the State accordingly have no rights over them, nor can they claim any share in their control; on the contrary, it is the duty of the State to respect and cherish them.[52]

Notably, Leo XIII was a student of Luigi Taparelli, the Jesuit scholar who (arguably) coined the term "subsidiarity."[53] Taparelli's influence is apparent in Leo's ideas that smaller and larger societies differ in their immediate purposes and aims, but they come together (i.e., *support* one another) for the common good of civil society.[54] Aquinas's influence is also clear: Leo XIII cites Aquinas on several occasions in paragraph 51, before noting that man, as a political and social being, must be allowed to form associations, and that when the state forbids such associations, "it contradicts the very principle of its own existence."[55]

Subsidiarity was also raised in Pope Pius XI's 1931 encyclical, *Quadragesimo Anno*.[56] In perhaps the most frequently cited paragraph in the subsidiarity literature, Pius XI argued: "just as it is gravely wrong to take from individuals what they can accomplish by their own initiative and industry and give it to the community, so also it is an injustice and at the same time a grave evil and disturbance of right order to assign to a greater and higher association what lesser and subordinate organisations can do."[57]

While Pius XI's motive behind the encyclical was to counter the rise of fascism and its interference in the church,[58] the sentiment has since expanded greatly, providing a platform for a much broader argument for nonabsorption and non-interference. Indeed, it manifests as a distinctly liberal argument against state interference in the affairs of social organizations, associations, and charities.[59] Thus, the Catholic model combines the strands of subsidiarity discussed above: authority should be decentralized and exclusive, in the sense that the state should not get involved in the affairs of social groups, but power should also be shared, because the state should exist to support and foster those organizations. In the words of Komonchak, "intervention ... is only appropriate as 'helping people help themselves.'"[60] However, the Catholic model is less insistent on decentralism than the way subsidiarity manifested in the Holy Roman Empire and Confederal America; instead, the "common good" is a relevant and often persuasive justification for centralism. In fact, the Catholic approach to subsidiarity is more prescriptive than earlier approaches to the principle: while the central unit should not interfere unduly, it is *obliged* to intervene, for the "common good," if the subunit cannot provide the required services.[61]

The Catholic view of subsidiarity is underpinned by the idea that the "human good" is to develop and fully realize one's potential.[62] As a result, the state must not intervene or absorb the functions of individuals or private associations, but at the same time must intervene when the public good is threatened, or to "help people help themselves." Notably, this means that the Catholic approach to subsidiarity "rests on contested views of the social order and of human flourishing,"[63] more specifically, the flourishing of realizing one's potential is based on achieving what God intended – living up to the potential God has instilled in them.[64] Naturally, from a secular perspective this assumption about "goodness" is problematic because it is not one that is universally shared. Nevertheless, the Catholic approach to subsidiarity is important because it provides a justification for central intervention (support), even if the exact application of that justification might be contested.

Subsidiarity in the Twentieth Century

Subsidiarity's adoption by the Catholic Church brought the principle to a wider audience. In the second half of the twentieth century, subsidiarity was invoked in two key ways, which Føllesdal describes as fiscal federalism and liberal contractualism. The fiscal federalism conception of subsidiarity operates from the premise that the power and burden of a public good should be held by the population that benefits from it. In other words, "the costs of public goods which benefit only a subset of the community should be borne by that subset."[65] There are two core arguments for this position. First, local decision-making is thought to be more efficient, as local decision-makers should have a better knowledge and understanding of the relevant needs, preferences, and alternatives.[66] Second, localized decision-making is better able to detect variations between localities in preferences, as opposed to a "one size fits all" approach from the centre. An example of this approach was economist Colin Clark's argument for fiscal federalism in Australia, which focused on lowering taxes but shifting more public costs onto citizens making use of government services.[67]

The fiscal federalism conception is less proscriptive than the previous approaches, for two reasons. First, central intervention may be necessary to overrule a free-riding subunit and to prevent a "race to the bottom." Secondly, a subunit's performance can be evaluated based on the quality of service provided, and central intervention may be required to address gaps in service delivery.

Liberal contractualist conceptions of subsidiarity recognize the importance of social orders, which provide the means of satisfying one's basic needs and conception of a "good life."[68] Thus, individuals have an interest in "control over the social institutions which shape values, goals, options and expectations."[69] Therefore, political influence is important, as it protects against subjection and control by others, and helps to manage and maintain legitimate expectations. According to Føllesdal, these conceptions allow for two cases for subsidiarity. The first relates to the regulation of political power, and is expressed as follows: "When individuals share circumstances, beliefs or values, they have a prima facie claim to share control over institutional change to prevent subjection and breaking of legitimate expectations. Those similarly affected are more likely to comprehend the need and scope for change."[70] This is something of a "classic" argument for subsidiarity, and it brings to mind a scenario where a small, possibly isolated, community holds very different values to a far distant capital. The application is much broader, however. Increased levels of individualism in many Western democracies in the latter half of the twentieth century, as a counterpoint to increasing globalization, strengthened the potency of this argument.

The second case is for the regulation of political deliberation. In requiring social orders to publicly justify the legitimacy of their use of power, and in bargaining with other orders (e.g., between levels of government), public deliberation of issues is heightened.[71] While Føllesdal acknowledges that public deliberation does not require subsidiarity per se, he maintains that it is useful in guiding the public debate.

The two conceptualizations of subsidiarity prominent in the twentieth century were therefore heavily decentralist, emphasizing the individual and the local. The conceptualizations also represent a step away from supportive elements of the principle.

European Union

Finally, attention turns to the European Union, where the principle was used to protect the rights and jurisdiction of the member states. The Preamble of the Treaty on European Union states that in the context of the Union, "decisions are to be taken as closely as possible to the citizen in accordance with the principle of subsidiarity."[72] Additionally, Article 5 of the treaty provides that the use of the Union's jurisdictional competencies is governed by the principle of subsidiarity: "Under the principle of subsidiarity, in areas which do not fall within its exclusive competence, the Union shall act only if and in so far as the objectives of the proposed action cannot be sufficiently achieved by the Member States, either at central level or at regional and local level, but can rather, by reason of the scale or effects of the proposed action, be better achieved at Union level."[73]

In some ways, we have come full circle here: the ancient Greeks probably would have included similar provisions in the covenants that created the Greek leagues. However, in the time since Aristotle, subsidiarity has changed, developed, and evolved. In particular, supportive elements of the principle, which are hinted at in subsidiarity's Latin roots and popularized in the Catholic social doctrine, barely feature in the EU usage. Additionally, the adoption of subsidiarity in Article 5 has created scope for even further development, both in terms of judicial interpretation,[74] and because the use of subsidiarity in the formation of the European Union has dramatically altered current conceptions of the principle. In particular, the modern understanding of the principle as a preference for local decision-making is drawn heavily from the decentralism emphasized in Article 5. The difficulty is that the principle's use as a political compromise, assuaging member states' concerns without imposing many particular requirements, meant that subsidiarity's meaning became untethered from its historical context.

RECOVERING SUBSIDIARITY'S MEANING

This account of subsidiarity's history highlights how the principle has become a confusing amalgam of ideas about decentralism, independence, non-interference, support, and political order. Subsidiarity is not alone among concepts and principles in political science that have a complex history, but it is clear that subsidiarity's history is often ignored by or unknown to those who would invoke the principle. As a result, when a scholar or policymaker refers to subsidiarity, it can be difficult to tell what they mean by it; do they have in mind the specific European Union application, the broader Catholic model, or some other combination of influences in the principle's history? Further, the confusion around subsidiarity's definition can lead to scenarios such as the Brexit debates, where both leave and remain campaigners thought subsidiarity supported their point of view, because each of them attached a different meaning to the principle.[75]

To assist in the understanding and implementation of subsidiarity, some scholars have sought to consolidate the debate over subsidiarity's meaning by identifying different categories and conceptions of subsidiarity. For some, this is as simple as arguing that subsidiarity has two parts. Brennan, for example, identifies a negative and a positive limb of subsidiarity: "Negatively, it is a principle of nonabsorption of lower societies by higher societies, above all by the state. This is the aspect of subsidiarity that is commonly invoked today, but it represents only half the story. Positively, subsidiarity is also the principle that when aid is given to a particular society, it be for the purpose of encouraging and strengthening that society."[76] Utz and Brouillet, who respectively considered the principle's resonance in natural law and Canadian federalism, also favour this dichotomous view of subsidiarity.[77]

Gosepath expands on the idea that "subsidiarity has a positive and a negative thrust"[78] by offering a three-pronged approach: the rule of assistance, the ban on interference, and "helping others to help themselves." The rule of assistance holds that larger or higher orders (society, the state, or a national government) ought to support smaller and lower orders if they are unable to perform a task/fulfill their responsibilities by themselves.[79] The ban on interference stands directly opposite the rule: larger social entities are prohibited from "interfering with the affairs of a smaller unit of affected individuals or of an individual."[80] These two conflicting principles are reconciled in the third principle, which holds that the only kind of support/intervention that is legitimate is the kind that "help[s] others to help themselves."[81] Gussen also endorses this threefold approach to subsidiarity in his analysis of subsidiarity in New Zealand.[82]

These two approaches do a good job highlighting the supportive and nonabsorptionist elements of subsidiarity, but are less well-suited to accounting for the emphasis on decentralization that has come to dominate thinking about subsidiarity. Accordingly, there is scope to extend these ideas.

Three Elements of Subsidiarity

This book proposes a new construction, which centres subsidiarity on three key ideas that thread their way through the development of the principle and the different conceptions listed above: decentralism, nonabsorption, and support. Crucially, these three elements are designed to bring together the competing approaches identified earlier, and reconcile them if possible. As such, they are deliberately broad, aiming to cover the field in understanding subsidiarity, although they do not necessarily preclude future research from identifying additional elements. Equally, while each element corresponds to a distinct way of conceptualizing subsidiarity in the literature, there will unavoidably be some overlap between the elements and some blurriness at the edges of each. The following descriptions therefore focus on the core of each element, and provide guidelines on the differences between them, rather than hard or fixed definitions and boundaries.

Decentralism

The first, decentralism, is perhaps the most easily recognizable principle in the modern subsidiarity literature. It is expressed in the idea that "functions of government should be performed at the lowest level possible."[83] For example, Bridge states that "decisions, whether legislative or administrative acts, should be taken at the lowest practicable political level,"[84] while Bednar gives subsidiarity a very decentralist meaning, defining it as "a systemic predilection for locating authority at the most local level feasible."[85] A decentralist preference is also evident in Pope Pius XI's statement that "it is an injustice ... to assign to a greater and higher association what lesser and subordinate organisations can do."[86] Perhaps the clearest real-world example is Article 5 of the Treaty on European Union. Subsidiarity as decentralism proposes a clear progression of authority: there is a presumption that power is held at the lowest level (the individual), but is then conceded upwards to private associations, and then to local, state, and finally national (or international) governments if the lower level is not competent to act. In that regard, "subsidiarity as decentralism" has a narrower focus than devolution, because it operates from a localized starting point, while devolution can refer to situations where power is gifted or ceded from the centre to a lower order.[87]

For the purposes of this conceptualization, what constitutes the "lower" or "lowest" level will be determined by context. Sometimes, this will be constitutionally defined, although even this may be ambiguous, as local governments (typically the level of government closest to the people) are often absent from national constitutions.[88] In the context of the European Union, the nation-state may be the lowest level. When considering relations between state and non-state actors (which are generally beyond the scope of this book), the "lowest level" might be driven by norms, such as the preference for individualism under a confederalist approach to subsidiarity, or claimed by particular groups, such as ongoing debates in Australia and Canada about Indigenous peoples' rights to land, self-governance, and self-determination.[89] While taking this contextual approach risks introducing yet more ambiguity to an already ambiguous topic, it is preferable when compared to the alternative, which would be to place rigid definitions on the term "lowest level." However, for the purpose of this book, which focuses on subsidiarity between levels of government within a nation, "lowest level" generally refers to local or state/provincial governments.

Nonabsorption

The second element, "nonabsorption," refers to the intolerance of central intervention or the takeover of responsibility. This was articulated in *Quadragesimo Anno* when Pius XI argued that higher orders should "never destroy and absorb" the functions of lower organizations. In arguing that decentralist interpretations of subsidiarity do not capture its full meaning, Chaplin states that "subsidiarity is a call for social functions to be fulfilled, not at *the lowest possible level*, but rather at *the right level*; that is, by the community properly fitted to fulfil them."[90] This view is therefore not inherently decentralist, because it is intolerant of any intervention or absorption of function by the "wrong" level, whether that be higher or lower. Hittinger agrees with this perspective, stating that subsidiarity "is proposed as a principle of nonabsorption, not a principle that necessarily requires devolution."[91] However, the decentralist and nonabsorptionist elements of subsidiarity are generally quite compatible. Take, for example, subsidiarity in the European Union. Article 5 provides both a decentralist presumption that individual member states should have jurisdiction rather than the Union, and holds that the Union shall only act if the member states cannot do so (i.e., that the Union should not absorb the functions of the states). What truly distinguishes nonabsorption from decentralism is that it can work both ways. It recognizes that some decisions or responsibilities are simply better handled by a more central government, and that in such cases, local levels should not interfere with the central authority. This duality is exposed in Australia, where state governments often argue for decentralism on the basis that the federal level has unduly interfered with their responsibilities, but in turn often refuse to cede power to local governments on the basis that the states are best equipped to make policy and govern on most issues (i.e., nonabsorption, where the states are the "right level").

According to Chaplin, subsidiarity only calls for authority to be held at the "right" level, it "does not tell us what the right communities are."[92] This contradicts Weinstock's claim that subsidiarity is a rule rather than a principle that allocates power within a federal system,[93] because (according to Weinstock) it takes the local level as a starting point and then evaluates whether responsibility should be centralized. The distinction also reflects debates about the political versus the legal nature of subsidiarity – whether a higher level can carry out a particular responsibility effectively, or whether the policy aims would be "better achieved," and will often be a subjective, political argument, rather than a legally enforceable rule.[94] While distinguishing between decentralism (which creates a presumption that the lower level will be preferable) and nonabsorption (which makes no claims about which level should be preferred) does not directly solve the ambiguity arising from these political decisions, it can provide an insight into how the political judgment was reached: are those who are invoking subsidiarity operating from a presumption of and decentralism, or is their approach informed by an argument that a particular level is "best placed" to handle responsibility?

This takes on special importance for the current study, as the debate provides a window of opportunity in which public attitudes can be vastly informative. Specifically, nonabsorptionist subsidiarity has the potential to preserve norms and attitudes about allocations of responsibility, because it argues against interference with a government's current functions. In contrast, decentralist views may call for reform and changing attitudes where existing power structures do not decentralize authority (especially in places such as Australia). Testing whether one element resonates with citizens more strongly than the other therefore offers useful insights into whether and how to approach structural reform.

Support

The third dimension, "support," might describe the kinds of interactions levels of government "should" have. According to Halberstam, the principle of subsidiarity holds that "the central government should play only a supporting role in governance,"[95] while Komonchak argues that "subsidiarity requires *positively* that all communities not only permit but enable and encourage individuals to exercise their own self-responsibility and that larger communities do the same for smaller ones."[96] Clearly, this fits neatly alongside a decentralist viewpoint; central governments are to play a facilitating role for smaller orders. However, subsidiarity as support can also work with nonabsorption. Just as the Roman legions and auxiliary troops each had different but complementary roles to play in battle, so too can governments support but not absorb or subsume one another in their exercise of power or rollout of programs or functions. Germany's functional or administrative federation, where policy setting is often conducted at the national level, but individual Länder are responsible for service delivery,[97] provides an example of this in practice.

Typically, support is taken to mean financial assistance. For example, a central government might provide funding to local communities but not dictate how the money must be spent, or set broad policy goals but allow lower levels the freedom to decide how to achieve those goals; this empowers the community to be responsible for itself, while not limiting their ability to self-govern. However, support need not always relate to funding. For instance, a national government might collect data from around the country, which subnational governments can access to better inform their own local decisions (easing some of the transaction costs Føllesdal describes in relation to fiscal federalism).[98] Higher orders might also play a supportive role by coordinating the deployment of experts, ensuring that skills are delivered where they are needed. Brennan correctly notes that the notion of support in subsidiarity is often neglected as discussion usually focuses on nonabsorptionist or decentralist interpretations of the principle instead.[99] The key distinction between support, and decentralism and nonabsorption, is best reflected in Brennan's "negative" and "positive" limbs,[100] or Føllesdal's "proscriptive" and "prescriptive" subsidiarity.[101] Generally, decentralism and nonabsorption are negative or proscriptive, because they require the central government or higher levels to not get involved or not interfere. Conversely, supportive subsidiarity places a positive burden on the centre, prescribing action that will empower the smaller or lower level. Thus, while "helping lower levels help themselves"[102] may seem decentralist because it is aimed at enabling lower levels to take greater control, the key difference is the obligation to support that it places on the centre or higher level. Supportive subsidiarity is therefore a crucial aspect to understanding subsidiarity as a whole, as it describes the kinds of interactions levels of government have with each other.

The Three Elements Combined

In essence, then, these three key elements offer slightly different things: decision-making at the lowest level possible (decentralism), "wrong" orders not interfering with the functions of "right" orders (nonabsorption), and higher levels supporting lower levels, with a view to empowering the local community (support). This tends to confirm there is no "one right answer" or "true subsidiarity" to be found. Rather, there are likely to be different dimensions of subsidiarity, with differences in the value placed on each dimension likely to result in different understandings, including – potentially – the vastly different examples and experiences of subsidiarity previously described. These elements should not be seen as pieces of a jigsaw, which fit seamlessly together. Instead, they are better understood as volume controls on a speaker; just as bass and treble can be adjusted independently of one another to affect the overall sound, decentralism, nonabsorption, and support can manifest and fluctuate separately from the others, producing different kinds of subsidiarity. Usually, endorsement of one element will be related to endorsement of one or both of the others, especially given the interrelatedness of the elements at their edges (discussed above). However, this does not have to be the case, and it is possible that endorsing one element and rejecting the other two can still be considered as viewing subsidiarity as meaningful. This is most often apparent in cases drawing on the narrow, decentralist interpretation of the principle: just because that particular conceptualization misses the principle's wider meaning, does not mean that its advocate does not see subsidiarity as meaningful.

Another key feature of this conceptualization of subsidiarity is that it understands the three elements as being equal in their potential relevance or importance, but recognizes that in practice the three elements will not be equal – sometimes a focus on decentralism will be the most important, while at other times supportive subsidiarity will take on the critical role. Layering public values on top, we would expect aggregate attitudes toward each element to differ in each country (thus producing a unique subsidiarity political culture), but the three elements are all potentially relevant. A useful analogy for this approach is the five-factor model of personality. This theory, which dominates modern psychology literature, holds that an individual's personality is the product of five core underlying factors: openness, conscientiousness, extraversion, agreeableness, and neuroticism.[103] A personality test would reveal an individual's tendencies across these five factors (e.g., highly extroverted, low on agreeableness, etc.) but it would also show which factor(s) provide the key driving force in their personality (e.g., a highly creative individual's personality might be defined by high openness, with other factors such as conscientiousness and extroversion influencing how that creativity manifests itself – say, as an industrious but withdrawn artist, or as a loud but disorganized performer). In that regard, each of the five factors is equivalent in the abstract sense, but at the individual level they will not be of equal importance. Further, it is in discovering the inequality of the factors that we find out the nuances of one's personality. The same is true of the new approach to subsidiarity presented in this book – in theorizing about subsidiarity, we must be careful not to emphasize one element over the others (cf. the recent focus on decentralism), but when it comes to understanding public attitudes toward the principle, or deploying it to guide policymaking, we must be sensitive to the fact that the three elements will not apply equally.

To demonstrate this effect, it is useful to consider some of the historical examples described in the previous section, situating them on top of the three dimensions just described. Althusian subsidiarity emphasizes all three elements, valuing the local unit as a means for empowering individuals (decentralism and support), and championing their immunity from central interference (nonabsorption). However, Føllesdal's observation that Althusius's conception of subsidiarity is "proscriptive not prescriptive"[104] can be understood now as supportive subsidiarity being less strongly emphasized than decentralism and nonabsorption. The Catholic model also draws on all three dimensions, but differs from Althusian subsidiarity in its stance on decentralism and support. While there is a clearly favourable attitude taken toward smaller scales, communities and associations, the real decider in Catholic subsidiarity is the common good and doing things at the "right" level; although decentralism may be the right allocation of power in many cases, it is not a default position, and the emphasis is on supporting and not absorbing associations, rather than decentralizing authority. The confederalist and liberal contractualist conceptions are, by contrast, strongly focused on decentralism and nonabsorption, but remain silent on support. Fiscal federalism, while also decentralist, is more flexible about nonabsorption, recognizing that there are times when central intervention will be the most efficient.

This approach views subsidiarity, not under a particular definition, or even as a set of competing conceptions, but rather as a manifestation of particular combinations of values. In the context of confusion about subsidiarity's meaning, such an approach is important because it allows us to be sensitive to variations in understanding the principle. Where previous approaches have either provided a narrow definition that does not capture the history of the principle, or have identified differing conceptions but offered little guidance on which conception is to be preferred, the approach developed in this book offers a middle ground that is both flexible enough to adapt to different perspectives, but definite enough to give meaning to subsidiarity. This perspective is also important to validly recognizing subsidiarity values amongst the general public. As covered in the following chapters, conceptualizing subsidiarity as the product of decentralism, nonabsorption, and support values means that it can be sensitive to the possibility that subsidiarity's meaning and importance vary between cultures.

CONCLUSION

This chapter examined how subsidiarity's meaning was lost, tracing the different values and ideas underpinning the principle through history. The chapter then explored how we might recover the principle's meaning by providing a new understanding of the principle. The three-element approach it developed reconciles competing conceptions of subsidiarity by identifying the fundamental values that underpin the principle – namely, decentralism, nonabsorption, and support. This chapter showed that these ideas have been part of subsidiarity since ancient times, but that their use and emphasis has varied over the centuries, with different thinkers bringing different perspectives and insights. Understanding these developments gives the principle new meaning, as it helps reconcile previous approaches to defining subsidiarity.

4

Charting a New Course

Measuring Public Value for Subsidiarity and Federalism

22 August 2015. Leader of the Canadian Liberal Party Justin Trudeau is preparing for the national election, which will be held in two months' time. He responds to a letter from Phillippe Couillard, premier of Quebec, in which Couillard outlined the major policy issues facing his province, and asked the leaders of the major parties what they proposed to do for Quebec if elected. Trudeau faces the same challenge all prospective prime ministers of Canada must confront: acknowledging Quebec's unique nationality and status within the Canadian federation without disrupting his appeal to the rest of Canada. In his response, Trudeau aims to highlight his and his party's respect for Quebec's uniqueness while still promoting national unity, and in doing so he invokes the federal spirit: "*We must constantly come back to the spirit of federalism*: the idea that we must work together – respecting our differences – in order to achieve our common objectives."[1]

Trudeau's reference to the federal spirit was not out of the ordinary; many world leaders have used the term. Take, for instance, Indian opposition leader Sonia Gandhi's criticism of the national government, saying "the spirit of federalism, which is an integral part of our constitution, is all but forgotten."[2] The problem is that, as Burgess identified, the term is "as ambiguous as it is seductive."[3] This ambiguity gives political leaders and policymakers flexibility to define the federal spirit and federal values in a way that suits them. But can we assess the vibrancy of federal values more objectively?

We can, but the key is to focus on public attitudes and values, rather than the actions of government or political elites. The core claim of federal political culture is that successful federalism is built on a commitment to federal values amongst citizens. Accordingly, this chapter focuses on the question of how we measure public attachment to federalism. Given debates about subsidiarity's closeness to federalism, this chapter also explores the relationship between the two concepts through the lens of developing a world-first measure of public attitudes toward subsidiarity. The previous chapter examined how subsidiarity's meaning was lost, and identified three underlying elements (decentralism, nonabsorption, and support) that we might use to find its meaning again. To echo Duchacek's analogy of a map of federalism,[4] we now have an "X" marking the spot where we might locate subsidiarity's value and meaning as a principle related to the federal spirit and that contributes to successful federalism. The challenge for this chapter is to chart a course to help reach that spot.

Therefore, this chapter focuses on examining how to study public attitudes in a federal context. The chapter begins by tracing the development of measures of federal political culture, charting the pathway from Duchacek's "blank space" to the creation of the measures used in this study. Next, the chapter details the design of a new measure of subsidiarity values, which is a world-first in subsidiarity research. The third section details the methodological considerations of the study on which this book is based, outlining the procedures by which the International Constitutional Values Surveys (ICVS) were administered. Finally, the chapter concludes with some initial comparative results. Specifically, it provides an overview of the levels of attachment to federal and subsidiarity values and tests the relationship between the two sets of values. It tests two questions central to understanding subsidiarity's meaningfulness in federal systems: (1) is subsidiarity more highly valued in federal than nonfederal countries, and (2) is there a significant relationship between subsidiarity and federal values? The key finding is that, while there is some association between federal and subsidiarity values, it is not strong and does not follow the same pattern everywhere, revealing that the relationship between these two principles is more nuanced than is often assumed. These results therefore set the scene for the detailed country-level analysis presented in Part II of this book.

MEASURING FEDERAL VALUES

As noted in chapter 2, there are a variety of ways to understand and measure federal political culture. Even the narrower focus on federal constitutional values taken in this book has an important history.

Cole, Kincaid, and Rodriguez pioneered the measurement of federal political culture in their 2004 survey of respondents from the US, Canada, and Mexico.[5] The authors sought to capture three aspects of federal political culture: (1) governmental ("a federal form of government … is preferable to any other kind of government"), (2) psychological/sociological ("a country with diversity is preferable compared to one without it"), and (3) decision-making ("bargaining with a wide variety of groups with different opinions is preferable to having a strong leader making decisions on what they think is best"). Cole and colleagues combined responses to the items to form a federal political culture scale, and found that the mean scores in the three countries conformed to their expectations, with Mexico on average having the weakest federal political culture, and Canada having the strongest.[6]

Brown took a different approach in the Australian Constitutional Values Surveys (ACVS), asking respondents to rate the desirability of different features of federal governances – namely, the division of power, having different laws in different parts of the country, being able to elect different parties at different levels of government, and different governments arguing over responsibility for an issue.[7] The four items did not scale, but nevertheless enabled the categorization of respondents along a six-point spectrum of federalists and nonfederalist counterparts that were "strong," "clear," or "conflicted." These items produced stable results across four surveys from 2008 to 2014.

The North American and Australian approaches were brought together as part of an international comparative project, starting with a workshop of experts in federalism at the 2014 International Political Science Association World Conference.[8] Subsequently, the 2014 iteration of ACVS included both the North American measures, as well as an expanded set of items based on the Australian model. Subsequent analysis helped produce a four-item measure of federal constitutional values (as a subcomponent of federal political culture),[9] listed below. These items were used in the 2016 and 2018 ICVS on which this study is based.

The measure asked respondents to rate the desirability of four features that are central to federal governance:

A Having power divided up between different levels of government ("divided power")
B Allowing different laws in response to varying needs and conditions in different parts of [country] ("different laws")

C Allowing the governments of different parts of [country] to get involved in decision-making on national issues ("participation")
D Different levels of government being forced to respect each other's roles and responsibilities when dealing with a problem ("respect")

Items A and B were retained from earlier versions of ACVS and are designed to capture what are often thought to be the fundamental features and benefits of federal governance, namely dividing power and sovereignty, and the capacity to adapt law and policy to reflect the needs of constituents.[10] Items C and D were new developments in the 2016 surveys, and were developed by Brown and colleagues following a series of workshops with international experts in federalism.[11] Item C was designed to cover the ability of federal systems to facilitate geographic representation and pluralism, while Item D taps into the German concept of *bundestreue*, a principle of "comity," "loyalty," "fidelity," or "faithfulness" in intergovernmental relations.[12]

Overall, the four items capture design features and values that are typical of or uniquely strong in federal systems. Each item individually taps into a distinct part of federal governance, but together the measures provide a deep insight into federal values as a whole. Notwithstanding the diversity of the items and the inherent challenge of "reconciling principles that are, *prima facie*, contradictory,"[13] a factor analysis of responses to ICVS confirmed that all four items load onto one dimension, in all countries. This means that, while the four items are aimed at a different element of federalism, participants answer all four items in consistent ways suggesting that their responses are driven by deeper federal values.

The items also used wording which does not rely on the term "federal," to avoid complications arising from any lack of familiarity with the term or potential conflicting meanings. Even in federal countries, the meaning of "federalist" may vary – from support for the coming or holding together of political units (i.e., "federationist"),[14] to support for stronger integration or national governmental powers, to support for stronger states' rights and decentralization (as is more often the case in Australia).[15] With any of these, the concept may have positive connotations or negative ones (e.g., Quebec citizens' view of a "federal" position as favouring integration, even when valuing the system itself as providing some defence against that).[16] Further, by avoiding the "federal" terminology, the survey could be readily deployed in nonfederal settings, thereby allowing an examination of federal constitutional values outside formally federal institutions. McGrane and Berdahl's study of Canadian federal political culture experimented with the inclusion of a specific reference to federalism (versus the more generic approach taken in ICVS), and found a moderate but significant effect.[17] While the authors made a compelling argument that in the Canadian case including the word "federal" is important to capturing the public's experience, for an international comparative study like ICVS the generic approach is more appropriate.

The approach taken, with its focus on federal constitutional values, clearly emphasizes citizens' attitudes and expectations of government. As discussed in chapter 2, this approach inevitably shies away from the bigger questions of the sociological elements of federal political culture. In terms of this book's study of the relationship between decentralization, subsidiarity and the federal spirit, the focus on constitutional values is the most appropriate because it keeps the focus on issues of governance. While broader sociological factors undoubtedly have some influence on federal values, these approaches contain too much uncertainty and abstraction to usefully test the connection between federal and subsidiarity values and meaningfully contribute to understanding federal success. This book therefore charts a safer course through these new waters, and leaves the broader sociological questions to future research.

MEASURING SUBSIDIARITY VALUES

The measurement of attitudes toward subsidiarity has a short history. Earlier versions of ACVS purported to capture subsidiarity values by asking respondents to choose between two statements: "It is better for decisions to be made at the lowest level of government competent to deal with the decision," or "It is better for as many decisions as possible to be made at the higher levels of government." This approach was consistent with the principle's narrow use as a guide for decentralism in the Australian debate.[18] However, recognizing the principle's meaning as broader than decentralism might have significant implications for the supposed relationship between federalism and subsidiarity. Accordingly, an expanded measure of subsidiarity was developed for the surveys used in this study.

A new, three-item approach was adopted for measuring attitudes to capture a wider scope of subsidiarity's meaning. This was fielded as part of the 2016 ICVS, and repeated in 2017 (Australia) and 2018 (Belgium, Canada, France, Germany, Switzerland, the UK, and the US) respectively. This new approach is one of the key empirical contributions of this book, as it presents a world-first holistic measure of public attitudes toward subsidiarity. Accordingly, considerable detail is provided to the methodology behind the measure. The surveys retained the item used in the 2008 to 2014 iterations of ACVS, which measures decentralist values, but then added two further items which are described after considering the broader approach.

As with the federalism measures, the surveys took the approach of avoiding express use of the word "subsidiarity." There were two reasons for doing so: first, there were concerns citizens would apply different interpretations to "subsidiarity," as scholars do, if they recognized it at all. Second, the consideration of the historical development of subsidiarity in chapter 3 showed that values of decentralism, nonabsorption, and support long predate the term "subsidiarity." Therefore, it is more useful to target these values directly, rather than attempting to tie them to the word "subsidiarity." Of course, this necessarily means that the survey items will be an approximation of attitudes toward the core values of subsidiarity, and in some ways prevents respondents from bringing their own meaning to the term. However, restricting respondents in this way allows for consistency in measuring attitudes toward the principle (and, in turn, its relationship with federalism).

The surveys retained the 2008–14 ACVS approach of presenting respondents with a pair of dichotomous options, and asking them to pick which one they prefer or aligns more closely with their views. This approach is easy to understand, because it takes complex ideas about subsidiarity and government responsibility, and turns them into a simple question: "would you rather government be more like X, or more like Y?" However, this approach is limited because it does not allow for much variation within the sample. To retain the benefit of the "X or Y" questioning, but still introduce some more variance in the sample, an "unfold" question was added. After participants nominated their preferred option (e.g., "it is better for decisions to be made at the lowest level") they were then asked whether they were "strongly" of that view, or "tend to be" of that view. Combining the two parts of the item produces a four-point scale of attitudes toward subsidiarity.

The three items used to measure subsidiarity values (tables 4.1 to 4.3) each targeted a different element of the principle, testing dif-

Table 4.1
Decentralist subsidiarity survey item

Thinking of the federal government as being the highest level of government, and state and then local as being lower levels of government, which one of the following comes closest to your view?			
It is better for as many decisions as possible to be made at the higher levels of government		It is better for decisions to be made at the lowest level of government competent to deal with the decision	
(Anti-subsidiarity)		(Pro-subsidiarity)	
1	2	3	4
(Strongly hold view)	(Tend to hold view)	(Tend to hold view)	(Strongly hold view)

Note: The wording is as per the surveys.

ferent aspects in which subsidiarity might be related to or entwined with the federal spirit. Respectively, the three items measure decentralism, nonabsorption, and support – each is considered in turn.

As discussed, the decentralism measure (table 4.1) matched the item already used in the previous surveys, although it added the new "unfold" question. There was good reason to retain the 2008–14 wording. This question captured the typical view of subsidiarity, and its consideration of governance at higher or lower levels cuts to the heart of the issue of whether decentralism and "thinking local" is an essential part of the federal ideal and spirit. While this chapter raised concerns above about using the item as a measure of subsidiarity as a whole, there is nothing to suggest that it does not work as a measure of decentralism. In fact, previous analysis of the Australian data suggested that this item performed reliably and produced valid results.[19] This item has also had the benefit of several rounds of pilot testing over the years.

The second item sought to measure attitudes toward nonabsorption (table 4.2), reflecting Hittinger's argument that subsidiarity "is proposed as a principle of nonabsorption, not a principle that necessarily requires devolution."[20] It asked participants to "imagine a situation where a lower level of government is responsible for a particular task, but a higher level of government thinks it could do a better job and wants to take over the task itself." They were then presented with the following options: "A higher level of government should not be able to just take over a task that is the responsibility of a lower level,

Table 4.2
Nonabsorptionist subsidiarity survey item

Imagine a situation where a lower level of government is responsible for a particular task, but a higher level of government thinks it could do a better job and wants to take over the task itself:			
The higher level should be able to just take over the task itself, whether the lower level likes it or not		A higher level of government should not be able to just take over a task that is the responsibility of a lower level, simply because it thinks it could do a better job	
(Anti-subsidiarity)		(Pro-subsidiarity)	
1	2	3	4
(Strongly hold view)	(Tend to hold view)	(Tend to hold view)	(Strongly hold view)

Note: The wording is as per the surveys.

simply because it thinks it could do a better job" (pro-subsidiarity); or "The higher level should be able to just take over the task itself, whether the lower level likes it or not" (anti-subsidiarity). Exploring the tension between a higher level taking over, or being prevented from doing so, addresses the potential of subsidiarity as attaching to confederal ideals of a strict division of power.

There are several crucial elements here. The first is that the higher level only *thinks* it could do a better job, as opposed to some omnipotent and objective knowledge that it could in fact do a better job. Had the item been worded where the higher level could objectively do better, there was a risk that participants would interpret the question as simply asking "do you want responsibility to go to the best government for the job?" or even "do you want government to do a good job?" While these questions of competence are certainly relevant to subsidiarity (and correspondingly, to public attitudes toward the principle), it is likely that respondents would almost all have answered in the affirmative, significantly reducing the utility of the item. In order to provide meaningful and practical responses, this item necessarily falls short of Chaplin's assertion that subsidiarity is about giving power to the "right level,"[21] since determining which level is the right one is itself a question that will be influenced by one's values and beliefs.[22]

In addition, the item was framed in terms of what the *higher* level thinks. This is important because, as Føllesdal notes, one of the defin-

Table 4.3
Supportive subsidiarity survey item

Which of these statements comes closest to your view?			
Lower levels of government should find their own resources to fulfil their responsibilities, without relying on support from higher levels of government		It is part of the job of higher levels of government to support lower levels with the resources they need to fulfil their responsibilities	
(Anti-subsidiarity)		(Pro-subsidiarity)	
1	2	3	4
(Strongly hold view)	(Tend to hold view)	(Tend to hold view)	(Strongly hold view)

Note: The wording is as per the surveys.

ing characteristics of subsidiarity (and key reasons for its complexity) is that there is confusion and debate as to who should get to decide whether a higher level is more competent or not.[23] As Føllesdal points out, this is something that is often not explicitly acknowledged, but rather develops according to the conception of subsidiarity in question.[24] The survey items tap into this debate by providing for it in the options: the anti-subsidiarity option prefers the higher level's judgment (allowing for intervention on the basis of what it thinks is best), while the pro-subsidiarity option favours lower-level assessment, essentially giving a veto against higher-level interference.

Finally, it is significant that the higher level wants to "take over," rather than simply "get involved." This is to distinguish this item from the notion of supportive subsidiarity, where the higher level might simply lend resources and expertise to assist the lower level in doing a better job.

The third measure addressed supportive subsidiarity (table 4.3), which is an often-overlooked element of the principle. It invoked Brennan's description of a positive limb of subsidiarity, which Evans and Zimmerman note as being tied to notions of "assistance or help."[25] Additionally, Komonchak's argument that subsidiarity is about "helping others help themselves" is also relevant.[26] Including a measure of supportive subsidiarity is critical, both to capture a holistic picture of subsidiarity values and to test subsidiarity's connection to federal values; a supportive relationship between governments is potentially far removed from federal ideals that emphasize competition between jurisdictions.

Capturing the notion of subsidiarity as "helping others help themselves" is difficult to convey in a manner suitable for a public attitude survey. On the one hand, it was desirable to keep what was meant by "support" fairly abstract (as outlined in chapter 3, while support is often financial, it can also be provided by sharing information and expertise, or by delivering other kinds of resources). On the other hand, respondents generally answer better to questions that are more concrete and "real-life oriented." Balancing the need to make the question as relatable as possible to participants, without unduly restricting their interpretation of "support," the question asked respondents to choose between: "Lower levels of government should find their own resources to fulfil their responsibilities, without relying on support from higher levels of government;" and "It's part of the job of higher levels of government to support lower levels with the resources they need to fulfil their responsibilities." The word "resources" is a good compromise, as it has enough financial connotations for respondents to see how support might be provided, but can also be understood in a broader sense: "resources" may refer to expertise or human resources to get a job done, or training or data collection – activities that Metzenbaum terms as "learning and leader roles" for federal agencies to help lower levels harness the benefits of policy innovation and learning.[27]

Notably, the three items are not intended to come together to form an overall "subsidiarity scale." This is because the three elements, while clearly related under the broad umbrella of the subsidiarity principle, are best understood in their individual components. Returning to the personality analogy from chapter 3, personality tests utilizing the five-factor model do not attempt to reduce to a single scale; instead, there are separate scales for each of the five personality dimensions. Similarly, we will be best placed to capture the nuances of subsidiarity's meaning by addressing each element individually, and looking at the overall pattern of values without consolidating them into a single scale. Reliability analysis on the data confirmed the appropriateness of this approach, as Cronbach's alpha (which tests the reliability of a scale) fell short of acceptable standards in each case. This finding is useful, as it confirms that the measures are well positioned to deal with the complexity of subsidiarity's meaning.

SURVEY METHOD

Having explained the core measures used, this section details the context in which those measures were deployed by providing an overview of the key survey instruments. This book primarily draws on data from ICVS 2016–18, which are nationally representative surveys of respondents in Australia (2016 and 2017); Canada, Germany, the UK, and the US (2016 and 2018); and Belgium, France, and Switzerland (2018). ICVS has its genesis in ACVS, which were established in 2008 and ran every other year to 2014. ACVS built on previous research by Brown and colleagues,[28] providing insights into the way Australian citizens perceive and value their political and legal structures.[29]

The 2008–14 Australian surveys were conducted as computer-assisted telephone interviews (CATI) and ran for approximately twenty minutes. Respondents were selected as a stratified sample, with nationally representative quotas set by region (states and territories), gender, and age. Landline telephone numbers within these constraints were randomly generated, and a screening question was used to randomly select participants over the age of eighteen within a household.

ICVS emerged from these Australian studies to harness international efforts to measure attitudes toward federalism.[30] To accommodate the expanded case selection, ICVS was fielded online. Online surveys are increasingly common,[31] driven by the fact that it is becoming easier to reach participants online rather than through traditional landline random-digit dialling; the pervasiveness of online technology makes participants more accessible. This is especially the case for young people, who are difficult to reach in phone surveys, although those over the age of sixty-five may remain easier to reach via landline than computer. Nationally representative samples for each country were obtained via stratified random sampling, with quotas set for region, age, and gender. Table 4.4 details the sample sizes for each survey and country.

In addition to their efficiency, online surveys also have the advantage of giving participants time to consider their answers. While ICVS was designed to take approximately fifteen minutes to complete, respondents were not bound by time, and could therefore take as long as they needed to answer each question. This gave participants the opportunity to read and re-read the items to ensure they understood what they were being asked.

Table 4.4
Sample sizes for ICVS (2016–18)

	Australia	*Belgium*	*Canada*	*France*	*Germany*	*Switzerland*	*UK*	*US*
2016	1,222	–	1,015	–	1,030	–	1,030	1,021
2018	1,526	1,021	1,034	1,021	1,011	1,000	1,019	1,041

Note: Belgium, France, and Switzerland were surveyed only in 2018.

Despite the benefits of online surveys, researchers have identified some limitations with the online format.[32] In addition to the difficulty of sampling from older generations discussed above, perhaps the biggest limitation is the motivation of participants and incentive structure for completing surveys. Where respondents to the CATI received no direct reward for participating, online surveys often provide a system where participants receive points, gift cards, or store credit for completing enough surveys. While these incentives are good for encouraging participation, they can distort results as some participants may simply complete the survey as fast as possible, and with no regard to their answers, in order to be rewarded. This is less likely with telephone surveys where there is no disincentive from withdrawing at any time, and where the presence of the interviewer also creates some social pressure to take the survey seriously. Thus, concerns about whether "what actors say is so, is so"[33] are amplified by the online format.

A particular issue here are respondents who selected "Don't Know" or "Can't Say" options on the items measuring federal and subsidiarity values described above. A comparison of the 2016 Australian dataset with the results from previous years (where the CATI method was used) revealed that respondents to the online surveys were more likely to choose a "Don't Know" option,[34] suggesting that the administration format did have an influence. While there were several options for dealing with these responses, including imputing data based on a participant's other responses or the mean score, the best option was to remove "Don't Know" responses to the items from the dataset. Doing so increases our confidence that participants who did answer understood the question; the substantial number of "Don't Knows" indicates that respondents were more than willing to select this option (as opposed to feeling pressure to give a "viable" response without understanding the question). By implication, then, participants who did answer probably felt that they were informed enough to do so, increasing the validity of the measures used.

ICVS used the same questions as ACVS, apart from some minor adaptations to local contexts (such as replacing "State" with "Region" in Belgium, "Province" in Canada, "Land" in Germany, "Canton" in Switzerland, and "Region" in the UK) and languages.[35] This ensures comparisons between the case countries are standardized and are therefore more reliable. Further, experts in federal studies translated the non-English versions to ensure the surveys accurately captured any special meanings. Importantly, in European countries, the survey included a number of cues specifically instructing participants not to consider the EU in their answers to avoid complications arising from attitudes toward the supra-state. This issue was especially charged in the UK in 2016, as the survey was conducted mere weeks before the Brexit referendum in June 2016. While the European Union will undoubtedly have some influence in respondents' perceptions, these specific instructions were designed to ensure that this influence is limited to diffuse political culture, rather than direct attitudes toward the EU.

SUBSIDIARITY IN THE MAP OF FEDERALISM: INITIAL RESULTS

This section sets out the initial comparative results of the surveys. It begins with the federal and subsidiarity values of each country, setting a foundation for the analysis to come. Next, this section turns to the two key questions from the beginning of this chapter: is attachment to subsidiarity higher in federal than nonfederal countries? And is there a significant relationship between subsidiarity values and attachment to federal design principles? This analysis reveals that the relationship between subsidiarity and federalism – in federal and nonfederal countries – is more complicated than often assumed. The nuances of these findings are therefore unpacked in subsequent chapters.

Federal and Subsidiarity Values in the Selected Countries

Table 4.5 sets out the proportion of respondents from each country who rated each of the four federal design principles as "desirable" or "undesirable." The table columns are ordered according to the average strength of attachment to federal values across the four items,[36] con-

Table 4.5
Attachment to federal design principles by country (ICVS 2017–18)

	BEL	AUS	UK	GER	FRA	USA	CAN	SWI
Having power divided between different levels of government ("divided power")								
Desirable	57.0	64.0	69.8	73.9	80.9	79.5	80.4	78.7
Undesirable	43.0	36.0	30.1	26.1	19.1	20.5	19.6	21.3
Allowing different laws in response to varying needs and conditions in different parts of [country] ("different laws")								
Desirable	53.8	57.9	55.7	47.0	66.3	68.7	70.7	64.2
Undesirable	46.2	42.1	44.3	53.0	33.6	31.3	29.3	35.8
Allowing the governments of different parts of [country] to get involved in decision-making on national issues ("participation")								
Desirable	53.6	74.6	72.3	80.8	78.8	74.2	78.3	88.0
Undesirable	46.4	25.4	27.8	19.2	21.2	25.7	21.7	12.0
Different levels of government being forced to respect each other's roles and responsibilities when dealing with a problem ("respect")								
Desirable	65.0	84.1	79.4	89.4	80.6	84.0	85.3	89.0
Undesirable	35.0	15.9	20.6	10.6	19.3	16.0	14.7	11.0

firming that the classically "successful" federations of Switzerland, Canada, and the US generally had the strongest federal values. At the other end, Belgians and Australians commonly saw less value in the four federal design features, which aligns with the ongoing debates about the suitability of federalism in those countries. Belgians in particular were relatively evenly divided on three of the four items. Most of the federal design principles were endorsed in Germany, although not as strongly as in other countries, which is itself remarkable given Germany's reputation as a classically successful federation. The other surprising result was the strength of attachment to federal design principles in the UK and France. In fact, the proportion of respondents who thought dividing power was desirable was higher in France than in any other country. This finding raises the important questions about how nonfederal countries should accommodate or address strong spirits of federalism amongst citizens.

Turning to subsidiarity values, figures 4.1, 4.2, and 4.3, respectively, present levels of attachment to decentralist, nonabsorptionist, and

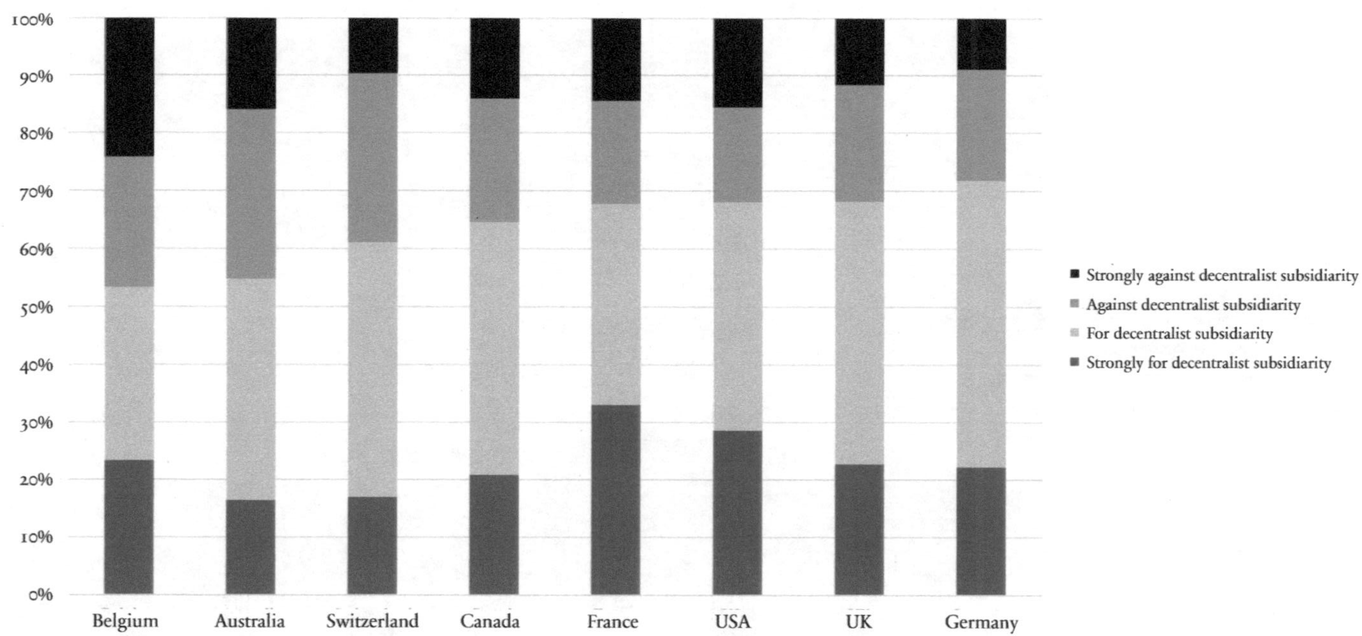

Figure 4.1 Attitudes toward decentralist element of subsidiarity (least to most support) – ICVS 2017–18

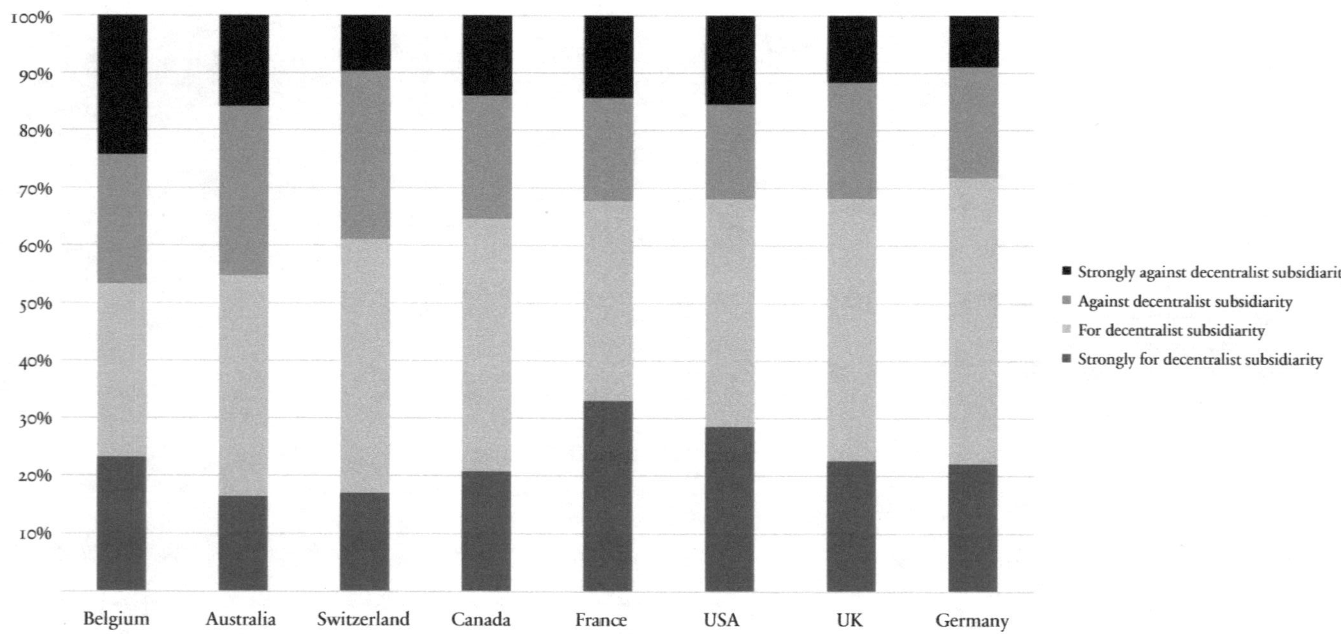

Figure 4.2 Attitudes toward nonabsorptionist element of subsidiarity (least to most support) – ICVS 2017–18

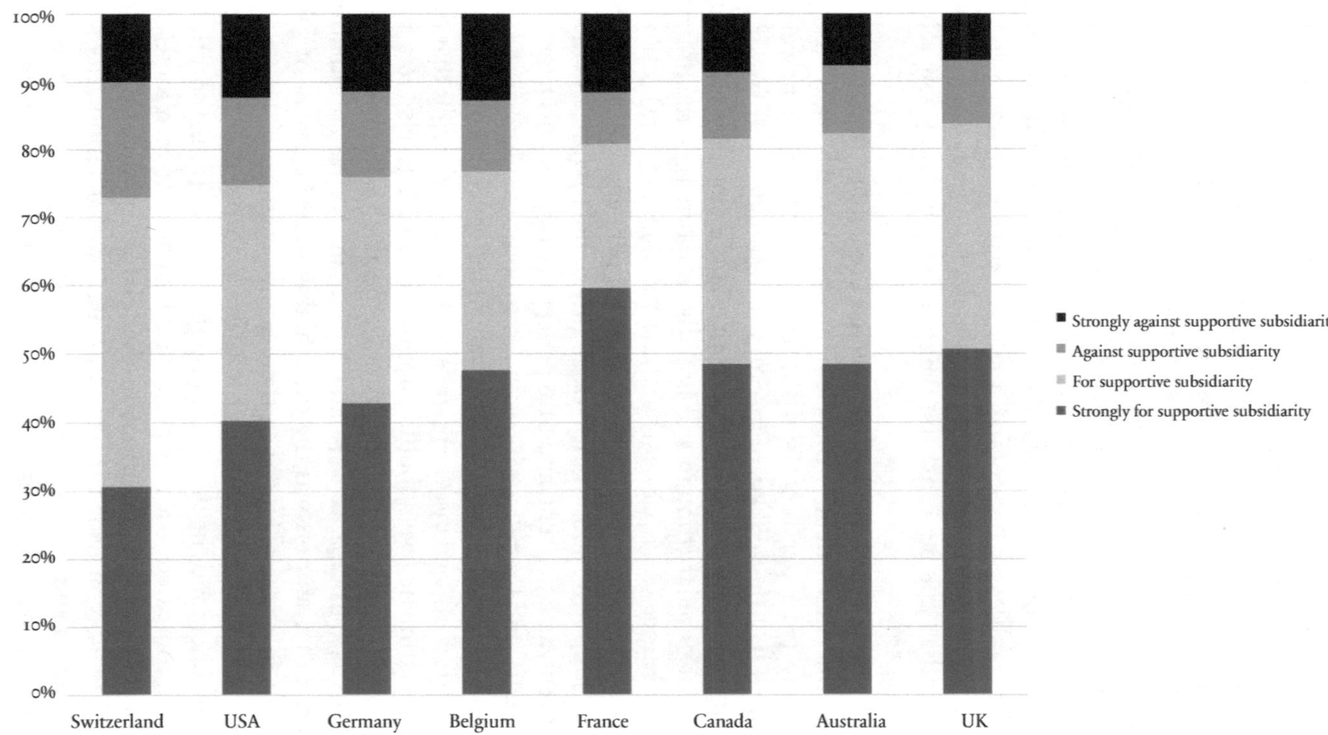

Figure 4.3 Attitudes toward supportive element of subsidiarity (least to most support) – ICVS 2017–18

supportive notions of subsidiarity. First, decentralism was broadly popular amongst respondents from all countries (although as seen in figure 4.1, it was generally the least popular of the three elements). In all eight cases, over half of respondents were "for" or "strongly for" government at the lowest level possible (figure 4.1). However, within this broad attachment, there are important variations. On average, Germans were the most likely to value the decentralist element of subsidiarity (71.8 per cent), followed by respondents from the UK (68.2 per cent), the US (68.1 per cent) and France (67.8 per cent). Comparatively lower levels of attachment to decentralism (though still high overall) were present in Canada (64.6 per cent) and Switzerland (61.1 per cent). Finally, only just over half of respondents from Australia (54.8 per cent) and Belgium (53.3 per cent) saw value in decentralism.

Second, nonabsorption was on average even more popular than decentralism. Attachment to this element was again especially strong in Germany (75.4 per cent) and the US (76.2 per cent); however, Switzerland had the highest proportion of respondents in favour of nonabsorption (77.9 per cent) (figure 4.2). This element of subsidiarity was least popular (though still broadly supported) in the unitary nations of France (61.7 per cent) and the UK (69.8 per cent), and the comparatively recently federal Belgium (55.4 per cent).

Finally, supportive subsidiarity was highly popular, with as many as 83.7 per cent, 82.3 per cent, and 81.6 per cent of respondents from the UK, Australia, and Canada seeing value in supportive subsidiarity (figure 4.3). This element was also highly valued in France (80.9 per cent). Three-quarters of Belgians, Germans, and Americans thought that the higher government levels should support the lower levels (76.9 per cent, 76.0 per cent, and 74.8 per cent, respectively). Lastly, 72.9 per cent of Swiss participants were attached to supportive subsidiarity. This meant that support was the most highly valued element of subsidiarity in most cases. However, there were variations in *how much* more it was valued. For example, there was a 7.2 per cent difference between support and the next most popular element (nonabsorption) in Canada, compared to a 21.5 per cent difference between these elements in Belgium. The variations in the relative importance of each element therefore provide further confirmation that subsidiarity as a whole is valued and understood differently in different countries.

It is possible that some respondents were drawn to supportive subsidiarity simply as a question of good governance; they interpreted the question as asking: do you want your governments to get along and help each other out? However, even if respondents did take this interpretation, this is still a valid understanding of supportive subsidiarity, as it reflects Komonchak's argument that higher orders should help lower orders to help themselves.[37] Thus, the strong attachment to supportive subsidiarity indicates that the item works as intended.

The results are unpacked in greater detail at the country level in the following chapters, exploring the factors unique to each case that might explain these findings. For the remainder of this chapter, the focus is on testing the two key questions about the relationship between subsidiarity and federalism – (1) are subsidiarity values higher in federal countries compared to nonfederal ones, and (2) is there a significant relationship between subsidiarity and federal values?

IS ATTACHMENT TO SUBSIDIARITY HIGHER AMONGST CITIZENS IN FEDERAL COUNTRIES THAN IN NONFEDERAL COUNTRIES?

To answer this question, responses to each of the three subsidiarity elements are compared. Doing so reveals that while there are important and significant differences between countries, these differences do not appear to be based on the federal constitutional structure of those countries.

A Games-Howell post hoc analysis of variance, which is designed to detect differences in mean scores and is robust against data that does not follow a normal distribution or bell curve (which is the case here), revealed that many of the differences between cases were indeed significant.[38] Starting with decentralism, Australia and Belgium stand apart, with mean attachment to subsidiarity significantly lower than all other cases (except each other). This confirms that subsidiarity, when viewed as a principle of decentralism, is not especially meaningful in Australia. Here, public sentiment echoes Evans's comment that the Australian High Court has "disregarded" subsidiarity as a constitutional principle.[39] Decentralism was also not overwhelmingly popular in Belgium, potentially reflecting the ongoing "search for a proper "centre of gravity" in Belgian federalism."[40] The third lowest case, Switzerland, also differed significantly from the higher-scoring Germany and France. This is an important finding, as it aligns with Dardanelli and Mueller's observations that despite its extremely decentralized foundations, Switzerland is becoming more centralized in some policy fields.[41] It suggests that either while decentralism is still reasonably highly valued, Swiss attitudes might be changing, or the majority of citizens remain attached to decentralism and policymakers should be wary of further centralization in the Swiss federation. While future longitudinal research is necessary to test and confirm either interpretation, this finding highlights the value and importance of measuring public attachment to subsidiarity.

The lack of any significant differences amongst the higher-scoring cases (Germany, the UK, the US, and France) is itself important. The fact that the UK and France, the two nonfederal cases in this study, scored about as highly on the decentralism item as the classic federal nations of Germany, the US, Canada, and Switzerland and significantly outscored Australia and Belgium, calls into question whether federal institutions or constitutions are necessary for subsidiarity to flourish. The alternative interpretation is that there is evidence of a federal political culture that could sustain federalism.[42]

To the extent that constitutional protection of the sovereignty of subnational units is a defining feature of a federal system, there appears to be a stronger connection between federalism and nonabsorptionist elements of the principle than the decentralist aspect, in that respondents from new (Belgium) or nonfederations (France, UK) were on average comparatively less attached to nonabsorptionist subsidiarity than those from established federal systems. This finding suggests that subsidiarity is important to federalism, but it is less about decentralization and "thinking local," and more about respecting the boundaries of responsibility between levels. This finding also aligns with Chaplin's comment that subsidiarity is about ensuring decisions are made at the right level, but is not about determining what the right level is.[43] In a federation, it seems subsidiarity is more important as an enforcer of the constitutional assignment of responsibility than in deciding how those responsibilities should be allocated.

Finally, the results for the supportive element suggest that subsidiarity is not valued more highly in federal countries: attachment to supportive subsidiarity in the UK and France was on par with Australia and Canada, with over 80 per cent of respondents in those four countries valuing the principle. At the other end of the spectrum, value for supportive subsidiarity did not significantly differ between German, Swiss, and American respondents.

Overall, the analysis therefore suggests that subsidiarity can be important anywhere – it is not necessarily uniquely important or valued more highly in federal countries. However, the principle's "negative limb," which emphasizes nonabsorption, does seem to be more relevant to federal constitutional values.

IS THERE A SIGNIFICANT RELATIONSHIP BETWEEN SUBSIDIARITY VALUES AND ATTACHMENT TO FEDERALIST PRINCIPLES?

Having demonstrated that subsidiarity values are not necessarily higher in federal countries, the question of the potential importance of a strong connection between subsidiarity and federal values (which may exist outside federal structure) remains. A factor analysis of the four federalism items and three subsidiarity items was conducted with the aim of testing whether subsidiarity and federal values appear to stem from a single common factor. However, the results indicate that this is not the case – in all countries, the exploratory factor analysis identified at least two underlying factors. In all countries, the four federal items always loaded onto a single factor. In the UK, Canada, France, Switzerland, Belgium, and Australia, the three subsidiarity items all loaded onto a second factor, while in Germany and the US, decentralism and nonabsorption formed a second factor while supportive subsidiarity featured as a distinct third factor, potentially reflecting ideas that subsidiarity has positive and negative limbs.[44] It is clear, therefore, that attitudes toward subsidiarity and federalism can be regarded as separate. But is there *any* relationship between them?

A bivariate correlation analysis between the subsidiarity and federalism items revealed weak but significant relationships between many of the items, but not between all of them and not in every country. Some relationships stand out as especially relevant or consistently significant – the detailed results of the analysis are available in table A1, available as part of an online appendix on the author's website.[45] First, the correlation between decentralism and dividing power – the "classic" core of the relationship between subsidiarity and federalism – was significant across all eight countries. Arguably, this provides some confirmation of Duchacek's idea that thinking in terms of local initiative is a sign of federalist values.[46] It also potentially reflects Weinstock's argument that "subsidiarity is a rule rather than a principle,"[47] in the sense that subsidiarity provides a (decentralist) guide for how power should be divided. However, this relationship was strongest in France and the UK ($r = .190$ and $.168$, respectively) – the two nonfederal cases. This suggests that, while citizens see a connected value in dividing power between the levels of government and decentralizing that power, this connection is not restricted to a formal or constitutional federal bargain.

The other consistently significant relationship across the eight countries was between supportive subsidiarity and respect between levels of government. This is a product of the strong attachment toward both items individually; the ideas that higher order governments should support lower order governments, and that all levels should be forced to respect each others' roles and responsibilities are popular sentiments. However, the connection between the two reflects the fact that these are not isolated ideals; higher levels can show their respect for the value and importance of lower levels by giving them the resources and support they need to fulfill their responsibilities.

In addition to these generally consistent relationships, some correlations in particular countries or groups of countries are worth highlighting. Notably, in Germany, Switzerland, and the US the strongest relationship was the correlation between nonabsorption and respect ($r = .140$, $.150$, and $.140$, respectively). In Germany and Switzerland, this potentially reflects notions of bundestreue (as described earlier). Histories of confederalism – which Føllesdal notes as being central to some conceptualizations of subsidiarity[48] – in Switzerland and the US are also relevant, where the different levels of government are expected to respect each others' roles and responsibilities by not absorbing their functions. These themes are further explored in the next chapter.

Another especially noteworthy result is the relationship in Germany between supportive subsidiarity and having different laws in different parts of the country. This was the only significant negative correlation observed, meaning that people who thought higher levels should support lower levels were less likely to think that having different laws is a desirable feature of a multilevel system of governance. This potentially reflects the "equivalent living conditions" clause in the German Basic Law, which operates as an exception to the subsidiarity principle – a plausible interpretation is that German respondents who thought the higher levels should support lower levels felt that this support should be done in the interests of promoting equal living conditions, rather than fostering or facilitating diversity. Overall, these results must be interpreted in the context of the weakness of these relationships – no correlation was stronger than $r = .190$. Accordingly, while there are some significant associations, at best we can only say that subsidiarity and federal values are related in a very limited sense. This has important implications for the debate in the literature and in practice over whether the two doctrines are to be regarded as linked or separate. Specifically, there is partial support for the hypothesis that the values are linked. This is a critical new discovery for better understanding how federations operate because it adds nuance to long-standing claims that the two principles are inextricably linked and that "thinking local" is necessary to the federal values that animate successful federations. Subsidiarity clearly has some relevance to federal values, but it is clear that we must adopt a broader understanding of its meaning to understand its full importance.

CONCLUSION

This chapter examined how we might fill in some of the blank spaces in the map of our understanding of federalism by exploring federal and subsidiarity values. It examined some of the ways of measuring public attachment to federal design principles, and showcased an innovative world-first measure of subsidiarity values. The chapter then presented some initial comparative results, and tested long-standing theories about subsidiarity's importance in federal countries and the relationship between subsidiarity and federal values. The analysis highlighted the complexity of the relationship between subsidiarity and federalism, with weak but significant correlations between subsidiarity and federal values emerging in federal and nonfederal countries. However, some clear patterns still emerge. Nonabsorptionist subsidiarity seemed to matter in federal countries more than nonfederal. Further, it seemed to have a stronger connection to federal values and was more highly valued in Switzerland, Germany, and the US – three "classic" federations. Conversely, supportive subsidiarity seems more important in Canada and Australia – two federations that have generally adopted a more cooperative approach to federalism (with varying degrees of success). Subsidiarity and federal values in the UK also often matched those found in Canada and Australia. Finally, Belgium and France stood out as anomalous in their own way – Belgians were generally the least attached to subsidiarity and federal design principles, even compared to respondents in nonfederal countries, while French respondents were surprisingly strongly attached to the two principles.

In the following three chapters, these observations are unpacked in detail, uncovering the complex role subsidiarity plays in a federation and exploring the nuances and variations unique to each country.

PART TWO

Survey Findings

5

Classic Federations

Germany, Switzerland, and the US

The US, Switzerland, and Germany stand tall as three archetypical federations "commonly viewed as successful" by scholars,[1] and as the oldest federations in the world, the US and Switzerland in particular serve as the models on which other federations are based. As discussed in chapter 3, Germany also has a rich history of federal principles dating back to the Holy Roman Empire. The results from ICVS, which revealed strong attachment to federal design principles among the citizens in these countries, are therefore unsurprising. These results confirm many assumptions about federal constitutional values and their role in a successful federation, highlighting that on average, citizens in the US, Switzerland, and Germany "think federal" in their approach to structural design principles, and do so to a higher degree compared to citizens from other federations. Similarly, attachment to subsidiarity values was also generally high in the three countries, supporting the view amongst many scholars and practitioners that subsidiarity and federalism are meaningfully linked. However, contrary to the common view that decentralist approaches to subsidiarity are the key ingredient in a successful federation, the results from the surveys indicated that the nonabsorptionist element of subsidiarity was more highly valued by respondents in these three countries. This finding stands out for two reasons. First, it challenges modern thinking about "subsidiarity as decentralization" and its role in federalism. Second, the comparison to other cases showed that in other federations (such as Canada and Australia), the difference between levels of attachment to each of the three elements was greater and supportive subsidiarity was held in higher esteem, suggesting that the federal and subsidiarity values that drive successful federalism in the US, Switzerland, and Germany are not universal. In turn, these findings raise important questions, which this chapter addresses: what factors contribute to the overall high attachment to federalism and subsidiarity values in these three countries? Why is nonabsorption the most highly valued element of subsidiarity, and what impact does this have on the federal political cultures of these nations? How can scholars and practitioners use this new understanding of federal and subsidiarity values in the US, Switzerland, and Germany, and particularly the emphasis on nonabsorption over decentralization, to overcome the significant social and political challenges facing each country?

This chapter answers these questions by examining the three cases in greater detail. The nuances of each case are unpacked in turn, but two themes cut across each country: a history of confederalism, and the influence of language. These two themes form an analytical frame for the chapter, guiding its analysis of federal values in each country.

UNITED STATES OF AMERICA

The US is a nation divided. Enduring tensions about partisanship, identity, and civil rights dominate political discourse in America, and the country is heavily polarized.[2] These divisions present significant challenges for US federalism. Public trust in political institutions, especially the federal government, is at a record low after decades of erosion.[3] Nevertheless, a majority (58.1 per cent) of respondents to ICVS felt that the federal system of having three levels of government was working well, and attachment to federalist design principles remains high. Further, while trust in the federal government is waning, trust in state and local governments has held steady, suggesting that a strong commitment to federalism offers a pathway for the US to navigate these turbulent times.[4] But first we must understand and appreciate the reasons behind the federal constitutional values and attachment to subsidiarity in the US. This section begins with a detailed analysis of the attitudes toward subsidiarity and federal design principles, revealing that political affiliation and race stand out as particularly important drivers of public attitudes. From the foundation of that analysis, this section then examines the potential reasons driving these findings, placing particular emphasis on America's confederal history as a nexus between subsidiarity and federalism.

Table 5.1
Federal and subsidiarity values in the US (ICVS 2016–18)

%	*2016*	*2018*
Decentralism	74.2	68.1
Nonabsorption	77.1	76.2
Support	71.1	74.8
Divided power	70.3	79.5
Different laws	60.5	68.7
Participation	57.9	74.2
Respect	73.1	84.0

Federal and Subsidiarity Values in the US

The results from the 2016 and 2018 ICVS reveal two important characteristics of public attitudes toward federalism and subsidiarity in the US – their overall strength (high levels of attachment on all elements) and consistency (little change between the two years). Table 5.1 presents the proportion of respondents who endorsed or desired each federal or subsidiarity value. Overall, between two-thirds and three-quarters of respondents were attached to each principle, revealing a clear and stable spirit of federalism and subsidiarity in both years. While two surveys conducted two years apart are not enough to demonstrate long-term stability, to have found any consistency between 2016 and 2018 given the massive upheavals in US politics during that time is an important finding. In a period marked by deep division and instability, most Americans appear to have common ground in seeing the value of federalist design principles and decentralism, nonabsorption, and support. But beneath the surface there are important differences between subgroups of the American population.

Most notably, a comparison of Republican and Democratic voters highlights an interesting dynamic at play (table 5.2). The timing of the surveys (June 2016 and April 2018) meant that we have data from when a Democratic (Barack Obama) and Republican (Donald Trump) president held office. While attitudes toward federal values were fairly consistent between voters of either party regardless of who was in power, attitudes toward subsidiarity differed substantially between party and year. In 2016 (under Obama), 85 per cent of

Table 5.2
Republican and Democrat federal and subsidiarity values, US (ICVS 2016–18)

%	*2016*		*2018*	
	Republican	*Democrat*	*Republican*	*Democrat*
Decentralism	85.2	56.8	67.1	68.5
Nonabsorption	85.1	63.5	72.9	79.9
Support	59.9	80.4	60.9	83.4
Divided power	83.6	86.6	77.8	82.1
Different laws	75.8	71.9	64.8	71.7
Participation	67.1	73.3	68.9	79.7
Respect	88.6	84.9	86.6	87.8

Republican voters thought that decisions should be made at the lowest level possible (85.2 per cent), and that a higher level should not be able to take over the responsibilities of a lower level (85.1 per cent). But in 2018 when Trump was president, this proportion decreased to 67.1 per cent and 72.9 per cent, respectively. The reverse pattern emerged among the Democratic voters, with the proportion of respondents who valued decentralism and nonabsorption increasing after Obama left office (56.8 per cent to 68.5 per cent, and 63.5 to 79.9 per cent, respectively). In other words, while attachment to subsidiarity was generally high across both sides of politics, respondents tended to prefer decentralist and nonabsorptionist elements of subsidiarity more when their preferred political party did not have power in the White House. This suggests that at least part of subsidiarity's appeal in America is its protective function – decentralization makes one less vulnerable to a president they dislike and nonabsorption prevents encroachment on state and local authority when the "other side" holds office at the federal level.[5] These are functions or benefits usually attributed to federalism, suggesting that there is a clear link between federal constitutional values and attitudes toward subsidiarity. Interestingly, however, when examining support for federalist design principles there were few notable differences between Republican and Democratic voters – federalist attitudes were stable across 2016 and 2018 (i.e., did not change much based on which president held office) and did not vary significantly between parties. A plausible interpretation of these results is that while baseline attitudes toward federalism (federal constitutional values) remain stable, subsidiarity's role in aid of federalism as a guide for allocating power fluctuates at the individual level but remains fairly constant in aggregate. For example, while most Americans see dividing power and having different laws around the country as desirable, when it comes to deciding *how* to divide power and *which* policies should be uniform/differentiated – questions to which subsidiarity offers guiding answers – partisan views have some influence.

Racial identity was also linked to differences in attitudes toward subsidiarity and (to a lesser extent) federal values. White respondents were more attached to every subelement of subsidiarity and federal values than African American, Asian American, and Hispanic respondents except for supportive subsidiarity (both years) and having different laws in different parts of the country (2018).

Two caveats apply to those findings: first, the sample was designed to include a nationally representative cross-section of the American population. In terms of race, this meant that the majority of respondents identified as white, while only small proportions identified with the minority groupings. While these proportions reflect census population data, it does mean that the smaller samples may not be completely reliable or representative. Second, comparison between years might be unreliable due to the smaller samples. Nevertheless, these findings do highlight potential differences in the subsidiarity values of ethnic groups in the US, with white Americans generally being more attached to subsidiarity than African American, Asian American, and Hispanic populations.

There are logical explanations for these results. While the treatment of non-white Americans has a poor history at all levels of government, state and local governments stand out as being especially prone to racist and prejudicial governance.[6] The Civil War, driven by southern states' desire to preserve slavery, is the most obvious example, but the Black Lives Matter movement, which focused much of its attention on state and county police departments' treatment of ethnic minorities, especially African Americans, offers a more recent example highlighting long-standing issues at the more local levels.

Of course, the influence of race and party affiliation on subsidiarity values are not completely independent of one another. Historical voting data shows that a higher proportion of racial minority voters favour the Democrats, while the Republican voter base is predominantly Caucasian. This was also true of ICVS respondents. Notably, however, the comparison between 2016 and 2018 showed a relatively constant effect for race, while the party affiliation variable revealed a stronger desire for decentralism and nonabsorption among voters whose preferred party was not in power. The most plausible interpretation of these results is therefore that, because the lived experience of race (especially for minority groups) is fairly constant, race has a stable influence on subsidiarity and federal values. By comparison, the fortunes of one's favoured party wax and wane – or conversely, an individual swings between parties – resulting in a two-paced set of attitudes where a certain baseline of citizens are attached to subsidiarity, but then above that subsidiarity values increase or decrease depending on which party holds office. This interpretation is confirmed by a linear regression testing the predictive value of race (white vs non-white) and party (Republican vs Democratic) on attitudes toward subsidiarity, with other demographic variables such as age, gender, education, and income added as controls. Racial identity emerged as the most important predictor, and party was the only other significant result.[7] The caveats about sampling different racial groups still apply, but, overall, these findings suggest that the strength of subsidiarity and federal values in America is driven by two of the most divisive issues in the US: race and politics. In this context, the fact that nonabsorptionist subsidiarity was the most highly valued element of subsidiarity makes perfect sense – it reflects a skepticism of "others" built into the American federation.

Nonabsorptionist Subsidiarity in US Federalism

The finding that US attitudes toward subsidiarity are influenced by divisive issues such as race and politics, while perhaps not surprising, is an important one. As this section discusses, this finding has critical implications for theories of subsidiarity, and for US federalism. Starting with subsidiarity theory, the strong attachment to the nonabsorptionist element of subsidiarity resonates with what Føllesdal describes as a "confederalist" interpretation of subsidiarity. As discussed in chapter 3, "confederal subsidiarity" takes its cues from the development of American federalism.[8] In particular, it is characterized by an emphasis on decentralized government as the best guarantee for liberty and protection against tyranny. This approach fiercely argues against undue interference from the centre and places few, if any, obligations on higher orders. Confederalism takes the individual as its main focus: "the principle of subsidiarity is, on this confederal account, thought to offer the best protection of individual liberty against tyranny."[9] Under this conception, subsidiarity is thus justified as a protection of individual freedom.

The US has a deep history of confederalism,[10] a legacy that continues into its modern federation. Before forming the United States of America, the thirteen colonies came together under the Articles of Confederation in 1777 to create a loose but unified American government. While the later US Constitution of 1787 expanded the role of the national government in the new federation, the Tenth Amendment (1791) retained much of the spirit of confederalism, providing: "The powers not delegated to the United States by the Constitution, nor prohibited by it to the States, are reserved to the States respectively, or to the people."

While the Supreme Court has declared the Tenth Amendment a truism that added "nothing to [the Constitution] as originally ratified,"[11] the amendment serves as an ongoing and explicit reminder of the confederalist approach behind the drafting of the Constitution. Calabresi and Bickford's analysis of the Supreme Court jurisprudence on subsidiarity also highlights the role and influence of nonabsorption in US federalism. The authors identify four key areas of US constitutional law where the Supreme Court has recognized and enforced subsidiarity: Congress' enumerated lawmaking powers, the dormant Commerce Clause, intergovernmental immunity, and federal jurisdiction case law.[12] Calabresi and Bickford's argument focuses on the common, decentralist interpretation of subsidiarity: in their words, "subsidiarity is the idea that matters should be decided at the lowest or least centralized competent level of government."[13] However, their analysis actually emphasizes the nonabsorptionist element of the principle, highlighting how in landmark decisions such as *United States v Lopez*, *Printz v United States*, *Gibbons v Ogden*, *McCulloch v Maryland*, *New York v United States*, and *Eirie Railroad Co v Tompkins*, the Supreme Court has consistently ruled in ways that protect states from having their power, responsibilities, or functions absorbed by the federal government.

The public attitudes results, together with analysis of institutional and jurisprudential features of federalism, points to division as a key driver of successful federalism in the US. Federalism works in America because of a strong desire amongst citizens to divide power and to staunchly defend against incursions on that division, and a judiciary that remains vigilant against potential absorptions of power. While this spirit of federalism and subsidiarity has made for a strong federation, its limitations are also apparent in the American society. The legacy of the Civil War and ongoing problems with the treatment of minorities highlights the devastating impact division can have on people, but other examples also abound, such as the slow national uptake of marriage equality, tenuous rights to abortion services for women, and a faltering response to the COVID-19 pandemic. In his inauguration address, President Joe Biden promised to write "an American story of … unity, not division."[14] Two pathways lead from this statement. The first is the possibility that division is so deeply ingrained in American society and its federal political culture that coming together is all but impossible. Accepting such a division as inevitable might further reinforce nonabsorptionist tendencies and subsidiarity's role in the federation, promoting state power against the federal government. The second possibility is that some divisions can be healed, and that Americans can come closer together, but at the cost of the nonabsorptionist approach to subsidiarity that drives the federation forward. The result would be a less divided America, but potentially also a less federal one. Whichever path is taken, it is clear that America faces significant challenges in the years ahead which will fundamentally alter its federal balance.

GERMANY

Academic opinion is divided on subsidiarity's status within the German federation. Some scholars such as Bröhmer argue that it remains the "flavour of the day,"[15] while others point to centralizing trends in some policy fields to raise concerns about subsidiarity's ongoing utility – for example, Taylor questioned whether subsidiarity was dying a slow death in Germany.[16] Subsidiarity is most clearly operationalized through Article 72(2) of the German Basic Law, which states that the federal government's ability to legislate in relation to concurrent powers is limited to situations where national legislation is in the national interest and necessary to establish "equivalent living conditions." This is a clear realization of both the decentralist and nonabsorptionist dimensions of subsidiarity. Specifically, the limitation on national control protects the Länder from central interference (nonabsorption), and codifies a preference for decentralized jurisdiction (decentralism). The third dimension is also evident in the form of power-sharing that *supports* poorer Länder. The provision that national

Table 5.3
Federal and subsidiarity values in Germany (ICVS 2016–18)

%	2016	2018
Decentralism	75.2	71.8
Nonabsorption	80.5	75.4
Support	74.1	76.0
Divided power	62.2	73.9
Different laws	39.7	47.0
Participation	69.2	80.8
Respect	76.9	89.4

legislation is permitted to establishing "equivalent living conditions" is reminiscent of Catholic notions of the common good and subsidiarity in the sense that it accepts centralization if it results in a better outcome. The German understanding of subsidiarity therefore encompasses all three elements of the principle, and its constitution explicitly provides a mechanism that makes subsidiarity meaningful.

However, reforms to Article 72(2) in 2006 reduced the scope of that provision (and consequently, of subsidiarity). Additionally, Taylor points to the increased use of the "equivalent living standards" clause as a signal that subsidiarity's importance in Germany is declining.[17] While the broader conceptualization of the principle developed in chapter 3 suggests that this clause still gives effect to subsidiarity, the divergence in perspective reinforces the importance of understanding public attachment to the principle: even if subsidiarity's position in the Basic Law is weakening, or changing, do the German people remain committed to decentralism, nonabsorption, and support? The results from chapter 4 suggest that they do, although in 2016 the decentralist and nonabsorptionist limbs were slightly more highly valued than the supportive element (see table 5.3). Further, in both 2016 and 2018, more German respondents placed value on decentralist subsidiarity than participants from any other country.

A Unified Approach to Subsidiarity

Unlike in the US, where race and party affiliation were significant predictors of subsidiarity values, analysis of the German results revealed no substantial differences in attitudes on the basis of voting preference, age, gender, level of education, or household income. This finding is important in itself, as it suggests that subsidiarity is highly valued across German society. In comparison to the US, German politics has been remarkably stable over the past two decades. Germany has had the same chancellor in Angela Merkel from 2006 to 2021, and its mixed-member proportionate electoral system lends itself to a more collaborative and less divisive approach to politics.

Further, attitudes toward subsidiarity did not vary significantly between Länder. Bavarians were on average strongly attached to the decentralist and nonabsorptionist elements of the principle, a result that aligns with Bavaria's long-standing identity as slightly separate from the rest of Germany,[18] but they were not necessarily more attached to the principle than respondents from elsewhere in the country. Further, there was no significant difference in attitudes between the former East and West Germany. This result is more remarkable, as political culture research in Germany continues to find differences between East and West well after the collapse of the German Democratic Republic. For example, in 2010, Dalton and Weldon observed significant differences between East and West Germans on indicators of national identity, and attitudes toward democracy and the role of the state twenty years after the reunification.[19] Thus, despite Germany's fractured history and strong local identities, citizens appear united in their appreciation for subsidiarity.

Analysis of the federal values in Germany revealed a similar pattern of no significant differences between Länder or the East/West divide. However, as highlighted in chapter 4, while 74 per cent to 89 per cent of respondents thought that dividing power, having multiple levels participate, and forcing different levels to respect each other were desirable features for a political system, less than half were drawn to the idea of having different laws in different parts of the country. This finding reflects a key design feature of the German federation. As mentioned above, Article 72(2) of the Basic Law provides for equivalent living conditions, presenting a challenge for German federalism and subsidiarity's role within it. In their analysis of dynamic decentralization in Germany, Kaiser and Vogel observed that, despite deep-rooted cultural orientations that favoured uniformity and central decision-making held by political elites post-1949, "socio-cultural changes, reinforced by the increasing heterogeneity of the Länder since the 1990s have resulted in Germany's emphasis on decentralism."[20] At the same time, however, they note that citizens and the media mostly prefer uniform policies. This contradiction at the heart of German federalism and decentralization is captured in the public attitude data analyzed in this book: German respondents are clearly in favour of decentralized decision-making and are highly resistant to higher levels taking over the responsibilities of lower levels, but at the same time are not especially enamoured with the idea of having different laws in different parts of the country.

There are two potential explanations for these ostensibly inconsistent values, both of which have significant implications for understanding federalism in Germany. The first possible interpretation is that the results provide evidence of what Charles Jeffrey and others refer to as the "devolution paradox," where citizens desire greater decentralization and want state or regional governments to have more responsibility, but simultaneously desire policy uniformity and equality.[21] This interpretation posits that German respondents place a high value on decentralist subsidiarity, but are more likely to balk at the possibility of having different laws in different parts of the country. The second potential explanation is that these values reflect Germany's administrative federalism, whereby authority for policymaking is given to the federal level while the administration and delivery of that policy is handled by the Länder. This structure differs from the typical model of siloing the policymaking and service delivery functions for a particular domain (e.g., health and education) to either the federal or regional level, or having both levels share aspects of both functions. Under this explanation, the results can be interpreted as a muted enthusiasm for having different laws in different parts of the country (thanks to the equivalent living conditions clause of Article 72(2)), but a clear preference for decentralization in the administration of policy.

Both of these interpretations are plausible, and indeed may be complementary. If the results are driven by the paradoxical desire to have both uniformity and diversity, then this will require a careful approach to policy on the part of political elites. Scheller delivers a compelling warning about a divide between mass and (political) elite ideas about German federalism, and he cautions that ignoring public views risks undermining the legitimacy of the federation.[22]

Heimat

The structure of Germany's administrative federalism and its provision for equivalent living conditions appears to be a perfect fit for the German spirits of federalism and subsidiarity. But from where do these values arise? One plausible answer is to consider the role of *Heimat* as a cultural phenomenon in Germany. There is no real translation in English that accurately captures the multidimensional nature of Heimat, although the closest approximation would be "homeland." Broadly, Heimat is a strong, socialized, and often emotional attachment and sense of belonging to a particular region. According to Applegate, "for almost two centuries, Heimat has been at the center of a German moral – and by extension political – discourse about place, belonging, and identity."[23] While the term was unfortunately misused as part of the Third Reich's propaganda to foster zealous attachment to the German nation,[24] for the most part (and in this book), Heimat usually describes attachment to a local area before Germany as a whole.

At its simplest, Heimat is a sense of attachment or belonging to a particular place, and identification with a particular group of people.[25] Heimat usually places the strongest attachment to the local or regional area, and progressively weaker attachment to the national (country) level. Schneller's study of German political values found that more respondents chose their local community as the place they identified with than any other scale (Land, Germany, or Europe).[26] These results align with the concept of Heimat, even though the item was not presented to respondents in those terms. The strong sense of Heimat and how it relates to German national identity is captured perfectly in Applegate's statement that "the survival and transformation of *Heimat* reveal to us the struggle to create a national identity out of the diverse materials of a provincially rooted society."[27]

Crucially, Heimat draws on and relies on early socialization experiences, and, in many respects, is an emotion as much as it is an identity. Ratter and Gee argue that "*Heimat* inevitably comes with a strong sense of place, but sense of place can also be experienced without the deeper emotionality and social connectivity which is inherent in the experience of *Heimat* ... *Heimat* creates more profound emotions than the technical term 'sense of place' which is predominantly used in science."[28] Additionally, Heimat typically has a romanticized or sentimental dimension.[29] It is, in many respects, an idealized version of one's childhood home, a "persistent German longing for a space of innocence."[30] In that regard, Heimat takes on an almost mythical quality: for Applegate, "*Heimat* has never been a word about real social forces or real political situations. Instead, it has been a myth about the possibility of a community in the face of fragmentation and alienation."[31] This mythologized and romanticized understanding of a local place, particularly the childhood home, might help explain why 73.3 per cent of German respondents who were born in Germany were attached to decentralist subsidiarity, compared to only 56.5 per cent of respondents who were born outside of Germany.

Conversely, however, Heimat is not just an idealized, fantastical picture of the homeland. It captures the very real, usually natural, elements of a region. These very tangible aspects of Heimat include forests, lakes and rolling hills, or the North Sea as in Ratter and Gee's study of Heimat in Niedersachsen and Schleswig-Holstein.[32] The apparent conflict in meaning, between a concept of place that is simultaneously mythical and tangible, "is in no way unsettling to German speakers. Just the opposite, it seems. *Heimat* is everywhere."[33]

In many respects, the complexity and multifaceted nature of Heimat is more important for subsidiarity (itself a complex term, as highlighted in chapters 1 and 3) than its actual meaning. To illustrate Heimat's elusive meanings, Blickle draws a parallel between Germans' inherent understanding of the concept, and an anecdote that in answering the question "what is time?" Saint Augustine stated "I think I know – as long as no one asks me. But as soon as someone asks and I want to explain, I don't know anymore."[34] Similarly, Ratter and Gee state that "to German speakers, the term has an almost intuitive meaning, with everyone knowing or feeling what is implied even though most would find it difficult to offer a hard and fast definition."[35]

The notion of an intuitive, complex, and deep sense of local homeland and regional identity that the English language simply fails to capture might go a long way to explaining why Germans appear to have a strong spirit of subsidiarity, particularly its decentralist and nonabsorptionist elements, compared to the other countries. Specifically, the connection between Heimat's preference for the local is likely to manifest as a strong attachment to decentralism, nonabsorption, and support, but because any German can have a Heimat, regardless of where it is, this would explain why no significant differences in subsidiarity values between regions were detected in the analysis. Additionally, to the extent that federal structures protect local or regional areas by dividing power and forcing governments to respect each other, it is logical that attachment to these features of federal governance were most strongly correlated with attitudes toward decentralism and nonabsorption. Thus, given subsidiarity's long and rich history there, Germany might be considered subsidiarity's Heimat – a place where the principle will always be at home.

SWITZERLAND

As the third and final case in this chapter, the analysis of the Swiss results unites some of the ideas raised in the discussion of the US and German cases. Specifically, like the US, Switzerland has a history of confederalism, while its significant proportion of German-speaking citizens might bring the concept of Heimat into play. On top of these two elements, Switzerland is multilingual and multinational – characteristics commonly considered to drive successful federalism. It therefore comes as little surprise that subsidiarity and federalism were highly valued in Switzerland. However, the comparatively low attachment to the decentralist element of subsidiarity casts doubt on the assumed necessity of decentralization to successful federalism. While Swiss respondents have vibrant federal constitutional values in terms of their attachment to a system of government that divides power, enables legislative diversity and participation, and fosters respect between levels, they may not "think federal" in the sense meant by Duchacek because they are not overwhelmingly decentralist in their attitudes. This section therefore explores Swiss history and political culture to unpack the complexities of decentralization in successful federalism.

Table 5.4 presents the results from the 2018 ICVS. On average, Swiss respondents were more attached to the nonabsorptionist element of subsidiarity than respondents from any other country – 77.9 per cent of participants thought that a higher level should not be able to just take over the responsibilities of a lower level. This deep connection to subsidiarity, especially its nonabsorptionist element, might be driven by a similar history of confederalism as was detected in the US. Specifically, from 1291 to 1848 the rural communities and cantons of the Central Alps entered a series of loose alliances to maintain peace and facilitate trade between them. While the region was nominally part of the Holy Roman Empire until 1648, from the sixteenth century the confederation was effectively independent from the empire.

Table 5.4
Federal and subsidiarity values in Switzerland (ICVS 2018)

%	*2018*
Decentralism	61.1
Nonabsorption	77.9
Support	72.9
Divided power	78.7
Different laws	64.2
Participation	88.0
Respect	89.0

Føllesdal's comments about confederal subsidiarity's lack of a positive element (i.e., a positive duty on the centre to provide aid or support) plays out even more strongly in Switzerland than in the US – while attachment to supportive subsidiarity was still high (72.9 per cent), this was both significantly lower than attachment to the other two subsidiarity elements,[36] and the lowest of any country studied.

Switzerland's varied linguistic landscape, with notable German-, French-, Italian-, and Romansh-speaking populations, is another potential driver of subsidiarity and federal values. Specifically, language is relevant in two ways. First, language is an important social divider within Switzerland. It is an ever-present reminder of heterogeneity within the Swiss nation, and, by extension, constantly reinforces the value of having a system of government that divides power and protects against unnecessary absorption. Second, the role and influence of the German-speaking majority may have a further influence on the federal spirit. The previous section identified the concept of Heimat as a likely factor in the strong subsidiarity and federal values in Germany. But some scholars of German culture argue that Heimat is more attached to the German language than the country,[37] raising the possibility that Heimat might also play a role in Switzerland. The limitations of the ICVS data – specifically, a lack of data on the languages spoken by respondents – make it difficult to definitively test whether German speakers have different subsidiarity and federal values to other language groups within Switzerland. However, a comparison of cantons that officially recognize German, French, Italian, Romansh, or some combination of languages serves as a rough approximation. Notably, respondents from German-speaking cantons had higher attachment to decentralism and nonabsorption than those in French-speaking cantons (decentralism: 62.1 per cent vs 52.7 per cent; nonabsorption: 78.6 per cent vs 68.6 per cent). Conversely, respondents in officially francophone cantons were significantly more likely than those in German-speaking cantons to value support. While not conclusive in themselves, these results suggest that there is something about the German language that emphasizes decentralist and nonabsorptionist approaches to subsidiarity, which may be the concept of Heimat.

The stars appear to have aligned for subsidiarity and federalism in Switzerland. It has a rich history of confederalism, a multilingual society that reinforces the value of federalism, and a significant proportion of the population who might understand and draw on the German concept of Heimat in their approach to the values they think their political system should reflect. However, this precise alignment of factors is so unique to Switzerland that it may prove a fragile foundation for other nations looking at Switzerland as a model federation. Further, the shifting structural forces within Swiss institutions may present fresh challenges. Scholars have observed a consistent centralization of policy in Switzerland, gradually taking the federation away from its confederal roots.[38] More importantly, much of this centralization has occurred with the explicit consent of Swiss citizens at referenda. ICVS detected this strong collaborative preference through the overwhelming (88 per cent) attachment to "allowing the governments of different parts of Switzerland to get involved in decision-making on national issues" as a desirable federalist design principle. While it is impossible to make a prediction about the trend of values from only one data point, the comparatively low attachment to decentralism might indicate that Swiss citizens are slowly turning away from decentralization in favour of a more collaborative federal model. Time will tell on this issue. Switzerland may have found the perfect balance in its federal system, or it might face a reckoning as different elements of its subsidiarity and federal values come into conflict.

Conclusion

The US, Germany, and Switzerland are successful federations with vibrant spirits of federalism and subsidiarity. However, each case highlights that so far as attachment to subsidiarity is part of valuing federal design principles, mere decentralization alone is not enough. While most respondents in all three countries thought that decisions should be made at the lowest level possible, a more complete picture uncovered by ICVS is that the American, German, and Swiss participants were highly attached to the full package of federal and subsidiarity values. Nonabsorptionist subsidiarity was almost always the most important element of subsidiarity in all three cases. Thus, while respondents appeared to "think federal" by prioritizing decentralization, they were even more committed to the federal division of responsibilities and preventing higher levels from absorbing the functions of lower levels.

The strong overall attachment to subsidiarity, and particular emphasis on nonabsorption, is likely driven by a complex array of deep-rooted historical developments, institutional and constitutional forces, and cultural factors. The negotiation of aligning the respective political systems of each country with the subsidiarity and federal spirits has resulted in a federal balance that generally seems to work for each nation. However, these same factors mean that attempting to follow the federal models of America, Germany, and Switzerland elsewhere is not guaranteed to succeed. Without the foundational federal and subsidiarity political cultures to emphasize nonabsorption and the division of power, the kinds of federal systems modelled by the US, Germany, and Switzerland remain steadfast examples of classic and successful federations, but they might also be elusive and unattainable archetypes.

6

The Case for Supportive Subsidiarity

Australia, Canada, and the UK

In 1991, a century after Pope Leo XIII incorporated subsidiarity into the Catholic social doctrine, Pope John Paul II reiterated subsidiarity's importance, stating: "a community of a higher order should not interfere in the internal life of a community of a lower order, depriving the latter of its functions, *but rather should support it* in case of need and help to coordinate its activity with the activities of the rest of society, always with a view to the common view."[1]

In the modern focus on subsidiarity as decentralism, the supportive elements of the principle often go overlooked. As Brennan notes, focusing on the decentralist or nonabsorptionist elements of subsidiarity "represents only half the story."[2] As discussed in previous chapters, acknowledging and understanding the positive or supportive limb of subsidiarity is critical to making the principle meaningful in any federal system. This chapter's examination of Canada, Australia, and the UK, where public value for supportive subsidiarity was at its strongest, reinforces this point. Where the previous chapter suggested nonabsorption was the critical driving factor in the success of "classic" federations, this chapter foregrounds the supportive element or positive limb. The three cases each bring a different perspective to the relationship between subsidiarity and federalism. Canada is often regarded as a very successful federation, and is fairly unique globally as a federation that has tended toward decentralization rather than centralization in recent decades. However, attempts to measure Canadian federal political culture have produced mixed results, leading to uncertainty about the strength of citizens' attachment to federal principles. This chapter explores how we can use attitudes toward subsidiarity to better understand Canadian federal values.[3] Specifically, while decentralization is important, the ICVS results presented in chapter 4 highlight that decentralism was the least widely valued subsidiarity element, suggesting that concepts of federal political culture that rely on or emphasize decentralization do not capture the full story. Further, unlike in the US, Switzerland, and Germany, supportive subsidiarity was the element to which most Canadians were attached. In contrast to Canada, Australia is often seen as a federation in desperate need of reform.[4] However, that judgment is often made on the basis of its highly centralized federal balance – this chapter uses public attitude data to argue that if Australia were to embrace a more supportive approach to subsidiarity, the principle might have a greater impact on Australian federalism. Finally, while the UK is not constitutionally a federal country, it has many elements necessary for a federation. This chapter therefore examines how federal and subsidiarity values can thrive outside formal federal structures.

CANADA

In contrast to subsidiarity's long history in countries such as Germany and the US, the principle is characterized as an emerging force in Canada.[5] The comparatively recent academic attention given to the principle has generally occurred in response to decisions of the Supreme Court of Canada referencing subsidiarity. While these decisions are undoubtedly important, subsidiarity in Canada must be understood in a much broader context of decentralization, which began well before mainstream mention of "subsidiarity." In contrast to many established federations, Canada has followed a path of decentralization, and "defies assumptions about the inevitability of centralization in modern federation."[6] Scholars have long observed that in Canada, "power has flowed towards the provincial governments at the expense of the central government, at times with the latter's approval or acquiescence."[7] This dynamic makes Canada a perfect case to study in testing the role of subsidiarity and decentralization in successful federations.

It is important to remember that Canadian federalism began from a very centralized position; in many ways, the only direction the system could go was to decentralize.[8] The British North America Act,[9] which forms the constitutional foundation of the Canadian system, provided many centralizing features, most notably the power of the federal government to reserve and disallow provincial legislation,[10] and to appoint judges to provincial courts. Further, Article 91 allowed the federal parliament to make laws for "the Peace, Order and Good Government of Canada," effectively giving residual powers to the centre. These features have led scholars such as Stevenson to conclude that the original intent was to create a centralized federation,[11] and Lecours has commented that Canada was indeed "very much centralized at its birth."[12] Part of the motivation for this centralism was the founders' concern about the conditions of US federalism that gave rise to the Civil War, which was raging as the Canadian federalist movement was gathering momentum.[13] Establishing a more centralized federation was therefore seen as a protection against the fractured US-style of federalism.

From this centralized starting point, Canadian federalism eventually took a decentralized turn. Observers have noted, especially since the 1960s, that Canada has become increasingly decentralized in both policy and fiscal arenas.[14] While there have been some notable exceptions in certain policy fields such as social welfare and language policy,[15] the overall trend is of the provinces taking on increased responsibility and fiscal capacity, a trend which is "exceptional" compared to the centralization of most modern states.[16]

Despite sixty years of decentralization, discussions of subsidiarity have only recently emerged. Indeed, in 2011 Brouillet asked whether discussions of Canadian federalism should "open Pandora's box" in considering subsidiarity, noting that subsidiarity in the Canadian context remained a relatively untouched topic.[17] However, the results of ICVS suggest that, regardless of academic opinion, Pandora's box is well and truly open in terms of public attitudes: most Canadians valued all three subsidiarity elements highly, although there was significant variation in attachment to each item. The attachment to supportive subsidiarity is especially striking. In both 2016 and 2018, over 80 per cent of respondents thought that that higher levels should support lower levels – in 2016 more than half of respondents strongly held that view (as opposed to "tending" to be of the view) (table 6.1). The particular attachment to supportive subsidiarity is important. The difference between mean attachment to support and decentralism was both statistically significant and moderate in effect;[18] in simpler terms, Canadians can generally be characterized as highly attached to subsidiarity on the whole, but to them the supportive element of the principle is especially meaningful.

Table 6.1
Federal and subsidiarity values in Canada (ICVS 2016–18)

%	2016	2018
Decentralism	67.3	64.6
Nonabsorption	74.1	74.4
Support	87.1	81.6
Divided power	70.8	80.4
Different laws	59.6	70.7
Participation	72.7	78.3
Respect	76.2	85.3

Apart from the overall strength of subsidiarity values in Canada, the most noteworthy feature of these results is that the decentralist and nonabsorptionist results do not significantly differ from those in the US, Germany, and Switzerland. How, then, has Canada become more decentralist while other federations have not, if Canadians are no more decentralist in their values? The answer seems to lie in two dynamics in the Canadian federation: an empathetic approach valuing supportive subsidiarity, and a divisive approach to national identity.

Empathy and Supportive Subsidiarity

Attachment to the supportive element of subsidiarity was the key difference between Canadian respondents and those from the US, Germany, and Switzerland. In comparison to respondents from the classic federations, Canadians were about as attached to decentralism and nonabsorption, but significantly more attached to supportive subsidiarity. This means that on average Canadians were more attracted to subsidiarity in its totality than respondents from other countries studied. This finding highlights the importance of supportive subsidiarity, not just in its own right, but as a complement to the "negative" limb of the principle. Specifically, it suggests that decentralization on its own is not as powerful as decentralization buttressed by a mechanism for supporting and empowering lower levels of government. Further, while respondents in Canada, the US, Germany, and Switzerland all felt it was important that a higher level be prevented from taking over from a lower level (nonabsorption), in the US, Germany, and Switzerland this was the most important concern, while in Canada a supportive relationship between higher and lower levels was even more widely endorsed. This different emphasis, with a stronger value for supportive subsidiarity, has worked extremely well for Canada, as decentralization of policy responsibilities previously held at the federal level is often accompanied by an adequate supportive structure (otherwise the provinces would not take on the responsibility). Conversely, in other federations where policy begins as constitutionally decentralized, problems of capacity (or lack of support) are solved by centralizing responsibility for the issue.

The evidence of strong attachment to supportive subsidiarity also has important insights for better understanding Canadian federal political culture. As already identified in chapter 4, the most important correlation between federal and subsidiarity values was between a desire for participation from around the country and supportive subsidiarity. This result naturally speaks to a value for a cooperative approach to federalism in Canada,[19] but it also offers a means of reconciling competing conceptions of Canadian federal political culture. McGrane and Berdahl's 2019 analysis of Canadians' value for federalism highlighted that different measures of federal political culture (including the 2016 ICVS results and McGrane and Berdahl's own original survey) yielded very different pictures of the strength of attachment to federalism in Canada.[20] In contrast to ICVS, McGrane and Berdahl specifically aimed to create a measure that balanced positive and negative features of federalism, on the grounds that federal political culture is best captured in understanding citizens' reactions to the trade-offs and compromises inherent in a federal system.[21] Unsurprisingly, McGrane and Berdahl found that Canadian respondents had a "utopian" view of federalism, in that they were attracted to the benefits of federalism (e.g., innovation and accountability), and did not readily accept its drawbacks (e.g., slow decision-making and differential levels of service). While those results undoubtedly capture citizens' federal political culture as McGrane and Berdahl defined it, the findings offer little direction in how we might use an understanding of federal values to strengthen or further improve the already-successful Canadian federation. However, adding ICVS's subsidiarity results into the equation, we can now take a closer step toward the "utopian" federal model. Specifically, the strong emphasis on supportive subsidiarity indicates that, from the perspective of the average Canadian, the trade-offs inherent in a federation are best managed through the lens of supportive subsidiarity. For example, on the issue of differential levels of service (a negative of federalism), a supportive approach to subsidiarity might ensure that an acceptable baseline level of service is met across the country, and that any differences in quality are therefore varying degrees of high quality, rather than a gap between good and poor service.

A further element of Canadian federalism that is important is Jedwab's observation of a high degree of empathy within the federation. Specifically, Jedwab notes that more than two-thirds of Canadians agreed that "as part of the federation people in my province should be responsible for helping those provinces that are most vulnerable."[22] While all the federations in this study have some form of horizontal fiscal equalization measures, Canada's is one of the most comprehensive. The horizontal element of the question reported by Jedwab is critical here: the fact that the item refers to "people in my province helping [other provinces]" highlights an interesting combination of decentralist and supportive elements of subsidiarity, as it refers to provinces (a lower level) supporting other provinces without necessarily needing to involve the central government. A recent, concrete example of this was Alberta's donation of excess personal protective equipment to other provinces at the outset of the coronavirus pandemic. Such an approach goes far beyond simply "thinking local" as a feature of federal political culture, and shows that the principles of collaborative federalism and subsidiarity are not just implicit in the Canadian Constitution – they are alive and well in the minds of citizens.

National Identity in Canada

Analysis of attitudes toward subsidiarity at the provincial level revealed that subsidiarity and federal values did not seem to differ significantly between the Canadian provinces. This is important for two reasons. First, it addresses Wiseman's critique that many studies tend to treat Canada as one united polity, rather than as comprising several smaller and unique political cultures.[23] On the issue of federalism and subsidiarity at least, Canadians can be regarded as united. Second, this means that Quebecois respondents were not more likely to hold these values than other Canadians, despite the province's autonomy. Instead, Albertans were consistently the most strongly attached to subsidiarity across the three elements, even if this attachment was not significantly different from other parts of the country. This finding is consistent with McGrane and Berdahl's study, which also found limited differences between respondents from Quebec compared to the rest of Canada.[24] Similarly, francophone respondents did not significantly differ from anglophones in their subsidiarity values. Again, this finding reinforces the interpretation that appreciation for subsidiarity is consistent across Canada, despite the common view that bilingualism is a driver of success in federations.

In fact, analysis showed that in both 2016 and 2018 there were no significant variations in subsidiarity values based on key demographic indicators. Simply put, there appears to be no systemic driver of subsidiarity values that would lead one part of the population to be more or less likely to endorse the principle. This finding is critical to better understanding subsidiarity's role in successful federations because it challenges much of the conventional wisdom in this space. Most notably, scholars of federalism often point to Quebec's unique status within the Canadian federation as a key driver of decentralization.[25] Quebec's position as a decentralizing force in Canadian federalism has led some scholars to argue that the federal spirit is stronger in Quebec than in the rest of Canada,[26] and based on those findings, it would have been reasonable to expect that respondents from Quebec would be more attached to subsidiarity. The fact that they were not suggests that Quebec's role and impact in the federation extends far beyond its own borders.

The answer may lie in conceptions of broader Canadian political culture. Specifically, while the ICVS data suggests that there is no meaningful regional variation in federal and subsidiarity values, it is possible that divisions in the broader political culture give rise to an appreciation for principles (subsidiarity and federal) that allow for that division. Debates over the existence of a "Canadian political culture" are well-established. Some, such as Wiseman, stress the importance of appreciating regional differences.[27] In other words, they take issue with attempts to aggregate the political orientations of people from, say, Manitoba, Nova Scotia, and Quebec. Nicol and Whalley are even more skeptical of a national political culture: "no other nation in the world can boast such a long and continuous tradition of doubt about the validity of its existence ... The result is a young nation that refuses to become involved with herself in case she turns out to be somebody else."[28]

Empirically, the question of whether Canada has a cohesive national political culture is contested. Simeon and Elkins's seminal study of provincial political cultures identified significant differences between the provinces,[29] and Beck,[30] Wiseman,[31] and Wesley[32] have reached similar conclusions in their studies over the years. Conversely, other studies have failed to find significant differences between the provinces,[33] or suggest that other variables such as socioeconomic indicators are more important.[34] Henderson has proposed that regional clusters, which sit between the federal and provincial levels, and may transcend provincial boundaries, may operate in conjunction with any provincial political culture that might exist.[35] McGrane and Berdahl also found significant regional variations in measures of overall political culture (in a separate study to their focus on federal political culture) even after accounting for sociodemographic differences.[36] The importance of these findings is that, if there are differences in political culture at a subnational level, federal institutions and the subsidiarity principle would facilitate them. Indeed, it was part of the reason for federating Canada in the first place. Accordingly, it is logical that a divided political culture would itself unite Canadians in their appreciation of federalism and subsidiarity, as revealed by the ICVS results.

This interpretation is further supported by the persistent theme in Canadian culture (to the extent that it can be regarded as nationally consistent) of Canada's apparent tolerance and accommodation of diversity. Bell and Tepperman point historically to the ethnic diversity of loyalist migrants to Canada during the American Revolution as the foundation for this diversity.[37] The authors argue that despite their varied cultural backgrounds, these migrants could (indeed, had to) unite under their loyalty to the British Empire while maintaining their ethnic identities. This laid the foundation for what has been called the "Canadian mosaic," where Canadian (political) culture is the product of many individual ethnicities and cultures.[38] As discussed in chapter 3, there are some important challenges to this description of Canadian society,[39] but it nevertheless has important implications for understanding subsidiarity values. The mosaic imagery presents Canada and Canadians placing a high degree of value on diversity and autonomy, values which sit comfortably alongside subsidiarity, especially its decentralist and nonabsorptionist elements. Indeed, it requires little stretching to conceptualize Althusius's or Pope Leo's arguments as calling for a mosaic of cities and private associations, respectively.

The Canadian mosaic therefore offers a powerful analogy for understanding how a fractured national identity contributes to successful decentralization and a strong federal political culture. It suggests that Canadians understand that the country lacks a cohesive or universal national identity. Instead, it is made up of many smaller identities. Just as a mosaic is purposely created to include different pieces to create an overall picture, so too is the Canadian federation designed to accommodate different identities, and Canadians seem to recognize this. Accordingly, when they think about the federation, their views recognize the value and importance of having a system that accommodates and protects the smaller pieces of the federal mosaic, even if they themselves are not necessarily beneficiaries of that system. Further, value placed on decentralism and nonabsorption is integral to the pieces of the mosaic, but it is aided by the strong attachment to supportive subsidiarity and the empathetic federal spirit described above – the mortar that binds the pieces of the mosaic together.

AUSTRALIA

In his analysis of Australian federalism, Riker observed "of all federations now in existence, Australia seems less in need of appeasing subordinate patriotisms than any other government. One wonders, indeed, why they bother with federalism in Australia."[40] Similarly, considering the social homogeneity of Australia, Livingston questioned "One is sometimes tempted to wonder why the Australians retain their federal system. The Australians often wonder this also."[41] Australian engagement with federalism is certainly a confounding one. At federation, the Australian Constitution set up a system more akin to the US and Swiss models in its decentralized division of powers than the Canadian example. Yet Australia lacked the diversity of Switzerland, or the divisions of the US, and since the 1920s has undergone a steady process of centralization. This centralization has largely taken place in the elite political and judicial areas, but has on occasion occurred with the direct approval of the Australian public in constitutional referenda. Calls to abolish the states, while not widespread, are nevertheless not uncommon, and previous ACVS data shows that a core block of citizens would do away with state governments.[42] Yet somehow, Australian federalism persists.

Subsidiarity is an equally challenging principle in Australia. Subsidiarity's uptake in Australia has been "long and difficult."[43] Attempts to realize the principle in Australia, such as Colin Clark's use of the principle to argue for economic reform in the 1950s,[44] and its use in federal reform debates in the 1990s,[45] and again in 2014–16,[46] did not prove especially fruitful. The principle is usually promoted to argue for decentralism (and the perceived benefits localized government will bring) and clarity of responsibility,[47] and it is also used to call for specific policy change, for example in schooling policy.[48] However, while the principle has received significant academic attention in Australia, it has had little real impact in practice. If subsidiarity can be described as a dull sword in Europe,[49] its blade in Australia is completely blunt.

The apparent disregard for subsidiarity and the broader context of Australia's highly centralized federal structure are naturally related. In fact, Australia is often not viewed as an especially successful federation because of its high level of centralization. As noted in chapter 1, Evans goes as far as arguing that the disregard for subsidiarity means that Australia is no longer an authentic federation at all.[50] Further, applying Burgess's criteria that a federation's success should be judged against the founding vision, Australia again falls short. It is widely noted that Australia's federal system has departed from its original expression in the Constitution in 1901.[51] But, as Kildea, Lynch, and Williams note, "if the current state of the federation would disappoint the founding generation, it is also of deep concern to the present one."[52]

For these reasons, Australia is a perfect counterpart to Canada for studying subsidiarity's role in a federation. Where Canada has a thriving federation and a recent recognition of subsidiarity, there is considerable scope to improve Australia's federal system, despite longstanding calls to adopt the principle.

Of all countries studied, Australians were the most varied in their attitudes toward each of the elements of subsidiarity. The immediately noticeable difference to the previous cases is the (relative) lack of attachment to decentralism. While a majority of Australians valued decentralism (53.2 per cent in 2016 and 54.8 per cent in 2017) (table 6.2), this number was far below the that in other federations studied.[53] The Australian decentralism results are very consistent with previous ACVS data; attachment to decentralism has remained at around 50 per cent since 2008.[54] This consistency reinforces the reliability of this item, and suggests that the item does in fact capture citizens' deeper political orientations, rather than more fleeting attitudes. The comparative ambivalence toward decentralism therefore appears well-set in Australia.

Table 6.2
Federal and subsidiarity values in Australia (ICVS 2016; ACVS 2017)

%	2016	2017
Decentralism	53.2	54.8
Nonabsorption	73.2	72.1
Support	83.8	82.3
Divided power	58.7	64.0
Different laws	52.1	57.9
Participation	67.3	74.6
Respect	75.3	84.1

In contrast to decentralism, supportive subsidiarity was extremely popular (83.8 per cent in 2016 and 82.3 per cent in 2017), while on the nonabsorption item, almost three-quarters of Australians thought that a higher level of government should *not* take over the responsibilities of lower levels. These differences are significant and important, and the difference between the way that decentralism and support is valued had the largest effect size of any of the within-country comparisons. These results indicate that, while Australians are evenly divided on the question of decentralism, they generally value the idea of higher levels of government supporting lower levels. However, it seems that this support should not be used as an opportunity to just take over responsibility. Instead, the support should be used to empower lower levels. These values align with (and were significantly correlated with – see chapter 4) attachment to participation from around the country and respect between governments as federal design features. Taken together, these findings paint the picture of a desire for a cooperative approach to federalism. This is a significant insight for the Australian debate, for two reasons: first, the subsidiarity literature in Australia has invariably focused on decentralist elements of the principle, and as such has difficulty accounting for the way the central Commonwealth government has used tied grants designed to support state governments as a means of expanding its power.[55] Second, while Painter and others have long observed a trend toward cooperative federalism in Australia,[56] in the Australian context cooperation has usually meant coordination to produce uniform policy, or cooperation with Commonwealth-led initiatives. In other words, cooperation has spiralled up in a centralizing manner. However, public values seem to align more closely to a cooperative approach that is more supportive of lower levels and more respectful of their roles and responsibilities. While there is not an overwhelmingly strong desire for decentralism in its own right, it seems that Australians have a value for empowering lower levels that the current system does not deliver.

National and Subnational Attachments

Analysis of subsidiarity values revealed some small variations in attitudes between the Australian states. Across the three elements, Tasmanians were the most attached to the principle, while Queenslanders and Western Australians switched between second and third across decentralism, nonabsorption, and support. This is an interesting finding, because these three states often find themselves on the periphery in Australian politics. As a small state detached from the mainland, Tasmania is sometimes isolated from Australian politics. Similarly, Western Australia's massive distance from the Eastern population centres has fostered a similar sense of separateness – the state was a latecomer to federation in 1901, held a referendum to secede in 1933 (which was quashed by the privy council), and to this day remains somewhat removed politically from the rest of Australia. As a large state with a significant population located outside the capital city, Queensland also operates from a politics of distance.[57] This was highlighted in the 2019 federal election, where the conservative Liberal-National Coalition won an unexpected third term, thanks to campaign rhetoric disparaging the "Canberra bubble" of national politics that resonated in Queensland, Western Australia, and Tasmania.[58]

While these results provide a useful insight, it is important to remember that they are only small differences – they are best thought of as variations on a common theme, rather than as completely disparate views. They tend to confirm Aroney and colleagues' characterization of Australian federalism as including slight differences, rather than strongly opposed perspectives.[59] Accordingly, in this book I continue to discuss "Australian attitudes" as a collective whole, rather than breaking all analysis down on a state-by-state basis.

In comparison to the divided political culture of Canada, Australian political culture is notable for its strong attachment to the nation, vis-à-vis the states. Denemark and Sharman note that "if regional social diversity in terms of ethnic, linguistic and religious factors were the mainspring of a federal form of government, Australian federalism would never have existed, let alone persisted."[60] More importantly, compared to Switzerland, Germany, and Canada, where subnational identities and cultures seem to play some role in fostering a high value for subsidiarity, the principle faces an uphill battle for the support of citizens in Australia.

That is not to say, however, that Australians have no attachment to their state. On the contrary, previous research has identified strong state and regional identities.[61] However, Smith suggests that these identities are fluid and "like quicksilver,"[62] manifesting in response to particular contexts, rather than being consistent, ever-present attitudes. Compared to the German Heimat, Australians likely have a very different approach to national versus subnational identity, and the tensions between centralism and decentralism that seem to come with those views.

Australia has no real contender for subnationhood along the same lines as Quebec in Canada. Historically, Western Australia may have had an equivalent status, to the point in 1933 where a majority of Western Australian voters voted in favour of secession.[63] However, in modern times there is little serious discussion of Australian states breaking away from the nation, and Smith observes that "Australian political culture contains a distinctive sense of national [(country)] identity."[64] Thus, while the existence of identifiable nations within other countries encourages citizens to prefer decentralism and nonabsorption, subsidiarity in Australia does not receive a similar boost. In explaining how federalism has persisted in Australia, however tenuously, we must therefore look to factors that do not rely on a widespread value for diversity or decentralism, as seen in other federations.

Egalitarianism and Pragmatism as Drivers of Supportive Subsidiarity

A core element of Australian political culture that may help explain Australian citizens' attachment to supportive subsidiarity and relative hesitance toward the decentralist element is its emphasis on equality and rejection of hierarchy. According to Smith, "equality is the most powerful defining cliché of Australian political culture,"[65] while Thompson argues that "egalitarianism has shaped our democratic institutions, our definition of democracy, and definition of ourselves."[66] While Australia is not unique in emphasizing egalitarianism, and its commitment to equality can be challenged on a wide array of indicators[67] (Australia has been described as a social welfare "laggard" when compared to many European countries),[68] Australians' value for equality, a "fair go" and a love of the underdog remains a powerful aspect of Australian identity and political culture.[69]

The Australian approach to egalitarianism has a distinct flair that may be incompatible with some elements of subsidiarity. While some, distinctly Catholic, conceptions of subsidiarity see the principle as facilitating equality,[70] subsidiarity can produce unequal outcomes when the decentralist element is preferred, as differences between subunits (e.g., local councils) will compound over time. Thus, the way subsidiarity and egalitarianism interact is potentially very influential on subsidiarity values in Australia, with a preference for supportive subsidiarity resulting in greater equality rather than decentralist subsidiarity.

A related and equally important concept is the notion of hierarchy in society. Subsidiarity very much draws on ideas about structure and order; the terms "higher" and "lower" levels of government alone prove this. Accordingly, societal perceptions of the value of structure and hierarchy are likely to be important to subsidiarity attitudes. Class is certainly relevant here, but it is not the only manifestation of hierarchy. Instead, it is more useful to consider broader notions of authority and power.

Australians' preference for equality can manifest as a rejection of authority and hierarchy. Accounts of Australian political culture and identity frequently draw on the "Anzac myth" born from Charles Bean's account of Australia's involvement in World War I[71] as the starting point of Australian attachment to equality. According to some, the national identity expounded in the Anzac myth is resistant to bonds between people and the state that normally create hierarchies of authority.[72] Instead, "mateship and egalitarianism are both horizontal bonds between people that leave little room for the vertical power relations between the state and people,"[73] or, one might add, between levels of government. These horizontal bonds do not fit comfortably with decentralist approaches to subsidiarity as they implicitly reject the notions of "higher" and "lower." The actions and rhetoric of the Howard government from 1996 to 2007 are particularly relevant here. As prime minister, John Howard was especially adept at centralizing power into the hands of the federal government,[74] but was also well-known for his strong discourse around "Australian values," and tied the language of "mateship" and a "fair go" to his controversial (and centralizing) reforms.[75] However, while mateship and egalitarianism may be incompatible with decentralism, they may resonate strongly with supportive elements of subsidiarity when framed as two orders of government supporting each other as equals with the resources, expertise and insight needed to govern effectively.

Another example was the public reaction to Prime Minster Scott Morrison's response to bushfires that ravaged the country in 2019–20. The federal government initially took an uncharacteristically hands-off approach to the state responsibilities of emergency services and fire management and was hesitant to get involved in the crisis response without explicit requests for assistance from the states. Despite its earlier cuts to rural fire service funding and public calls for national leadership as fires raged across the country,[76] the prime minister infamously quipped "I don't hold the hose" to justify the lack of involvement from the national level. This statement prompted significant public backlash. It reflected an uncharacteristically decentralist and nonabsorptionist approach from the federal government, and ostensibly did not sit well with citizens' preferences for a supportive federal level rather than a nonabsorptionist one.

Another useful insight comes from previous research indicating that Australians with experience in the public service may be "pragmatic" in their attachment to subsidiarity; that is, while they see value in decentralism, they weigh this against other principles and values (equality being the most dominant), and practical concerns such as distributions of resources and expertise.[77] These observations fit within a broader context of claims of a pragmatic streak in Australian political culture and a utilitarian approach to equality.[78] While arguments that Australians take a utilitarian view of equality have been the subject of a number of critiques,[79] the idea that Australians are pragmatic in their political outlook has proven more robust. Indeed, it has been used as a vehicle to explain Australian federalism ("pragmatic federalism"[80]). Pragmatism in this context can be defined as "a direct engagement or confrontation with pressing problems, an engagement unmediated by larger theoretical concerns."[81] High Court judge Patrick Keane famously described the Australian Constitution as a "small brown bird," meek in its pragmatic and uninspiring language compared to the soaring eagle of the American Constitution.[82] Importantly, this pragmatism is not an outright rejection of principled decision-making, however its apparent pervasiveness, at least in intergovernmental relations,[83] suggests that it can be difficult for principles such as subsidiarity to gain traction. This may be especially the case when subsidiarity is perceived as being inconsistent with other values (such as equality), or with practicalities.[84] This phenomenon may also have accelerated the Anzac myth, especially aspects that challenged authority. Bean noted that, during World War I, "the best officers were those who knew and were known by the ordinary troops."[85] This was especially the case when officers were promoted from amongst the rank and file, which, according to Smith, created a culture of "personal and direct authority, rather than bureaucratic authority."[86] Such relations presented a challenge to the state's need for legitimacy of office-holders regardless of their individual qualities. As a result, Smith suggests that "rather than cementing the Australian people and state together, then, the Anzac experience may have developed expectations of authority that the Australian state (or any other modern bureaucratic state) could not meet."[87] Without a strong institutional basis for authority, political elites were forced to adopt a more pragmatic approach to governance, which in turn led to greater centralization. This pragmatism might then also help explain why policymakers assume that Australian citizens are resistant to or fearful of federal reform, when the results presented in this book suggest that Australians place a high value on nonabsorption and supportive elements of subsidiarity.

Supportive subsidiarity, which emphasizes community empowerment, offers a means of reworking the federation that is more likely to succeed than previous attempts to invoke subsidiarity in its decentralist sense. The overwhelming attachment to supportive subsidiarity amongst Australian citizens demonstrates public approval for such an approach. Apart from being politically expedient, recognizing public attitudes in this space should allow for and even emphasize the community empowerment citizens support – the results from ICVS suggest that Australia is not as successful as it could be as a federal system because its structures do not align with public values, an important lesson that extends beyond the land "Down Under."

UNITED KINGDOM

Subsidiarity has taken on a new importance in the UK in light of the 2016 Brexit referendum. While subsidiarity is a critical driving force in the EU generally, it has a particular prominence in the UK because of the country's historical reluctance to commit to the EU. Margaret

Thatcher in particular was skeptical of the emerging union,[88] but subsidiarity served to allay some of her concerns, although some argue that the difficulties in defining the principle may have meant that even then the UK was out of step with the EU's version of subsidiarity. Indeed, French politician Jean Pierre Cot quipped that "only subsidiarity could manage to put [President of the European Commission] Jacques Delors perfectly in tune with Mrs Thatcher … on a misunderstanding."[89] Confusion about subsidiarity's meaning continued through the 2016 Brexit referendum, where both "leave" and "remain" campaigns argued that subsidiarity supported their side of the debate.[90] Such confusion further reinforces the importance of developing a clear understanding of subsidiarity's meaning.

However, the understanding and realization of the principle goes beyond the relationship between the UK and the EU. The devolution of power to Scotland and Wales in the 1990s represented, according to the then prime minister Tony Blair, a move to governance closer to the people (decentralism),[91] and a recognition of the separate and important histories and identities of Scotland and Wales (arguably nonabsorption, but of culture rather than governance). Subsidiarity was also invoked in the 2014 referendum on Scottish independence, both in the sense that the referendum empowered the Scottish people to make the decision to stay or leave for themselves,[92] and because voting to become independent would have decentralized more power to Scotland.[93]

The issue of devolution and the status of the regions within the UK has meant that the question of whether the UK would be better served by a federated political system is never far from the surface.[94] Even in 1952, Livingston theorized that the UK had a federal society, although he concluded that the processes and traditions of the British government were sufficient to negate the need for federal institutions.[95] However, in the decades since Livingston reached that conclusion, federalism has arguably grown in attractiveness. The "holding together" argument for federalism, where a unitary country federates in order to placate secessionist regions, has a strong case in the UK given agitations for Scottish independence, which never really went away following the 2014 referendum and were further heightened following Brexit. Further, the case for federation in the UK might be strengthened by a resurgence of English national identity. Observers of British political culture frame the renewed sense of "Englishness" in the context of a "crisis of identity" in the 1990s among the English

Table 6.3
Federal and subsidiarity values in the UK (ICVS 2016–18)

%	*2016*	*2018*
Decentralism	69.9	68.2
Nonabsorption	74.0	69.8
Support	83.0	83.7
Divided power	61.1	69.8
Different laws	49.8	55.7
Participation	65.2	72.3
Respect	71.4	79.4

population, where the English way of life was seen as under threat from Europe and from devolved power granted to Scotland and Wales. According to Kenny, "different figures, from a variety of genres, contributed to this anxiety fuelled conversation … all dissecting the national predicament and identity confusion from which the English were often said to be suffering."[96]

Some scholars see the devolution to Scotland and Wales in 1999 as being especially relevant here, viewing it as the trigger for a backlash among English citizens.[97] While the causality of these claims is questionable,[98] the importance of this power shift has not lessened. In some conservative circles, this devolution represented a reckless break from the conventions underpinning the United Kingdom, and has led some to call for the introduction of an English parliament.[99] For some, such action would protect the English from interference from the non-English territories, while others see it as the first step toward a more radical dissolution of the UK "and a retreat to the English heartland."[100] Regardless of the specific endgame in mind, the concerns that underpin them could be addressed, or might be worsened, through federation. Further, such reform sits comfortably with decentralist notions of subsidiarity. Accordingly, it is important to developed a renewed understanding of federal and subsidiarity values in the UK.

The results of ICVS indicate thriving federal constitutional values in the UK, despite the lack of formal federal institutions (table 6.3). In 2018, about 70 per cent of respondents thought dividing power and allowing participation from around the country were desirable features of government. Fewer (55 per cent) respondents thought that it was desirable to have different laws in different parts of the country, but more (79 per cent) thought that different governments should be forced to respect each other. While not the highest of the cases studied, these values are very high for a country that does not constitutionally guarantee the delivery of any of those features. The results suggest that many citizens in the UK "think federal," and, in doing so, they challenge the notion that a spirit of federalism is predicated on federal institutions.

Public attachment to subsidiarity values was also consistently high. In 2016, 69.9 per cent, 74.0 per cent, and 83.0 per cent of participants respectively valued decentralism, nonabsorption, and support. Attachment to decentralism and support remained stable in 2018 (68.2 per cent and 83.7 per cent, respectively), but the proportion of respondents who valued nonabsorption dropped by 4.2 per cent to 69.8 per cent. This drop might be driven by the language and rhetoric around Brexit. The 2016 ICVS was fielded two weeks before the 23 June referendum and respondents were more than likely exposed to arguments about European absorption of UK policymaking. While respondents were instructed to think about domestic politics in answering the survey, it is likely that many participants' views were influenced by their perception of the UK-Europe debate. By 2018, much of the rhetoric about protecting the UK from European takeover had eased as the logistics of negotiating leaving the European Union came to the fore instead.

The high value placed on supportive subsidiarity further highlights the importance of understanding the principle's broad meaning. Crucially, however, the finding has broader implications for understanding subsidiarity in a federal setting. Specifically, the results confirm Golemboski's argument that subsidiarity is not restricted to being meaningful in federalist systems – the values that underpin it can be appreciated by anyone.[101] While this is naturally an important finding for the principle's role in the UK, it also reveals an important lesson for policymakers in federal countries: it should not be assumed that political values and attitudes toward subsidiarity and federalism will passively follow institutions structures. Instead, it is crucial that policymakers ensure that the federal system aligns with the unique subsidiarity values of each country.

Subsidiarity in the Union – Beyond Devolution?

There is a general level of consistency between the four territories of the United Kingdom – England, Scotland, Wales, and Northern Ireland.[102] This is important because, as Henderson and colleagues noted in their recent study of the role of national identification in Brexit, researchers often adopt a "whole of Britain" approach using a dataset dominated by English respondents, without critical consideration of their approach, or of particularly "English" attitudes.[103] Reliable comparison between the four territories is difficult, because the UK dataset was designed to be representative of the whole United Kingdom and therefore included the small numbers of respondents from Wales and Northern Ireland. Nevertheless, analysis did not detect any significant differences in attitudes toward subsidiarity between English, Scottish, Welsh, and Northern Irish participants.[104] Accordingly, at this stage there is no reliable basis for distinguishing between attitudes from the four territories. However, further research with larger samples from Wales and Northern Ireland is necessary to more comprehensively test the differences in subsidiarity values within the UK.

Uncovering a consistent value for federalism and subsidiarity across the country has crucial implications for the UK. On the one hand, it means that federal values are not limited to or driven by Scotland, Wales, and Northern Ireland; English respondents are generally just as attached to these values. On the other hand, it also means that the results are not a product of English demand for greater recognition in the system and apathy from Scottish, Welsh, and Northern Irish respondents. It seems there is a strong enough federal spirit throughout the UK to sustain a system that looks more federalist than the current model.

CONCLUSION

Canada, Australia, and the UK offer three important variations in the relationship between federalism, subsidiarity, and decentralization. Canada is a fairly decentralized federation with a strong theme of cooperation between levels. Australia is a highly centralized federation which has struggled to balance federal and state responsibilities, And the UK is not a federation at all, but is nevertheless expected to overcome many of the same challenges as a federation because of its diverse regions. Revisiting citizens' perceptions of how well the current system is working presented in chapter 1, 74.1 per cent of Canadian respondents thought their system was working well. This compares very favourably to 58.8 per cent and 57.7 per cent of Australian and UK respondents, respectively, who felt the same way about their systems. The results analyzed in this chapter suggest that the reason for this disparity might be that Canada's system is more closely aligned with the federal and subsidiarity values of its citizens than the Australian and UK systems are with theirs. Canadians placed a high value on all three elements of subsidiarity and the four federalist design principles, and the Canadian federation delivers on these values and principles admirably. By comparison, Australia's centralized federation does not deliver on the Australian people's strong desire for supportive subsidiarity. Similarly, the UK might not deliver enough decentralization to meet the expectations of citizens, and its devolved unitary structure falls short of the federal spirit in the UK.

The three cases are linked by the extremely high value placed on supportive subsidiarity. This finding reinforces the value of understanding subsidiarity's "positive limb." More importantly, however, while supportive subsidiarity was valued roughly equally highly in Canada, Australia, and the UK, the institutional operationalization of those values differs significantly. Accordingly, Australian and UK policymakers will likely benefit from incorporating a greater emphasis on supportive subsidiarity in their policy outlook.

Together, these three cases highlight that federal political culture is important in a successful federation. However, they reveal that there is no one universal federal spirit. Instead, federal institutions must be adapted to the unique perspectives and values of the citizens of each country. Here, subsidiarity values play an important role, although the question is not as simple as establishing whether citizens "think local" and are attached to a decentralist interpretation of the principle.

7

To Federate or Not to Federate?

Belgium and France

One of Burgess's criteria for a successful federation is to look at the founding purpose of the federation[1] – why did this country federate? What did its founders hope to achieve? Why was federalism chosen over some other form of government? These are important questions in themselves, but they take on an even greater significance when viewed in conjunction with ideas about the role of federal political culture in successful federalism. As Burgess notes: "Federations evolve but the underlying purposes for which they were originally formed do not necessarily fade from view; they are often kept alive as sources of legitimacy even if history becomes legend or myth."[2] The founding vision for a federation must therefore align with its federal political culture at the time of federation, and must be powerful enough to sustain federal values in the long term. In the cases examined in this book, we have seen this logic prove true. In successful federations such as Germany and Switzerland, the federal spirits – while different between each case – align with the respective founding aims of the federation. The two cases examined in this chapter, Belgium and France, offer a unique opportunity to extend this analysis. Of all the countries studied in this book, Belgian and French respondents were the least likely to think that their current system was working well (figure 1.1), suggesting that there would be the greatest gap between public values and the operating institutions in those two cases. Of course, the systems are very different; Belgium is a federation and France has a unitary system. But when analyzed together, these two cases reveal much about the role of federalism and subsidiarity, and public value placed on these principles. Specifically, they offer two clear examples of what can happen when the formal structures and founding visions of a country do not align with public attitudes toward federalism and subsidiarity.

This chapter starts by examining Belgium, a new federation with a complex – perhaps even unclear – federal spirit. It then turns to France, a comparatively unhappy unity with a clear federal spirit. By analyzing these two cases, this chapter examines the fundamental questions that operate at the start of a federation – why federate? Is federalism a good fit for this country and its political culture? What role does subsidiarity and decentralization play in this threshold stage, and what can this tell us about subsidiarity's ongoing meaning and importance in a successful federation?

BELGIUM

On 5 November 1967, 30,000 activists marched in Antwerp, the capital of the Flemish region of Belgium. Their protest was directed at the Catholic University of Leuven, a historically francophone university that became bilingual in 1930, located in Dutch-speaking Flanders. The Flemish protestors in Antwerp and Leuven demanded a formal split of the French and Dutch components of the university, carrying banners with slogans such as *Walen buiten* ("Walloons out") and *Leuven Vlaams* (Flemish Leuven). The government of the day attempted to find a compromise but was unable to do so. This in turn sparked a collapse in the governing coalition, and, in March 1968, Gaston Eyskens was elected as the new prime minister. In June 1968, Eyskens declared that the university would be splitting – the Flemish institution (Katholieke Universiteit Leueven, or KUL) stayed in Leuven, while the new French institution (Université catholique de Louvain, or UCL) moved to the newly created town of Louvain-la-Neuve (New Leuven) in Wallonia.

The split in the Catholic University of Leuven served as a microcosm for wider cultural tensions between Flemish and Walloon Belgians in the second half of the twentieth century. In 1970, Prime Minister Eyskens passed the first state reform, which created three autonomous communities within Belgium with responsibility for cultural matters. It was the first step on Belgium's pathway to federalism, which culminated in becoming a formal federation in 1993. Belgium is therefore unique among the federations examined in this book in that it only federated comparatively recently, and federalism was designed to keep Belgium united by conceding power to the regions, rather than taking power from subnational governments to create a national level. Federalism was therefore very much a concession to address cultural and economic divisions within Belgium. However, the three decades of federalism since 1993 have not been smooth sailing. Belgium is plagued by ongoing disputes about the direction it should travel[3] and problems locating an appropriate centre of gravity within it.[4] These disputes seem to also be reflected in public attitudes. ICVS revealed that most Belgians do not think the current system is working well, and they are roughly evenly divided in their support for or resistance to basic federal design principles. This section unpacks those results, examining the nuances of regional variation in attitudes and the broader phenomena of Belgian political culture as potential drivers of federal and subsidiarity attitudes.

The Federal Paradox

On the surface, Belgium appears to embody the paradox of federalism whereby decentralization encourages subnational communities to demand even greater autonomy, hollowing out the federation in a devolutionary spiral that threatens the federation itself.[5] In Belgium, political elites play on regional identities, especially the divide between Flemings and Walloons, and Dutch and French speakers, for political advantage.[6] These tactics are evident in the fact that twice in the past decade it has taken over a year to form a governing coalition following an election. Recent years have also witnessed a rise in Flemish parties advocating (Flemish) nationalist and even separatist positions – in the 2019 election, the two parties that received the greatest share of the votes were right-wing parties advocating greater autonomy for Flanders.[7]

However, Thijssen, Arras, and Sinardet suggest that the discourse among the political elites is out of step with public opinion.[8] Based on a survey of Belgian respondents who were asked about the desirability of regional autonomy for different policy fields, the authors concluded that "on the exterior, as it shows from elite and media discourse, Belgium may appear to be completely divided; however, Belgian society does not reflect such a division."[9] Instead, the authors observed that across seven policy domains, over a third of respondents would give no autonomous responsibility to Flanders, Wallonia, or Brussels (i.e., the territorial communities within Belgium).[10] Conversely, just over a third of respondents would give autonomous responsibility on four or more of the seven policy domains.[11]

Accordingly, when Thijssen and colleagues say that Belgium is "not divided," they mean that the discourse of division and demands for greater autonomy are not as widespread and do not run as deeply among the general public compared to political elites. However, their results do show a division in public attitudes in that there is no clear popular consensus about the federal balance – over a third of respondents seem to want a unitary system, while almost a fifth want complete autonomy for the regions.[12]

The results of ICVS provide further insights to Thijssen and colleagues' findings. Specifically, Belgian respondents were fairly evenly split between viewing federalist design principles as desirable or undesirable (table 7.1). They were similarly divided on the decentralist and nonabsorptionist elements of subsidiarity. These results set Belgium completely apart from all other cases studied in this book. In all cases except Belgium, three or even all four federal design principles attracted the support of at least two-thirds of respondents. The product of those high levels of support means that in each of the other nations studied, there is a clear set of federal constitutional values. While there are variations in those values unique to each country – as discussed in the previous chapters – it is possible to develop an overall picture or characterization of federal political culture that seems to fit with the views of a majority of citizens in each country. For instance, the US and Switzerland were characterized by their confederalist roots, with a strong emphasis placed on divided power and nonabsorptionist subsidiarity, while Canada had a more cooperative federal spirit as citizens placed a high value on having different laws in different parts of the country and supportive subsidiarity. Unlike these other cases, the picture in Belgium is not clear. It would be unfair to say that federalism is not popular in Belgium – each of the four design principles were seen as desirable by at least 50 per cent of respondents. But simultaneously, more respondents viewed these principles as undesirable than anywhere else, including two nonfederal countries. Accordingly, based on the ICVS results, we might say that while federalism has some support in Belgium, there is a lack of a clear attachment to federal constitutional values.

The unclear federal values in Belgium have an interesting parallel to the fallout from the split of the Catholic University of Leuven. In particular, Taub describes the process of dividing the university's library collection between the two institutions, as administrators had

Table 7.1
Public attitudes toward federalism and subsidiarity in Belgium (ICVS 2018)

%	2018
Decentralism	53.3
Nonabsorption	55.4
Support	76.9
Divided power	57.0
Different laws	53.8
Participation	53.6
Respect	65.0

to work out how to allocate several hundred centuries' worth of accumulated knowledge. According to Taub, the majority of items were divided by shelf mark, an "oddly prosaic solution to a fundamentally emotional conflict."[13] Odd-numbered items stayed in the Flemish KUL university, while even-numbered items were moved to the new French institution, UCL. Mark Derez, an archivist for the Catholic University of Leuven, described the approach as a "typical Belgian solution,"[14] but this comment might also speak to the broader Belgian federal political culture. Specifically, scholars of federal political culture emphasize that a successful federation is built and maintained by the belief among citizens in federal principles and ideals, and their continued support for federalism as a system of government.[15] In the classic federations such as the US and Germany, federal political culture flows from a popular consensus that unification as a country is desirable, but that individual regional differences ought to be preserved, whether that be because of linguistic, cultural, geographic, or economic factors. As reported above, the ICVS results from Belgium do not demonstrate a widespread or deep commitment to federal principles. Instead, much like dividing the Leuven university's library, the path to Belgian federalism was pragmatic, grounded in political compromise more than popular belief and emotion. UCL's chief librarian, Charles-Henri Nyns, described that students, faculty and staff at the two universities were "working in the same place, but not together,"[16] a description that seems just as applicable to the wider Belgian federation today.

Regional Differences

Another potential explanation for the lack of a distinct Belgian federal spirit might be divergences in the federal values of Flemish and Walloon respondents. Belgian political culture is often defined by its relatively weak national identity compared to stronger regional identities, facilitated by growing cultural divisions between French- and Dutch-speaking communities and the development of separate party systems in Flanders and Wallonia.

Again, the story is nuanced and complex, however. In 2006, Billiet, Maddens, and Frognier noted that many of the observed differences between Flemish and Walloon respondents in public attitudes surveys were transient and driven by contextual factors, rather than deep-set divisions in the national character.[17] Similarly, on issues of multilevel governance, Thijssen and colleagues found that the similarities between Flemish and Walloon respondents were greater than the differences in attitudes toward policy autonomy for the regions.[18]

The ICVS findings were again consistent with those of earlier studies. While there was some regional variation amongst Belgian respondents, it was not enough that would suggest that there are distinct Flemish or Walloon federal political cultures. On all three subsidiarity items, and the "divided power" and "different laws" features of federal systems, there was no significant difference between Flemish and Walloon respondents. However, Flemish respondents were significantly less likely than their Walloon counterparts to desire participation from all regions on national policymaking (41.5 per cent vs 71.8 per cent) and less likely to desire a system where different levels are forced to respect one another (51.8 per cent vs 74.9 per cent). On average, Flemish respondents were the least likely to "think federal," however they did endorse decentralized subsidiarity in slightly greater numbers (56 per cent) than Walloons (50.4 per cent) and respondents from Brussels (48.8 per cent). This finding is consistent with Deschouwer and Sinardet's 2009 study which also found that Flemish respondents were slightly more likely to favour autonomy than respondents from elsewhere in Belgium.

Further analysis also confirms minor variations in regional attitudes, and the disconnect between public attitudes and elite discourse that Thijssen and colleagues identified. Respondents to ICVS were asked whether they would prefer a system of government that:

Table 7.2
System reform preferences of Belgian respondents (ICVS 2018)

%	*Brussels*	*Flanders*	*Wallonia*
Single national government	48.2	23.9	36.1
Regional governments, but with *fewer* powers than they have now	23.5	14.6	15.1
Regional governments with the *same* powers they have now	9.4	25.1	23.8
Regional governments, but with *more* powers than they have now	11.8	27.9	19.4
A system that allows a region to become its own independent nation	7.1	8.5	5.6

- Has a *single national* government
- Has regional governments, but with *fewer* powers than they have now
- Has regional governments that have the *same* powers they have now
- Has regional governments with *more* powers than they have now
- Allows a region to become an *independent* government

A comparative analysis of this question across all eight cases is provided in the next chapter. For now, however, a close examination of the Belgian results reveals important regional differences (table 7.2). Notably, very few respondents would prefer the status quo, indicating a large public appetite for reform. However, there are significant differences as Flemish respondents were more likely to favour greater regional autonomy or even independence than respondents from Wallonia or Brussels. Nevertheless, a strong proportion (38 per cent) would prefer unitary government, or a decrease in the powers of regional governments, highlighting that the issue is far from one-sided in Flanders. The question was more settled among the respondents from Walloons and Brussels, with a clear preference for decreased autonomy. These findings align with Thijssen and colleagues' observation that substantial portions of the public do not see their opinions reflected by political elites who push for greater autonomy for the regions.[19] An analysis of reform choices by party voting preferences did reveal that supporters of the right-wing Nieuw-Vlaamse Alliantie, and Vlaams Belang were significantly more likely to favour independence (reflecting an extreme position of these parties' policies), but apart from this minority, political views had no significant relationship with reform preferences.[20]

Overall, the Belgian results are the most internally conflicted of any country studied in this book. In comparison to the other cases, even nonfederal countries, there is no clear federal political culture. Amongst some respondents, especially those from Flanders, the paradox of federalism appears in full force, whereby concessions of power to the regional level spiral into a devolutionary cycle culminating in demands for independence. Simultaneously, however, many respondents have little attachment to federal design princples and would prefer a more centralized or even unitary system. One thing that is clear is that the status quo is not seen as a viable option for most Belgians.

The future of Belgian federalism therefore hangs in the balance. Reform seems inevitable, but the type and direction are far from settled. Further decentralization may simply feed the federalism paradox in Flanders, undermining rather than fixing the federation in the long term. Conversely, centralization does not appear to be a satisfactory remedy either, as a slim majority of respondents to the survey expressed a preference for decentralist subsidiarity and nonabsorption. The only value that was clearly highly valued across the country as a whole was supportive subsidiarity, and it may be supportive subsidiarity that holds the answer to the challenges of Belgium's federation. In particular, supportive subsidiarity might capture a middle ground by giving a stronger role for the national government as an institution that bridges divisions between Flanders and Wallonia, while simultaneously empowering the regions. This approach to supportive subsidiarity is quite different to that proposed for Australia, which was driven by strong horizontal bonds between citizens from different parts of the country. Instead, what is suggested here is an adoption of supportive subsidiarity that reinforces attachment to the "common good," a distinctly, though not exclusively, Catholic approach to subsidiarity.

FRANCE

As the final case study in this book, France offers a unique perspective on the ideas of subsidiarity and federalism analyzed in this book. Despite substantial devolutionary reforms, especially in the 1970s,[21] France is steadfastly nonfederal. Nevertheless, respondents to ICVS displayed a strong attachment to federalist design principles. By way of comparison, more French respondents thought dividing power between different levels of government was desirable than respondents from any other country in the study, and support for having different laws in different parts of the country was only stronger in Canada and the US. A clear majority of respondents also expressed attachment to each of the subsidiarity values of decentralism, nonabsorption, and support.

Detecting strong federal and subsidiarity values in France pulls the analysis in two directions. On the one hand, it could suggest the kind of public sentiment necessary to sustain reforms in France that would take the nation in a more federal-like system. On the other hand, it potentially challenges the theoretical role and importance given to conceptions of federal political culture. If strong federal constitutional values are present in a staunchly unitary country, how "federal" are those values? This section addresses these two potential forces through a detailed analysis of the ICVS results and recent developments in French politics.

In 2018, Cole and colleagues observed that four in ten French survey respondents did not trust any level of government.[22] Distrust was most heavily concentrated at the national level, while local councils were the most trusted. Those findings are consistent with those uncovered by ICVS, which found that a staggering 70 per cent of respondents do not trust the national level of government, compared to 53.9 per cent who do not trust local councils. Cole and colleagues explain the low levels of trust in French institutions as a product of two conflicting drivers of public confidence. On the one hand, proximity is an important visible manifestation of authority, and a more proximate institution is more trusted than a distant one. Through this lens, it makes sense that local councils are more trusted than the national government. On the other hand, policy pertinence (confidence in appropriate action by an authority) attaches more strongly to the national level. In a unitary country, this makes sense because the national government is ultimately the only level with unconditional authority to act. In a federation, the disjunction between these kinds of trust is carefully managed because lower levels of government are given (usually constitutionally) authority to take appropriate policy action, therefore increasing policy pertinence that complements proximity trust. But in France, as a unitary country, it is impossible to completely put these two kinds of trust in harmony.

The results from ICVS add further weight to that explanation by revealing that French political structures are poorly aligned with federal constitutional values in France. Specifically, ICVS detected a sur-

Table 7.3
Federal and subsidiarity values in France (ICVS 2018)

%	*2018*
Decentralism	67.8
Nonabsorption	61.7
Support	80.9
Divided power	80.9
Different laws	66.3
Participation	78.8
Respect	80.6

prisingly high amount of support for federal design principles – four in five respondents approved of dividing power and forcing different levels to respect each others' roles and responsibilities (table 7.3). Strong majorities also thought a system allowing different laws in different parts of the country (66.3 per cent) and different regions being able to participate in national decision-making (78.8 per cent) would be desirable.

The obvious counter-interpretation is that these results reflect elements of France's existing nonfederal structure, where power is divided between the national government, and municipal and local authorities, rather than federalism per se. However, while it is true that dividing power, having different laws in different parts of the country, and participation from around the country and respect between governments can also be desirable features of devolved unitary governance, these design features are most closely associated with federalism and federal constitutional values. Indeed, according to Elazar, "successful federal systems are characterized not only by their constitutional arrangements in the narrow sense of the word but by their permeation with the spirit of federalism."[23] Elazar maintained that political institutions common to different political systems, such as divided power, took on a "distinctive character" when enlivened with a federal spirit.[24]

Detecting a federal spirit in France is a significant new step in understanding how values operate in a successful federation. Specifically, it demonstrates that federal values can exist and thrive even in the absence of formal federal structures and institutions. This is important because it highlights that public attitudes do not

Table 7.4
Bivariate correlation between federal and subsidiarity values and trust in government – France (ICVS 2018)

	Trust in national govt	*Trust in municipal govt*	*Trust in local govt*
Decentralism	.330***	.104**	.000
Nonabsorption	–.268***	–.151***	–.051
Support	.126***	–.012	–.097**
Divided power	.044	.125***	.163***
Different laws	.112***	.151***	.136***
Participation	.027	.104**	.110**
Respect	.061	.115**	.105**

$^{*}p < .05$, $^{**}p < .01$, $^{***}p < .001$

simply passively follow existing (federal) structures. Instead, the interaction between institutions and public sentiment is complex and two-directional.

Trust and Subsidiarity Values

As described earlier, ICVS's measurement of French respondents' trust in national, municipal, and local authorities to "do a good job" replicated Cole and colleague's finding that the national government was the least trusted level, and local councils were the most trusted. With the federal and subsidiarity measures, we can go a step further and examine how trust in government relates to the attitudes that build and maintain a desire for federalism. Of course, such questions are relevant to any federation, and will be revisited in chapter 8. But the French case warrants special consideration because its national government was the least trusted of any national government in the eight countries studied, and yet as the most formally centralized case, in theory the French national government also wields the most authority. Accordingly, the stakes are even higher because ascertaining whether federalism or a federated system is viable for France could go a long way to addressing the ailing trust in the French government.

A simple bivariate correlation analysis is extremely revealing (table 7.4). Specifically, it shows significant correlations between trust in the national government and the three subsidiarity elements (with lower trust being associated with higher attachment to subsidiarity). However, the only federal design principle associated with trust in the national government was "having different laws in different parts of the country" (higher trust was associated with a stronger desire for a system that allows for different laws). Conversely, trust in the local level was only associated with supportive subsidiarity (higher trust correlated with a stronger attachment to supportive subsidiarity), but was significantly correlated with all federalist design features. Trust in the municipal level was significantly correlated with all subsidiarity and federal values except for supportive subsidiarity. In plain terms, these results suggest that when answering the subsidiarity items, respondents' views were at least somewhat influenced by their opinion of the trustworthiness of national and municipal governments. For those respondents, a preference for decentralism might be less of an endorsement of local decision-making, and more a reaction against a perceived untrustworthy centre. Simultaneously, responses to federalist design features seems to be more likely driven by the trustworthiness of lower levels – can respondents trust municipal and local governments with the power to make laws for their own region? Can they trust their municipal and local governments if these levels were to be given the opportunity to participate?

These findings for France matter because they arise independently of existing power structures which allocate only a limited authority to lower levels, and even then, this authority has conditional autonomy. Conversely, trust in national and subnational governments in other cases operates within the context of significantly, usually constitutionally enshrined, powers allocated to lower levels.

LESSONS FOR FEDERATIONS AND NONFEDERATIONS

Of the eight countries studied in this book, Belgium and France are the most different. Belgium is a federation under strain, with a divide between discourse from political elites and the average citizen, and unclear or conflicting public attitudes toward federal principles. Conversely, France is a unitary nation with clear public support for federalist design principles and further decentralization. Together, these cases offer several useful insights for the broader study of federal political culture and the role of subsidiarity and decentralization in successful federal countries.

First, the Belgian case seems to confirm that a federal spirit is necessary to sustain a federation. While other cases in this book such as Australia have rebutted the notion that federal constitutional values must include "thinking local," a clear picture of the unique federal political culture of each country emerged in each previous case. However, as discussed earlier, Belgian respondents were evenly divided on most of the federal and subsidiarity values, making it impossible to develop a clear picture of the Belgian federal spirit. The broader question, however, is whether these are simply growing pains that all new federations face, or whether this is an unresolvable tension within the Belgian polity. It is common for new political cultures to take time to develop after federation. Australian discourse places considerable emphasis on the Anzac myth and Australia's involvement in World War I fourteen years after it federated as the turning point in developing a national identity. In Canada, the process arguably took even longer, as Nicol and Whalley observed that there was still little sense of a national identity even 100 years after federation.[25] Public attitude surveys in other new federations such as Ethiopia and Nepal might therefore help identify whether public opinion is deeply split in the years following federation.

Second, the Belgian results might instead serve as a warning about "holding together" federations and the federal paradox. By their nature, holding together federations may be at greater risk of falling into a devolutionary spiral because they begin life by granting concessions to regional governments. While other holding together federations such as India show that the devolutionary spiral is far from inevitable,[26] Belgium might nevertheless provide a useful lesson. Other unitary countries looking at reform involving federation would do well to closely examine the Belgian case and examine whether the federal spirit and public attitudes are aligned with supporting and maintaining a federation.

Third, and in contrast, the French (and the UK) results highlight that strong federal constitutional values can emerge even in the absence of formal federal institutions. In terms of broader federal theory, that finding suggests that federal political culture does more than simply maintain a successful federation – it can be the spark that creates a federation in the first place. While the results do not in themselves mean that France and the UK should federate, they do suggest that there is enough popular public sentiment to warrant taking federalism seriously in those countries. The finding also has significant implications for established federations – namely, they confirm that citizens are not simply passive receivers of political institutions, and their attitudes toward federalism do not have to merely reflect existing governing arrangements. This lesson is twofold – it encourages policymakers to pay attention to public values to ensure that federalism captures the federal spirit of the country, and it highlights that where there is a disconnect between public values and the operation of federalism, citizens can be active agents of change.

Fourth, the results from Belgium and France add further insight and nuance to the relationship between federalism and subsidiarity values. It was already clear from the correlation analysis in chapter 4 that federal and subsidiarity values are not inextricably linked, and that instead they have only a small to moderate relationship. The Belgian and French results add further layers to this observation. The Belgian results showcase that a strong attachment to subsidiarity might help overcome the paradox inherent in federalism whereby greater subnational autonomy risks spiralling into a devolutionary cycle. The French results highlight that trust in government is relevant to subsidiarity and federal values, but that the two principles are impacted most heavily by trust (or a lack of) in different levels – subsidiarity values seem even more strongly related to trust in the national government, while federal values appear to have a stronger association with trust in subnational levels. These themes are taken up further in the next chapter, which takes a closer look at the ways in which policymakers can harness subsidiarity and decentralization to help make federalism more successful.

CONCLUSION

The analysis of Belgian and French responses to ICVS rounds out the eight cases studied in this book. Measuring federal political culture in each country alongside a world-first measure of attitudes toward subsidiarity has revealed significant insights into the factors that drive successful federalism. It has highlighted federal and subsidiarity political cultures in each country (or lack thereof, in the Belgian case), and uncovered a nuanced and complex relationship between these two sets of values. In that regard, decentralization may not be as important to the federal spirit as is often assumed. Instead, the nonabsorptionist element emerged as even more important in the "classic" US, German, and Swiss federations, while supportive subsidiarity was more important in Canada and Australia. This is not to say that decentralization has no role in a successful federation. Instead, its importance is tempered by a more holistic approach to the subsidiarity principle. The next chapter takes up this challenge, exploring how subsidiarity can be used to maintain or create successful federal institutions.

PART THREE

Research Implications

8

Decentralization and Successful Federalism

What Is the Role for Subsidiarity?

One of the most important debates in any federation is the tension between centralization and decentralization. A federation that can successfully balance these competing forces will thrive, while too much centralization or decentralization undermines the federation itself and will ultimately result in poor outcomes for citizens. Subsidiarity is frequently invoked as a principle of decentralization that can help maintain this balance.[1] Scholars of federal political culture also emphasize that citizens' collective values and beliefs about their federal system, especially a tendency to "think local" is a critical component of achieving the right balance of de/centralization.[2] However, the results from ICVS presented in the previous three chapters demonstrate that the picture is more nuanced. Specifically, while the decentralist element of subsidiarity was on average more highly valued in more successful federations such as Switzerland and Canada than federations experiencing serious reform pressure such as Belgium and Australia, it was rarely the most highly valued element. Instead, nonabsorption and support were valued by greater numbers of respondents in each country.

These results provide several important insights into the relationship between federalism, subsidiarity, and decentralization. First, there is clearly more to successful federalism than a federal spirit of "thinking local." Second, and conversely, it is clear that decentralist values still have at least some role to play. Accordingly, the critical question is how decentralist values matter *in context*, rather than simply whether they are present or not. Third, because evidence of strong federal constitutional values was present in both federal and nonfederal countries, we must reevaluate the importance we assign to decentralism as a defining feature of federalism and federal political culture. Fourth, the results show that the ideas about reforming the system and trust in various levels of government also play a role.

This chapter explores these new ideas, approaches and challenges for subsidiarity and federal political culture. The first section engages in a detailed comparison of citizens' trust in government and examines how trust influences attitudes toward federalism and subsidiarity. The second section analyzes how the federal and subsidiarity values in each country shape citizens' views about how the system should look in the future. This explanation leads into the final section, which seeks to apply the lessons of this book to each of the eight countries, revealing a new and meaningful role for subsidiarity in each case.

TRUST

Successful federations must adapt to changing circumstances if they are to remain successful. According to Burgess, this "adaptation and innovation" criterion for success refers to the challenge of evolving the federal state to keep with the times and remain flexibly to fresh problems.[3] In previous chapters, we have considered some of the key challenges faced in various countries, and the attempts to develop innovative solutions to those problems. For example, one of Canada's responses to dissatisfaction among the francophones was to recognize French as an official language in 1969. This section goes a step further, using ICVS's measures of trust in national, regional, and local governments as a weathervane to identify where there might be a need for that country to adapt.

Trust in any political institution or system is crucial. But in federations, the interaction between trust in different levels of government takes on a new dynamic. On the one hand, trust or distrust in one level can threaten trust in other levels, either because citizens are unaware of which level of government to hold accountable, or because a failure of one level undermines confidence in the system as a whole. Faith in political institutions is not a zero-sum game, and a loss of trust in one level will not necessarily be made up by gains in trust in another level. On the other hand, federal systems can promote trust, even when one level of government is perceived as failing, because other levels can step in and save the day. Trust in government is also especially relevant to subsidiarity and subsidiarity values, because at a fundamental level, much of the principle can be seen as a wariness of other orders of government. Thus, decentralism and nonabsorptionist ideas reflect distrust of the centre and concerns about the "grave evils"[4] of centralism, while those who resist supportive subsidiarity may do so based on the view that lower orders are untrustworthy or undeserving of special help.

Accordingly, it is clear that trust is potentially relevant to federal and subsidiarity values and the role of decentralization, although the direction of influence is difficult to pinpoint. While we would expect participants who are pro-subsidiarity to have greater trust in lower levels and less trust in higher levels, it is hard to tell whether respondents' trust in different levels influences their subsidiarity values (e.g., "I prefer decentralism because I do not trust the national government, either generally, or on a particular policy issue"), or whether their values shape the perceived trustworthiness of governments (e.g., "I do not trust the national government because they try to interfere with/absorb the functions of lower levels"). The analysis presented below is therefore restricted to correlation analysis, as bivariate correlations do not test for causation (i.e., they are open to multiple directions of influence between the variables, rather than attempting to determine whether one variable *causes* another).

A further challenge is that the measures of general trust deployed by ICVS cannot detect specific (dis)trust of a particular government, compared to generalized (dis)trust of the level of government. In other words, a respondent might distrust a particular level of government because they do not agree with or have confidence in the government of the day, but a change in government to a preferred party might restore confidence in that level. We have already seen this phenomenon at play in chapter 5, where attitudes toward subsidiarity and federalism differed between Republican and Democrat voters and between 2016 and 2018, depending on which party was in power. Unfortunately, controlling for party affiliation is a fairly unsatisfactory solution, as trust and voting behaviour can be circular – it is impossible to tell from the data whether someone (dis)trusts a level of government because of the party they intend to vote for, or whether they intend to vote for a particular party because of their (dis)trust of the governing party. As such, the analysis and interpretations that follow must be treated with some caution, as there is an inevitable degree of partisanship that will influence the results, but which cannot be accounted for in the current data.

Table 8.1
Perceived trust and confidence in each level of government to "do a good job" by country (ICVS 2017–18) (ordered from least to most trust in federal/national level)

	FRA	BEL	USA	UK	GER	AUS	CAN	SWI
Federal/national								
Trust	28.3	38.7	40.9	41.4	49.0	50.3	59.4	66.6
Distrust	71.7	61.3	59.1	58.6	51.0	49.6	40.6	33.3
State/province/region/land/canton								
Trust	35.8	38.3	54.0	46.6	56.3	50.5	54.5	**69.6**
Distrust	64.2	61.7	46.0	53.4	43.7	49.6	45.6	30.4
Local								
Trust	**48.7**	**46.1**	**62.4**	**48.5**	**59.7**	**50.7**	**64.5**	68.5
Distrust	51.3	53.9	37.6	51.5	40.3	49.3	35.6	31.5

Note: **Bold** denotes the most trusted level within each country.

Table 8.1 opens the analysis of trust in federal systems by showing the trust and confidence in each level of government, ranked from least to most trust in the national level. Several observations are immediately apparent. First, there is substantial variation between countries – Swiss respondents were more than twice as likely to have trust in the national government as French respondents. While there is less variation at the local level, there is still a large gap between the least trusted local government (Belgium, 46.1 per cent) and most trusted local government (Switzerland, 68.5 per cent). Second, the national government was never the most trusted level. In all countries except Switzerland, local governments were the most highly trusted, while in Switzerland cantonal governments were most trusted (though local governments were only 1.1 per cent lower). Third, there is also considerable differences in the trust patterns of each country. In Australia and Switzerland, trust in the three levels of government is very similar – in Australia, the most trusted (local, 50.7 per cent) and least trusted (federal, 50.3 per cent) levels are separated by only 0.4 per cent. Conversely, there is more than a 20 per cent discrepancy between trust in national and local governments in France and the US.

Together, these observations confirm the importance of examining trust as related to decentralization and subsidiarity within federations. It is clear that public confidence is concentrated at more local levels, although the exact amount varies between countries. Accordingly, it is possible that there is a strong connection between trust in lower levels, attachment to subsidiarity values – especially decentralism – and federal constitutional values.

A regression analysis was conducted to test this potential relationship. The regression model was constructed to include trust in each level of government, as well as demographic controls such as gender, age, political outlook (measured on a self-identified ten-point scale, with one being the far political left and ten being the far political right), and self-rated interest in politics. The detailed output of the regression model for each dependent variable (the three subsidiarity items and four federalism items) in each country are presented in an online appendix (table A2).

Three key findings will be discussed in turn – the importance of trust in national governments to decentralist and nonabsorptionist values, the variation between decentralized federations and centralized federations (and unitary nations) in the importance of trust to supportive subsidiarity values, and the general lack of relationship between trust variables and federalist values. Overall, these findings shine a new light on the role of decentralization and subsidiarity in federalism, suggesting that citizens and political elites have different roles to play in contributing to a successful federation.

Trust and Subsidiarity Values

In seven of the eight countries, trust in the national government emerged as the most important predictor of attachment to decentralism, with lower trust in the national government being associated with a stronger desire to see as many decisions made at the lowest level. The only exception here was Australia, where trust in the national government was narrowly upstaged by trust in the local level as the most important predictor (higher trust in local government was associated with a stronger attachment to decentralization). Trust in local government was also a significant predictor of decentralist values in all other countries. These findings affirm the above theory that the perceived trustworthiness of the highest and lowest levels of government is related to the value placed on decentralization, although it is impossible to attribute causation on this data alone.

One possible interpretation is that subsidiarity values and the preference for decentralization is quite pragmatic – beliefs about how power should be allocated are based less on principled ideas about the "right" or "wrong" level of government to hold power and more on the practical perspective that power is better wielded by a more trustworthy level of government than a less trustworthy one. Across the eight countries, local government was more highly trusted than the national level, and therefore was thought of more deserving of authority. This interpretation is plausible, and fits with the general expectation that people place more trust in local governments because they are closer and therefore easier to hold to account.[5] It also places greater emphasis on trust driving subsidiarity values, rather than the other way around (i.e., "I want local governments to have more power because I trust them," rather than "I trust local governments because I think they are more deserving of power"). Interpreting the important relationship between trust and decentralist subsidiarity values in this manner would have significant implications for conceptualizing decentralization in a federation, because it suggests that decentralist reform is more likely to come from increasing trust in lower levels than it is from principled appeals to the "rightness" of localized authority.

However, three caveats rebut or at least caution against that interpretation. First, while the pattern that trust in national and local governments were the two most important predictors of decentralist values was consistent across all eight countries, the strength of their predictive value differed between countries. Specifically, trust in the national government accounted for 5.5 per cent (US) and 6.3 per cent (Germany) of the total variance in reform preferences, but only explained 1.8 per cent of the variation in Australia. Australia has a reputation as being especially pragmatic in its political culture and approach to federalism,[6] while the US in particular is renowned for its strongly principled approach to subsidiarity (as discussed in chapter 3 and 5 and the "confederal" interpretation of subsidiarity). The fit between the results from the regression and broader observations about political culture in these countries therefore favours an interpretation of the results that accommodates a principled approach to decentralism, rather than the pragmatic one described above.

Second, political outlook (left vs right) was only a weak predictor in Canada and Australia, and nonsignificant in all other countries. While only a rough approximation for partisanship, we would expect this variable to show up as a stronger predictor if participants were pragmatically basing their decisions about whether decisions should be made at higher or lower levels on which side of politics currently holds power. This is not to say that partisanship has no effect – results for the US clearly showed that it is at least somewhat relevant. But the fact that this variable was generally an insignificant predictor of decentralist attitudes suggests that its influence is not especially strong. In turn, this finding guides us away from the pragmatic interpretation of the regression results, and toward an explanation that better accommodates a deeper engagement with subsidiarity values.

Third, the ongoing nature of the Australian version of the Constitutional Values Survey, which has been run every other year since 2008, offers further insight. In particular, ACVS has tracked a steady decline in trust and confidence in the federal government since 2012 – trust in the federal government has declined from a high point of 83.5 per cent in 2008, to a low of 44.1 per cent in 2016. This decline spans across both major parties having terms in government, and the rules of four prime ministers (two from each side of politics). The steadiness of the decline despite these political fluctuations indicates that, while there is indeed movement in the general trust in government, it reflects a deeper and growing disenchantment with government, rather than specific dissatisfaction with a particular party or leader. However, while trust in the national government has declined, the proportion of respondents who are attached to decentralism has not increased significantly over the years.[7] The discrepancy between these two trends suggests that even though trust in government – especially the national government – does matter for decentralist values, the decentralist item taps into deeper sentiments and a potential subsidiarity spirit, rather than simply being a reflection of a respondent's current feelings toward the national government.

Therefore, the most appropriate interpretation of the results of the regression is that trust in national and local governments is related to decentralist values, but the relationship is multilayered. Part of the relationship is deep-set and based on principled ideas about the "proper" level of government which can be trusted to make a decision, while part of the association is driven by more immediate concerns, such as the performance and political alignment of a particular current government. While on this data alone it is impossible to determine the exact proportion of each layer at present, it is clear that the balance is different between countries, with some tending toward a more principled approach, and others being more pragmatic.

We can carry this interpretation over to the nonabsorptionist element of subsidiarity, where trust in the national government was again the consistently most important predictor of attachment to nonabsorption. Conversely, trust was rarely a significant predictor of attachment to supportive subsidiarity. This finding tends to confirm the separation between the negative (decentralist and nonabsorptionist) and positive (supportive) limbs of subsidiarity. In this instance, the trustworthiness of a level of government seems to be relevant to whether it should hold power and be protected against infringements of that power, but is not related to whether that government should receive support from higher levels to do its job.

Trust and Federal Constitutional Values

The regression analysis showed that in contrast to subsidiarity values, trust was a much more varied as a predictor of the strength of federal constitutional values. In Canada, Switzerland, and Germany, trust in the federal, regional, or local government was rarely a significant predictor of attitudes toward federalism. Conversely, in Australia, trust in local government was a significant predictor of all four federal attitude variables and trust in state governments emerged as significant for three of the four (divided power, different laws, and participation). Trust in regional and local governments also tended to be significant in Belgium. The two nonfederal countries also differed – in France, the only significant result was trust in local government as a predictor of attachment to divided power, while in the UK trust in the national and local governments predicted the desirability of participation, and trust in local government further predicted attachment to respect between levels.

The three distinct groups of results seem to fit closely with scholarly expectations about the role of federal values in federations. In successful federations such as Canada, Switzerland, Germany, and the US, trust in any level of government has little bearing on the value citizens place on federal design features. This result suggests that the federal constitutional values measured go beyond temporal politics and do indeed capture deeper aspects of federal political culture. While the exact makeup of that federal political culture differs from country to country (e.g., Canadians are generally attached to having a system that enables different laws in different parts of the country, while a majority of Germans see that aspect as undesirable), the findings appear to confirm that there is a strong and deep commitment to federal principles in those successful federations.

Conversely, trust did seem to matter in Australia and Belgium. The result is striking, given the concerns raised in previous chapters about federalism's traction and success in those countries. The significant relationship between trust in lower levels of government and federal values indicates that commitment to federal principles might not be as strong or as deep in Australia and Belgium as in other federations.

Finally, the results from the UK and France formed an interesting middle ground between the two groups of federations, as trust was a significant predictor of some values but not others. These results must be reconciled with the finding in chapter 7 that trust was significantly correlated with federal values. A regression analysis builds on the correlation model, accounting for the fact that some of the variance associated with a particular measure (e.g., desirability of divided power) can be explained by several overlapping predictor variables – for example, where trust in federal and local governments is correlated with federal values, but the correlation is actually a product of a consistent skepticism of *both* levels of government. A regression therefore assesses the unique contribution of each variable. In the French case, while trust in each level was correlated with federal values, often it made little or no significant unique contribution, suggesting that the relationship is better explained by some other factor, such as overall trust in the institution of the political state, or political outlook or even age.

REFORM

The role of federal and subsidiarity values in making federalism successful is put to the ultimate test when we consider how public attitudes can drive or influence reform. The broader role of public attitudes in political reform is a complex one. On one hand, reform is often conducted by political elites with little or no public input or consultation. In a federal context, most change in federations occurs slowly, such as the gradual acquiescence of power from national to provincial governments in Canada,[8] or the steady centralization of individual policy responsibilities in Australia.[9] Even when federal reform is part of a deliberate agenda, as in Switzerland and Germany in the 2000s,[10] negotiations between political elites from different levels of governments take years, often with little engagement from the general public.

On the other hand, citizens are not entirely cut out from the process altogether. In countries that hold referenda to change constitutional aspects of the federal bargain, such as Switzerland and Australia, public involvement is clearly necessary. Other notable examples of public-driven reform include the Quiet Revolution in Canada, and the protests in Flanders (including the University of Leuven) that triggered the pathway to federalism in Belgium. But public involvement in federal reform need not always be this spectacular. For example, responses to various governments' handling of the coronavirus pandemic have provided a good platform to showcase how reactions to individual policies feed into larger federalist ideas. Globally, we have seen citizens rally behind governments who are perceived as doing a good job managing the crisis. For instance, in Australia, Queenslanders supported Premier Anastasia Palaszczuk's handling of the virus, and elected her to a historic third term in October 2020. Similarly, Canadians responded positively to Albertan Premier Jason Kenney sending excess personal protective equipment to other provinces. As we saw in the previous section, trust in a particular level is related to the value placed on decentralization and nonabsorption. For state and local governments seen to be doing well responding to coronavirus, there was an opportunity to capitalize on and convert popular sentiment to a more diffuse trust and confidence in that level of government.

Accordingly, understanding citizens' reform preferences and ideas about what their federal system should look like in the future are critical to evaluating the role of the federal spirit in a successful federation. As described in chapter 7, ICVS assessed participants' views about the future by asking whether regional governments in their country should (1) not exist, (2) have fewer powers, (3) have the same powers as they currently have, (4) have more powers, or (5) be able to become independent. The purpose of the question, and the analysis that follows, is not to dictate reform policy according to the will of the masses, although bringing institutions into alignment with public attitudes might improve satisfaction with the system. Instead, the question is used to add further context to the federal and subsidiarity spirits, and to help predict future trends in those values.

Brown, Deem, and Kincaid have presented some analysis on this measure elsewhere.[11] Specifically, they highlighted significant differences between the countries in terms of the proportion of respondents seeking reform versus those who would prefer the status quo.

Table 8.2
Reform preferences (%) and federal constitutional values (means), ordered by most to least support for status quo

Question: Now a question about [COUNTRY]'s system of government in the ***future*** *– say, 20 years from now. Thinking about the structure of [COUNTRY]'s system of government, which one of the following systems do you personally think would be the best system in the future?*

A system ...	BEL % (FCV mean)	FRA % (FCV mean)	UK % (FCV mean)	GER % (FCV mean)	AUS % (FCV mean)	USA % (FCV mean)	CAN % (FCV mean)	SWI % (FCV mean)
with *a single national government but no state* governments*	22.9% −3.06	8.9% −4.36	9.0% −3.66	9.1% −3.70	17.2% −3.59	4.5% −4.79	6.1% −3.68	7.5% −3.94
in which state* govts have *fewer powers* than they do now	11.8% −3.5	9.3% −4.04	12.4% −3.87	14.1% −3.87	14.6% −3.86	10.8% −3.87	14.7% −4.27	15.2% −4.17
where the state* govts have *same powers* as they do now	17.1% −3.73	20.0% −4.08	22.0% −4.06	29.9% −4.19	30.5% −4.05	32.0% −4.58	36.2% −4.57	44.6% −4.75
in which state* govts have *more powers* than they do now	17.4% −4.04	34.2% −4.75	25.3% −4.25	21.7% −4.33	21.3% −4.42	22.6% −4.80	16.5% −4.73	15.7% −4.71
that allows a state* to become an *independent nation*	5.5% −3.10	3.9% −4.11	6.5% −4.53	6.0% −4.55	3.3% −4.37	4.5% −4.29	5.4% −4.52	3.7% −4.48
Don't know / can't say	25.3%	23.7%	24.8%	19.2%	13.1%	25.6%	21.1%	13.3%
Total	100	100	100	100	100	100	100	100

*In Canada, "province/provincial"; Germany, "Land"; UK, "region/regional."
Source: Table reproduced from A.J. Brown, Jacob Deem, and John Kincaid, "Federal Constitutional Values and Citizen Support: Explaining the Viability of Federalism and Federalist Reforms in Eight Countries," *Publius* 52, no. 1 (2022): 1–25.

Table 8.2 replicates that analysis here, showing that Swiss and Canadian respondents were more likely to want to keep regional governments' responsibilities as they are now, while 57.6 per cent of Belgians and 56.3 per cent of French respondents would change the current system. This chapter extends that analysis, examining whether and how subsidiarity and federal values contribute to respondents' views on reforming the system. The results of a multinomial logistic regression analysis using the same variables described in the trust section, plus the federal and subsidiarity values items, are presented in table 8.3.

Trust in the federal government was a significant variable in all eight countries, affirming the importance of the insights raised in the previous section. However, these results seemed to be largely driven by the extreme scenario of preferring a "single national government with no [regional] governments," with those with higher trust in the federal government unsurprisingly being more likely to select this option. Accordingly, it is clear that, while important, trust does not tell the whole story. Participants' self-reported political orientation (left to right) also featured as significant in all cases except the US, although analysis of the response categories revealed few consistent patterns. The exception here was Belgium, where political orientation was a significant factor in responses calling for a single unitary government, fewer powers for the regional governments, and more powers for regional governments. As discussed in chapter 7, this is a live issue in Belgian politics, and was a key policy platform for some parties in the 2019 election. The influence of political orientation therefore aligns well with those findings. The US results also bear further discussion, given that analysis in chapter 5 highlighted differences in values of Republican and Democratic voters. Further analysis did demonstrate that Republicans were slightly more likely to favour decentralizing reforms (and Democrats the opposite). However, the differences were not pronounced. One interpretation, given the observed differences in subsidiarity values between 2016 and 2018 ostensibly based on partisan views (chapter 5), is that politically-driven respondents could not be sure which party would be in power in twenty years' time, and their political views therefore played a smaller role in their reform preferences.

Notwithstanding these variables, subsidiarity and federal values were also often identified as significant in the model, confirming that better understanding these values can help guide reform to achieve greater success in a federation. At least one federal value emerged as a significant predictor of reform preferences in every country except Germany, but the pattern differed between cases. Most straightforwardly, rating divided power as a desirable feature

Table 8.3

Multinomial logistic regression analysis of reform preferences in eight countries (ICVS 2018)†

	UK	Germany	US	Canada	France	Switzerland	Belgium	Australia
	χ^2	χ^2	χ^2	χ^2	χ^2	χ^2	χ^2	χ^2
Gender	6.385	17.516**	11.270*	9.070	8.154	8.915	7.290	3.632
Age	57.581*	44.229	49.545	65.211**	47.567	82.608***	63.343**	63.815
Political view	59.858*	64.298**	45.827	61.619*	61.161*	67.754**	69.747**	68.578**
Interest in politics	30.864*	19.676	21.600	14.621	19.756	23.791	9.258	19.765
Trust in federal govt	28.772**	41.553***	28.163**	45.972***	48.186***	68.418***	30.949**	37.885***
Trust in "regional" govt	16.059	16.502	13.523	30.002**	11.902	18.569	22.980*	36.533***
Trust in local govt	7.286	32.644**	10.520	9.020	17.008	14.623	22.972*	5.080
Decentralism	47.031***	61.983***	44.624***	20.402	20.034	46.160***	56.015***	29.148**
Non-absorption	29.857**	20.257	28.269**	29.128**	25.079*	25.850*	26.301*	11.762
Support	11.028	14.644	19.142	15.654	34.322**	13.577	10.723	32.691**
Divided power	15.764	14.119	21.457*	20.960	14.636	19.968	11.479	45.899***
Different laws	32.326**	14.651	6.603	21.769*	23.154*	24.872**	23.486*	11.820
Participation	8.988	9.897	25.068*	11.739	22.669*	10.031	14.877	32.233**
Respect	19.192	11.813	24.031*	14.867	21.155*	26.496**	29.135**	7.609
N	509	594	500	523	555	596	511	903
McFadden Pseudo R^2	.328	.293	.312	.258	.275	.308	.306	.204
Df	224	212	216	216	216	216	216	228
χ^2	495.930***	509.389***	421.534***	372.347***	420.709***	469.196***	477.587***	534.837***

† Full parameter estimates provided in table A2, available in an online appendix at the author's website: https://jacobdeem.com/rethinking-decentralization.

* $p < .05$; ** $p < .01$; *** $p < .001$

predicted stronger support for reform options giving state governments greater autonomy in Australia and the US. There is a very logical fit between these two variables, but the pronounced result in Australia compared to other countries is especially important because of the centralized context of the Australian federation – giving state governments more autonomy would be a reversal of the trend in Australian federalism and would be a concrete means of giving effect to the widespread endorsement of dividing power in the Australian federal constitutional values. Conversely, in the already highly decentralized Swiss federation, the value placed on dividing power did not predict reform preferences, but valuing having different laws in different parts of the country, and respect for each others' roles and responsibilities, was significant. Again, this result aligns with the context of federal political culture in Switzerland, where multilingualism and deep regionalism thrive.

In Canada, having different laws in different parts of the country was the federal value that emerged as a significant predictor of reform preferences. Given provincial autonomy to create different laws in many key policy domains, especially in Quebec, is a fundamental principle of modern Canadian federalism, this result is unsurprising. Further, this result also ostensibly aligns with Canada's "empathetic federalism" discussed in chapter 6.[12] Interestingly, however, having different laws was also significant in the UK. This finding also aligns with desire for subnational autonomy in the UK, and must be interpreted in the context of a substantially higher appetite for structural reform in the UK compared to Canada. Accordingly, respondents who valued having different laws around the country were significantly more likely to desire giving more power to subnational orders of government.

Belgian and French respondents were the least satisfied with their current system (figure 1.1) and the most likely to want structural reform (table 8.2). Federal constitutional values provide further insight here. In France, value for "having different laws," "participation from around the country," and "respecting the roles and responsibilities of other levels of government" were all significant values, although having different laws was the most consistent across the reform options. Respondents who valued it were more likely to favour giving more power to subnational governments, and those who did not value it were less likely to do so. However, the variable was also significant in the "status quo" response category, with respondents who valued having different laws being more likely to think that subnational governments should have the same powers as they do now. In the context of values for dividing power and decentralist subsidiarity (which were not significant), these findings would suggest that France's dissatisfaction with the current system is driven by a pragmatic desire to allocate responsibility at the more trusted (lower) orders of government and to protect their authority, rather than a deeply principled desire for governance at the lowest possible level. Attitudes toward nonabsorptionist and supportive subsidiarity, which were also significant (especially support), further reinforce this interpretation: to the extent that French respondents want decentralizing change, it seems to be the product of a desire to protect existing differentiation (having different laws, respecting roles and responsibilities, and nonabsorption), and to ensure that the central government facilitates and empowers the better-trusted lower orders (support and participation).

In Belgium, respect and having different laws emerged as significant. These are two core goals, and currently key challenges, for the Belgian federation. However, these variables were outshone in their importance by decentralist subsidiarity. While not surprising, this result highlights the wider point that federal constitutional values are best understood in the context of attitudes toward subsidiarity.

In contrast to federal constitutional values, where specific values were important in specific countries, decentralist and nonabsorptionist subsidiarity values were consistently significant across all the cases. Of course, the options in the reform item do lend themselves to questions of decentralism and nonabsorption especially at either extreme – a single national government and no regions (complete centralization and absorption) and the ability to become independent (significant decentralization and guaranteed nonabsorption). To confirm that these options, which in most cases are extreme and not realistic, were not unduly influencing the importance of nonabsorption as a predictor variable, a second regression was conducted excluding the two extreme reform options, which produced similar results. This finding therefore reinforces the perspective that subsidiarity must be understood as more than simple decentralization. Especially in the context of reform in a federal country, nonabsorption is a critical element of the subsidiarity principle, further confirming the observations set out in chapter 4.

FINDING SUBSIDIARITY'S MEANING – GOING BEYOND DECENTRALIZATION

Chapter 3 explored how subsidiarity's meaning was lost, both definitionally and in the sense that it is perceived to be meaningless as a principle of governance. Subsequent chapters highlighted how we can recover subsidiarity's definition by adopting a broad understanding that includes elements of decentralism, nonabsorption, and support. The public attitude evidence from ICVS also demonstrated that there is a strong attachment to subsidiarity values, even if the pattern of that attachment varies from country to country. This section consolidates the lessons from the analysis presented above to show that subsidiarity is still a meaningful principle, and presents a guide to its use in successful federalism.

Most importantly, the results confirm subsidiarity's place as a bridge between federal political culture and the institutions of federalism. While the relationship is more complicated than simply "thinking local" or valuing decentralist subsidiarity, there are clear and logical ways of explaining the federal values expressed in each country when we consider the measured attitudes toward subsidiarity. Critically, this means that understanding "success" in a federation involves taking full account of subsidiarity values. The classically successful federations of Germany, Switzerland, and the US are aided by a strong public value for nonabsorptionist subsidiarity, which complements the strong separation of responsibilities between jurisdictions in those federations.

While each of those federations can be regarded as successful in their own way, the evidence from Canada shows that emphasizing nonabsorption is not the only way to build a successful federation. In Canada, supportive subsidiarity was the most valued element, a result that aligns well with its long history of cooperative federalism implicit in its constitution. Further, this finding demonstrates that modelling a system after the "classic" federations is no guarantee of success, especially if public value for nonabsorption is not strong. The results from Belgium and Australia, which both face ongoing debates about the suitability of the federal model, confirm that the federal system will have difficulty succeeding if it does not align with subsidiarity values as well as federal ones. In Australia, repeated attempts to use subsidiarity to reform the federation have failed because they have focused on decentralization, but the results of ICVS suggests that this approach does not align with Australian subsidiarity values. Instead, a more supportive approach is likely to result in a more successful federation. Similarly, the Belgian results show that, while political elites have viewed increasing decentralization as the silver bullet to problems in the federation, citizens are evenly divided on whether decentralization is valuable or not. Conversely, supportive subsidiarity attracts a much higher proportion of the general public.

The results also showed a strong value for subsidiarity in the non-federal countries of France and the UK. While not surprising in themselves, the results confirm that even though subsidiarity might be especially important in federations, it is still important outside federal settings. The findings therefore lend empirical weight to Golemboski's theoretical argument that subsidiarity is broader than a mere subcomponent of federalism.[13]

Using Subsidiarity in Six Federations

As a final demonstration of subsidiarity's ongoing importance and meaningfulness, this section concludes by briefly highlighting the role subsidiarity can play in the future for the six federations studied in this book.

Subsidiarity's continuing strength in Germany is a vital component of its policy outlook, and Germany's strong public appreciation for subsidiarity reinforces the importance of the principle. Nevertheless, this research does raise some important questions about the future of subsidiarity values. On the one hand, it is difficult to envisage subsidiarity as anything other than a core principle in German federalism and culture. Its rich history of subsidiarity dating back to the Holy Roman Empire, and the more modern institutional protections against central power, as well as the strong notion of local identity in the form of Heimat, presents a picture of strong and stable subsidiarity values complementing a clear federal spirit. While Germany has strong institutional provisions for the principle (e.g., Article 72), Germany's increasing international role[14] may demand the erosion of some of the localized emphasis. Equally, while the Federal Constitutional Court has protected the subsidiarity principle, it remains responsive to public attitudes:[15] if these attitudes change, so too may the court's outlook. Accordingly, it is important that applications of the principle in Germany are sensitive to potential changes in subsidiarity values in coming years.

Switzerland remains a shining example of successful federalism. However, the strong emphasis on decentralization that earned Switzerland its reputation of success may be shifting, and policymakers must be alert to the potential shift in the federation if it is to remain successful. Specifically, Mueller and Dardanelli have noted a clear shift toward policy centralization in Switzerland in the recent decades.[16] The results from ICVS paint a bigger picture around those observations of institutional and policy change. While recent centralizing reforms have been endorsed by Swiss citizens at referenda, ICVS showed that value for decentralization remains high and respondents expressed strong satisfaction with the way the system is working and a comparative lack of appetite for further reform. Thus, even though it is impossible to predict the trend subsidiarity values will take in coming years from only one datapoint, there seems to be a general contentedness with the state of the federation, and further centralization may not be met with the same enthusiasm as previous reforms.

In Canada, identifying strong public attachment to subsidiarity and federal values offers a timely chance to stop and take stock of subsidiarity's role in the federation. While the country is rather unique globally in its trend of decentralization, it is important to remember that subsidiarity encompasses more than just a preference for local decision-making. Importantly, while Canadians placed a high value on decentralism, they were even more attached to nonabsorptionist and supportive subsidiarity. In the context of recent controversies around oil and pipelines in British Columbia[17] and Alberta,[18] it is important that both federal and provincial governments are guided by the nuances in subsidiarity's meaning, rather than defaulting to traditional arguments about decentralization. Equally, it is worth noting that citizens' preferences for subsidiarity are strong right across Canada, not just in Quebec and Alberta. It is possible that subsidiarity values in Canada are the product of long-standing divisions over national identity, and they also might confirm observations of an "empathetic federalism" in Canada.[19] If future research proves this theory, it will demonstrate the vitality of subsidiarity values as an integral and enduring part of the Canadian political landscape and the success of its federation.

The US is at one of its most divided periods in its history. While much of that division is driven by hyperpartisanship and populist rhetoric, the results from ICVS suggest that deeply held values of nonabsorptionist subsidiarity and an appreciation for divided power might also play a part. This finding complicates the pathway to the more unified America outlined by President Biden. Specifically, there seems to be a unique challenge in improving political and social harmony without undermining the value for decentralization and nonabsorption that sustains the US federation and makes it successful. Taken to the extreme, it might even be possible that successful democracy and successful federalism are not compatible in the US in its current state. The way forward is therefore likely to emphasize a tolerance and appreciation for diversity, rather than to attempt to unify Americans toward a particular viewpoint. Of course, doing so is easier said than done.

While subsidiarity may have been "disregarded" in Australia,[20] it is certainly not dead to citizens, but its meaning to them differs from the way the principle is used in policy debates. Specifically, Australians are not especially attached to decentralism, especially when compared to respondents from other federations (and even nonfederations). Instead, they are far more attached to supportive notions of subsidiarity, potentially because it better aligns with Australia's broader culture of egalitarianism and "mateship." As a result, citizens may be more likely to endorse reform, or, more cynically, politicians will gain more popularity, if subsidiarity is used as a tool for community empowerment, rather than as a decentralizing principle as in past reform attempts.[21] Attempting to replicate federal reforms seen in Germany and Switzerland in Australia – which have previously served as inspiration[22] – will continue to prove difficult, if not impossible, as this book has identified vastly different attitudes toward subsidiarity in these countries. Instead, the data suggests that subsidiarity's realization in Australia will be more successful if attention is focused on the supportive elements of the principle, for example by addressing vertical fiscal imbalance to give the states greater financial capacity and independence.[23]

As with Australia, the Belgian results suggest that subsidiarity can be a useful guide to help the federation become more successful, but a focus on decentralization is unlikely to attract widespread support. Instead, turning to supportive subsidiarity might be the key to bridging the divide between Belgians who are unhappy with federalism because they want a more centralized system, and those who are unhappy because they want more regional autonomy. Specifically, supportive subsidiarity was the only subsidiarity or federal value that more than two-thirds of respondents saw as desirable, highlighting it as the most viable pathway for reform. In practice, placing a greater emphasis on supporting lower levels could appease both sides of the debate because Belgians wanting more autonomy for their region would find that region better supported, while those desiring greater centralization would be satisfied that the national government plays a greater role in distributing resources fairly around the country.

CONCLUSION

The analysis in this chapter has demonstrated that subsidiarity can play a meaningful role in helping federations to succeed. However, it will only do so if we embrace a broader understanding of the principle's definition, and it must be pursued in a manner that fits with the unique subsidiarity and federal values of each country.

9

Conclusion

Subsidiarity on the Map of Federal Political Culture

Opening his seminal book, *The Federal Principle*, Solomon Rufus Davis pondered: "How many times has it been said that concepts, abstractions, and words are like living things; they come into life, they grow, they change, they die like the humans that live by them."[1]

Davis's consideration of the human element of federalism perfectly captures the focus on federal political culture in the current study. A federation supported by a strong federal political culture will flourish, but without public belief in federal values and principles, federalism is doomed to die. While Davis concluded that federalism as a concept was living vibrantly in 1978, there is no doubt that federal systems have faced many challenges in the decades since. In the past few years alone, most federal systems have contended with increased political polarization and decreased trust in institutions, and the social and economic challenges of dealing with a pandemic. In the face of these adversities, understanding the conditions for successful federalism, or the factors that can lead to greater success, is critical. This book has examined the role subsidiarity can play in fostering thriving federal systems, with a particular emphasis on understanding subsidiarity as being broader than mere decentralization. This fresh perspective is important because subsidiarity faces its own hurdles. We might even apply Davis's quote to subsidiarity: after coming to life in ancient Greece in the works of Aristotle, the ideas and values that underpin subsidiarity have grown and changed, and according to some scholars, the principle is now dead or dying,[2] or at the very least has been rendered meaningless.[3] However, this book has argued that subsidiarity is alive and well and has real value in helping ensure that federal systems succeed. The principles that underpin subsidiarity –

decentralism, nonabsorption, and support – continue to be relevant and helpful and are recognized as such by people living in eight countries: Australia, Belgium, Canada, France, Germany, Switzerland, the UK, and the US.

This book sought to address concerns that the principle is only of limited use or importance by examining subsidiarity's meaning. Here, "meaning" was used in two senses. First, what does "subsidiarity" mean and how are we to define or at least understand it? Second, is subsidiarity meaningful, in the sense that it is an important principle in government and that everyday citizens value it? While some parts of the existing literature have grappled with these questions, the major contribution of this book has been to answer these questions through conceptualizing and measuring the collective attitudes and orientations of citizens toward the values underpinning subsidiarity. Thus, the question of how subsidiarity is understood was considered from the perspective of citizens, and the book demonstrated important variations in the way the principle is viewed in each country. Similarly, the meaningfulness of the principle was assessed, not according to strict policy terms, but by measuring whether citizens saw value in the ideas central to subsidiarity, and it was revealed that decentralism, nonabsorption, and support are indeed seen as valuable.

These insights have significant implications for long-standing questions about the relationship between federalism and subsidiarity. Specifically, the analysis presented in this book highlighted that subsidiarity values do seem to play at least some role in maintaining federal political culture which in turn drives success in a federation. Further, however, because those subsidiarity values differ from country to country, it was possible to draw clear connections between the way decentralism, nonabsorption, and support are respectively valued in each federation, and the successes (and challenges) unique to each federation studied. For instance, we can distinguish between the divisive brand of federalism in the US, complemented by strong civic attachment to nonabsorptionist elements of subsidiarity, and the more cooperative "empathetic federalism" of Canada,[4] assisted by a greater emphasis on the supportive element of subsidiarity. While both federations are considered successful in their own right, the federal political cultures supporting that success are very different, and will require different policies and rules to maintain or extend that success.

This chapter summarizes the key findings of this book by returning to the four criteria for successful federalism outlined in chapter 1 and explaining how the insights of the current study help us understand subsidiarity's role in a successful federation. It then considers the lessons and broader implications of this study, and identifies avenues for further research, before concluding with a final statement on subsidiarity's continued importance and meaning and the utility of understanding public values.

USING SUBSIDIARITY TO UNDERSTAND SUCCESSFUL FEDERALISM

This book has referred to Burgess's four criteria for judging the success of federalism as a touchstone for understanding the importance of federal political culture and the potential role for subsidiarity in making federalism work.[5] Considering the (1) primary or founding goals, (2) subjective views of citizens, (3) values, interests, and ideals, and (4) ability to adapt, adjust, and innovate of a given federation provides an insight into the ways in which it is succeeding and the areas in need of improvement. This section summarizes the key findings of the book, explaining how subsidiarity contributes to federal political culture and success of a federation on each criterion.

Primary Goals

We have seen that the primary aims and objectives of federating can have a profound influence on whether a federation thrives or not. A key challenge for subsidiarity is that most of the federations studied in this book were founded before the term "subsidiarity" reached popular usage. Accordingly, locating subsidiarity's meaning in successful federalism faces a problem at the outset, as, in many federations, "subsidiarity" could not have been an explicit primary goal or value. Nevertheless, as demonstrated in chapter 3, the ideas underpinning subsidiarity date as far back as ancient Greece. Thus, we can still find evidence of subsidiarity in the primary goals of some of the world's oldest federations. Further, when we take a broader approach to subsidiarity's meaning, conceptualizing it as being made up of decentralism, nonabsorption, and support, we can find even more impact for the principle in the founding aims of successful federations. Germany stands out as an especially good example here: as discussed in chapter 5, we can find evidence of decentralism, nonabsorption, and support in the German Basic Law. Embracing a broader approach to subsidiarity's meaning when we look for the principle in a federation's primary goals is also important when we are concerned that the federation might not be living up to its full potential. For example, scholars of Australian federalism have gone to great lengths to imply decentralist and nonabsorptionist subsidiarity into the text of the Australian Constitution.[6] However, now armed with the knowledge of Australians' strong attachment to supportive subsidiarity, it might be more useful to look at the founders' primary goals of building a supportive federation which sought to achieve a common good across the Australian continent.[7] It is clear, then, that including subsidiarity as one of the primary goals of a federation can be a factor in understanding the success of that federation, but in order to detect that influence we must be open to subsidiarity's full meaning.

Subjective Views of Citizens

The results from ICVS highlighted extraordinary differences between countries in terms of citizens' perceptions of whether their federal system was working well or not. At one extreme, respectively 82.3 per cent and 74.1 per cent of Swiss and Canadian respondents thought the system was working well, reinforcing scholarly opinion that these are successful federations. At the other end of the spectrum, only 39.1 per cent of Belgians were satisfied with how their system was working. A similar pattern emerged when respondents were asked about structural reform options – most Swiss and Canadian respondents would keep the status quo, while there was a strong appetite for change amongst Belgians.

Further analysis showed that federal and subsidiarity values were an important predictor of these reform preferences. Nonabsorptionist and decentralist values in particular were often the best predictor of a respondent's views on whether regional governments should have the same, more, or fewer powers. While it is impossible to make a causal inference here, it is evident that understanding subsidiarity values is critical to making sense of citizens' subjective views about the success of their federation. Whether subsidiarity values are a standard by which they judge the federal system, or whether dissatisfaction with the system breeds a desire for more decentralization and/or nonabsorption, it is clear that there is at least some relationship between these variables.

Additionally, these results highlight that there is a general alignment between citizens' subjective views about whether the federation is succeeding and expert opinions about the health of that federation. This is an important confirmation of Burgess's criteria,[8] but it also reinforces the value of studying public attitudes toward federalism and subsidiarity. Despite concerns that citizens are uninterested or unaware of their federal systems,[9] it is clear that most citizens can still identify when the system is working (and when it needs improvement), indicating that they are at least somewhat aware of the health of their federation.[10]

Values, Identities, and Ideals

The values, identities, and ideals of citizens are critical to understanding the success of federal systems. This book has placed a clear emphasis on this criterion, aiming to uncover attitudes toward federal design features that might evidence federal political culture, and providing a world-first measure of subsidiarity values. The unique comparison of eight countries (six federal and two nonfederal) revealed important insights into the role of federal and subsidiarity values. It is clear that each country has its own unique federal and subsidiarity spirits, which plausibly tie into the wider values, histories, traditions, and political cultures of those nations. For example, on average Canadian and Swiss respondents value the principle highly, but Swiss participants tend to value nonabsorption more highly than the other elements, while Canadians are more attached to supportive subsidiarity. This divergence reflects a tradition of confederalist nonabsorption in Switzerland, compared to an "empathetic federalism" in Canada.[11] The implication of this finding is that there is not just one federal or subsidiarity spirit, and no single meaning of "subsidiarity." Instead, subsidiarity takes on a unique meaning in each nation. Accordingly, while we can say that a strong federal political culture and "thinking federal" on the part of citizens is crucial to the success of that federation, the precise makeup of that federal political culture will vary between contexts. Further, while "thinking federal" will sometimes include "thinking primarily in terms of local initiative"[12] and emphasizing decentralist subsidiarity (e.g., Germany), that will not always be the case. For instance, the evidence from the Australian results suggests that thinking more in terms of supporting lower levels (rather than simply expecting them to be capable on their own) is more likely to produce better outcomes.

While there is some relationship between subsidiarity and federal values, it is not overwhelmingly strong, and valuing subsidiarity does not inevitably lead to strong federal constitutional values and vice versa. Further, strong attachments to federal and subsidiarity values were detected in France and the UK, the two nonfederal nations. These findings confirm that the relationship between these principles is nuanced and complex. While subsidiarity and federalism have a logical connection and subsidiarity should continue to play a meaningful role in policy design in federations, we should not assume that subsidiarity and federalism are the same. Rather than being the "soul of federalism,"[13] subsidiarity might be better understood as its close friend – useful and relevant, and frequently seen together, but nevertheless independent, and valuable in its own right. Additionally, while a value for decentralization is an important feature in successful federations, focusing on the decentralist element of subsidiarity alone is not enough. Instead, appreciating nonabsorptionist and/or supportive elements is usually an even more important ingredient for a subsidiarity spirit that contributes to successful federalism.

Ability to Adapt, Adjust, and Innovate

Some federations are better than others at adapting to new challenges and contexts. Canada stands out as a particularly good example of a federation that is successful because it has managed to adapt and grow over the years. Conversely, the Belgian federation is often viewed as struggling. One way we can make sense of Canada's success and Belgium's challenges is to explore how reforms and adaptations in the two countries have aligned with federal and subsidiarity values. In particular, both federations have had to manage subnational identities and the challenges of geographically concentrated linguistic groups. Both federations have also undergone significant decentralization in order to accommodate those subnational groups. And yet, Canada's adaptation has been more successful. This might be because its reforms better align with the subsidiarity values of its citizens. As a base comparison, decentralization is more widely valued among Canadians than Belgians, so we would expect decentralist reform to be more popular there. But the lesson goes further than that. Canadians also strongly value supportive elements of subsidiarity, and Canadian policymakers have been careful to preserve the spirit of cooperative federalism in their reforms. By contrast, Belgian reforms have tended to focus on granting Flanders and Wallonia more autonomy, and have paid less attention to supportive structures that go with that reform. Such an approach jars the strong attachment to supportive subsidiarity also evident among Belgian respondents.

This is perhaps the most important lesson from this study. The typical focus on subsidiarity as a principle of decentralism, in the context of – and as a pushback against – increasing levels of centralization in most federations, means that devolving power to lower levels of government is often viewed as the solution to problems within a federation. However, the evidence presented in this book shows that focusing on decentralization alone will rarely be an effective adaptive strategy in the long term. Instead, if policymakers want to help their federation succeed, or ensure that it continues to do so, they must pay attention to subsidiarity's broader meaning, and align policy and reform with the federal and subsidiarity values unique to each country.

WIDER IMPLICATIONS AND FURTHER RESEARCH

As discussed in chapter 8, this book has aimed to translate the insights from measuring federal and subsidiarity values into practical lessons and reform options to help ensure federalism succeeds and thrives in the federations studied. The utility of this approach demonstrates its worth, and also implies that similar benefits can be achieved in other countries. However, because the study uncovered unique federal and subsidiarity values in each country, it is clear that any attempt to draw wider insights must be alert to the importance of appreciating the nuances of federal political culture. Thus, while the generalizable lesson from this book is that federal political culture is important and that subsidiarity can be meaningful in driving or increasing federal success, the exact lesson will differ from country to country. The findings detailed in this book therefore also present three broad avenues for further research. First, additional research is needed to address some of the limitations of this study. Most notably, there might be some benefit in expanding the measure of subsidiarity values to include multiple items per dimension, and to test whether particular aspects of decentralism, nonabsorption, and support resonate especially strongly. For example, are citizens particularly drawn to higher levels providing financial support to lower levels, or do they also see value in support in the form of lending expertise or guidance? Further, constructing a bottom-up sample would allow for a more rigorous examination of subnational differences in federal and subsidiarity values, and could also provide clearer insights on the attitudes of migrants, Indigenous citizens, and other identifiable communities within a country.

Second, expanding on the research already conducted in the eight countries studied, the next step is to explore how to better reconcile the importance citizens give to the principle, with formal institutional arrangements that do not necessarily reflect these values. The attitudes and views of policymakers are key here, as one reason for the divide between public values and institutional practice might be that policymakers are concerned that citizens do not see the principle as meaningful. Additionally, investigation of a devolution paradox – where citizens desire greater decentralism and want state or regional governments to have more responsibility, but simultaneously desire policy uniformity and equality[14] – may also help identify where and how subsidiarity can be better realized. Subsidiarity appears highly valued, but under what circumstances, and in which policy areas, do these values have to compete with citizens' preferences for more centralized control? Such an investigation would also speak to the salience of subsidiarity values in federations – while this book has identified that citizens view subsidiarity as meaningful, does the principle remain meaningful when it comes into conflict with other values (such as egalitarianism in Australia)?

The third avenue for further research is to investigate subsidiarity attitudes in a broader range of countries. Clearly, the current study has only focused on established Western democracies. This was a deliberate and important choice, given the deep histories of subsidiarity and federalism in Western thought. But as federalism becomes more widespread throughout the world and the subsidiarity principle is adopted and acknowledged elsewhere (such as in Brazil[15]), studying the relationship in a non-Western context is increasingly important. Expanding the study is especially important in the context of Thomas Franck's remarks that the common thread linking many failed federations was in fact the "failure of traditional federalism" applied in non-Western contexts.[16] Studying subsidiarity values in a non-Western context would add particular insight: exactly how do broader Western values and institutions relate to or influence subsidiarity values and its role in a federation?

SUBSIDIARITY ON THE MAP OF FEDERAL POLITICAL CULTURE

This book began with Duchacek's observation that, like captains of old, we have a map of federalism, with a blank space where we might locate federal political culture. Through the analysis presented here, we have now charted subsidiarity's role in that space, identifying how understanding subsidiarity (and public attitudes toward the principle) can help drive successful federalism. Conceptualizing subsidiarity through the three elements – decentralism, nonabsorption, and support – provides an approach that is sensitive to and able to account for the important developments of the principle, but also provides enough clarity that we no longer need to ask, "what does 'subsidiarity' mean?" Freed from debates over how to define subsidiarity, the literature can focus its attention on how to give effect to the principle and how best to realize its potential as a principle of good government in a successful federation.

In doing so, we also need not ask "is the principle meaningful?" at least in the context of Australia, Belgium, Canada, France, Germany, the UK, and the US. The citizens of Canada, Germany, Switzerland, and the US see considerable value in the principle, as do citizens of the nonfederations – France and the UK. Australians and Belgians are also positively inclined toward subsidiarity, albeit not in the ways it has previously been used in policy debates. Evidence of distinct subsidiarity spirits in these countries highlights public appetite for the principle, even where there are concerns that institutions disregard or threaten subsidiarity's meaningfulness. In that regard, understanding subsidiarity values might be considered a whetstone to re-sharpen the dulled sword of subsidiarity,[17] providing evidence that the principle remains important and can play a critical role in the helping federal systems succeed.

While there is scope to refine the theory underpinning subsidiarity's relationship to federalism, and to explore the values of citizens in other nations as described in this chapter, the important challenge now is to take the lessons and insights revealed by this book and translate them into policy practice. In the context of key policy debates and issues of structural reform where subsidiarity can offer useful insight or benefit in Australia, Belgium, Canada, France, Germany, Switzerland, the UK, and the US, as well as elsewhere, subsidiarity's quest for meaning must take a new direction: now that it is clear that the principle is important and useful, especially in federal settings, we must turn our attention to how best to give effect to that meaning. Bermann's caution from almost thirty years ago still rings true: taking subsidiarity seriously is not an easy task.[18] But equipped with the insights of widespread public value for the principle, using subsidiarity to meaningfully help federations succeed is an achievable challenge.

Notes

CHAPTER ONE

1 Steven G. Calabresi and Lucy D. Bickford, "Federalism and Subsidiarity: Perspectives from U.S. Constitutional Law," in *Federalism and Subsidiarity*, ed. James Fleming and Jacob Levy (New York: New York University Press, 2014), 123–89. See also Michael Burgess, *In Search of the Federal Spirit: New Comparative Empirical and Theoretical Perspectives* (Oxford: Oxford University Press, 2012).

2 "Countries," Forum of Federations, accessed 11 June 2020, http://www.forumfed.org/countries/.

3 Greg Goelzhauser and David M. Konisky, "The State of American Federalism 2018–2019: Litigation, Partisan Polarization, and the Administrative Presidency," *Publius* 49, no. 3 (2019): 379–406.

4 See, e.g., Elizabeth Goodyear-Grant and Kyle Hanniman, eds, *Canada: The State of the Federation 2017* (Montreal and Kingston: McGill-Queen's University Press, 2019).

5 Michelle Evans, "Subsidiarity and Federalism: A Case Study of the Australian Constitution and Its Interpretation," in *Global Perspectives on Subsidiarity*, ed. Michelle Evans and Augusto Zimmermann (London: Springer, 2014), 185–205, 186.

6 Thomas Vandamme, "From Federated Federalism to Converging Federalism? The Case of EU Subsidiarity Scrutiny in Spain and Belgium," *Regional and Federal Studies* 22, no. 5 (2012): 515–31, 525.

7 See, e.g., Burgess, *In Search of the Federal Spirit*.

8 Burgess, *In Search of the Federal Spirit*, 235.

9 William S. Livingston, "A Note on the Nature of Federalism," *Political Science Quarterly* 67, no. 1 (1952): 81–95, 90.

10 Cheryl Saunders, "Dividing Power in an Age of Globalization," in *Beyond the Republic: Meeting the Global Challenges to Constitutionalism*, ed. Charles Sampford and Tom Round (Federation Press, 2001), 130.

11 Paolo Dardanelli, John Kincaid, Alan Fenna, André Kaiser, André Lecours, and Ajay Kumar Singh, "Conceptualizing, Measuring, and Theorizing Dynamic De/Centralization in Federations," *Publius* 49, no. 1 (2019): 1–29, 1.

12 See, e.g., Jenna Bednar, "Subsidiarity and Robustness: Building the Adaptive Efficiency of Federal Systems," in *Federalism and Subsidiarity*, ed. James Fleming and Jacob Levy (New York: New York University Press, 2014), 231–56, 231; A.J. Brown, "Measuring the Mysteries of Federal Political Culture in Australia," in *Tomorrow's Federation: Reforming Australian Government*, ed. Paul Kildea, Andrew Lynch, and George Williams (The Federation Press, 2012), 310–31, 317; John F. Kenney, "The Principle of Subsidiarity," *The American Catholic Sociological Review* 16, no. 1 (1955): 31–6, 31; Loren King, "Cities, Subsidiarity, and Federalism," in *Federalism and Subsidiarity*, ed. James Fleming and Jacob Levy (New York: New York University Press, 2014), 291–331, 291; Robert A. Sirico, "Subsidiarity and the Reform of the Welfare of the Nation State," in *Global Perspectives on Subsidiarity*, ed. Michelle Evans and Augusto Zimmermann (London: Springer, 2014), 107–27, 109; Patrice Ranjault, "On the Principle of Subsidiarity," *Journal of European Social Policy* 2, no. 1 (1992): 49–52, 49; Anne Twomey and Glenn Withers, *Federalist Paper 1 – Australia's Federal Future: Delivering Growth and Prosperity* (Council for the Australian Federation, 2007) 4, 28; Daniel Weinstock, "Cities and Federalism," in *Federalism and Subsidiarity*, ed. James Fleming and Jacob Levy (New York: New York University Press, 2014), 259–90, 261; Augusto Zimmermann, "Subsidiarity, Democracy and Individual Liberty in Brazil," in *Global Perspectives on Subsidiarity*, ed. Michelle Evans and Augusto Zimmermann (London: Springer, 2014), 85–106, 85.

13 See, e.g., Daniel Halberstam, "Federal Powers and the Principle of Subsidiarity," in *Global Perspectives on Constitutional Law*, ed. V.D. Amar and M.V. Tushnet (Oxford: Oxford University Press, 2009), 34; Robert Schütze, "Subsidiarity After Lisbon: Reinforcing the Safeguards of Federalism?" *Cambridge Law Journal* 68, no. 3 (2009): 525–36, 526.

14 Bednar, "Subsidiarity and Robustness," 231.

15 Burgess, *In Search of the Federal Spirit*, 3.

16 Daniel J. Elazar, *Exploring Federalism* (Alabama: University of Alabama Press, 1987), 192.

17 A.J. Brown, Jacob Deem, and John Kincaid, "Federal Constitutional Val-

ues and Citizen Attitudes to Government: Explaining Federal System Viability and Reform Preferences in Eight Countries," *Publius* 52, no. 1 (2022): 1–25.

18 This data was collected as part of the Australian Research Council Discovery Project "Confronting the Devolution Paradox." I am grateful to the ARC and to my project colleagues for making this research possible. Ethics approval for this project was granted under reference number 2013/9.

19 See, e.g., William S. Livingston, *Federalism and Constitutional Change* (Oxford: Clarendon Press, 1956), 269–72.

20 See, e.g., Richard Cole, John Kincaid, and Alejandro Rodriguez, "Public Opinion on Federalism and Federal Political Culture in Canada, Mexico, and the United States," *Publius* 34, no. 3 (2004): 201–21; John Kincaid and Richard Cole, "Citizen Attitudes Toward Issues of Federalism in Canada, Mexico, and the United States," *Publius* 41, no. 1 (2010): 53–75.

21 Ivo D. Duchacek, *Comparative Federalism: The Territorial Dimension of Politics* (Maryland: University Press of America, 1987), 344.

22 Ibid. See also Burgess, *In Search of the Federal Spirit*, 254.

23 Burgess, *In Search of the Federal Spirit*, 221.

24 See, e.g., Burgess's critique of Riker's survivorship approach to federal success. Ibid., 224; W.H. Riker, *Federalism: Origin, Operation, Significance* (Boston: Little Brown and Company, 1964), 136.

25 Harry Eckstein, *A Theory of Stable Democracy* (Princeton: Princeton University, 1961); Harry Eckstein, "Congruence Theory Explained," 1997 Centre for the Study of Democracy working paper, accessed 8 August 2021, https://escholarship.org/uc/item/2wb616g6.

26 Jan Erk, *Explaining Federalism: State, Society and Congruence in Austria, Belgium, Canada, Germany and Switzerland* (New York: Routledge, 2008), 1–2.

27 Burgess, *In Search of a Federal Spirit*, 246.

28 Michael Burgess, "Success and Failure in Federation: Comparative Perspectives," paper presented at the *Festschrift* for Ronald L. Watts, October 2007, Queen's University, 1–21, 2. Notably, in his later work, Burgess offered a longer list of conditions for successful federation, based on his summary of the works of Wheare, Riker, and Franck. The list includes conditions such as liberal democracy, and a written constitution – factors which are indeed ostensibly critical to successful (as opposed to failing) federalism, but which are not especially helpful for the present task of exploring factors which contribute to success in federations that are democratic and have a written constitution, etc. Notably, even in

this expanded list, Burgess found an important role for "the need to keep alive "the federal spirit," a sentiment better aligned with the scope of this book. For further discussion, see Burgess, *In Search of the Federal Spirit*, 232–6.

29 Burgess, "Success and Failure in Federation: Comparative Perspectives," 2.

30 See, e.g., George Bermann, "Taking Subsidiarity Seriously: Federalism in the European Community and the United States," *Columbia Law Review* 94, no. 2 (1994): 332–456.

31 See, e.g., Halberstam, "Federal Powers and the Principle of Subsidiarity," 34; Schütze, "Subsidiarity after Lisbon," 526.

32 See, e.g., Nicholas Aroney, "Federalism and Subsidiarity: Principles and Processes in the Reform of the Australian Federation," *Federal Law Review* 44, no. 1 (2016): 1–24.

33 Halberstam, "Federal Powers and the Principle of Subsidiarity."

34 Bermann, "Taking Subsidiarity Seriously."

35 Calabresi and Bickford, "Federalism and Subsidiarity," 148.

36 Evans, "Subsidiarity and Federalism," 188. Italics as per original.

37 Bronwyn Hinz, *Schooling Federalism: Evaluating the Options for Reform* (University of Melbourne School of Governance, 2015).

38 Alessandro Colombo, "Principle of Subsidiarity and Lombardy: Theoretical Background and Empirical Implementation," in *Subsidiarity Gov ernance: Theoretical and Empirical Models*, ed. Alessandro Colombo (London: Palgrave Macmillan, 2012), 3–17. See also Charles L. Glenn "Subsidiarity and Education in Lombardy: Limits and Possibilities," in *Subsidiarity Governance: Theoretical and Empirical Models*, ed. Alessandro Colombo (London: Palgrave Macmillan, 2012), 113–33; Helen Haugh "Regional Governance of Health Services in Lombardy," in *Subsidiarity Governance: Theoretical and Empirical Models*, ed. Alessandro Colombo (London: Palgrave Macmillan, 2012), 135–46; Gerard Van Bortel "Social Housing and Subsidiarity in the Lombard Model of Governance," in *Subsidiarity Governance: Theoretical and Empirical Models*, ed. Alessandro Colombo (London: Palgrave Macmillan, 2012), 157–70.

39 R.A.B. Leaper, "Subsidiarity and the Welfare State," *Social and Economic Administration* 9, no. 2 (1975): 82–97, 82.

40 Editorial Comment, "Subsidiarity: Furthering the Confusion," 5 Europe 2000, Executive Review (1992), cited in Bermann, "Taking Subsidiarity Seriously."

41 Philip Howard, "Philip Howard Column," *Times*, 15 October 1992.

42 Andreas Føllesdal, "Competing Conceptions of Subsidiarity," in *Federal-*

ism and Subsidiarity, ed. James Fleming and Jacob Levy (New York: New York University Press, 2014), 214–30, 215.

43 Gabriel A. Moens and John Trone, "The Principle of Subsidiarity in EU Judicial and Legislative Practice: Panacea or Placebo?" *Journal of Legislation* 41, no. 1 (2015): 65–102, 65.

44 Thomas McDonagh, "Subsidiarity: Sop or Substance," *Galway Student Law Review* 65, no. 1 (2003): 83.

45 Christopher Ritzer, Marc Rutloff, and Karin Linhart, "How to Sharpen a Dull Sword – The Principle of Subsidiarity and its Control," *German Law Journal* 7, no. 9 (2006): 733–60.

46 Bermann, "Taking Subsidiarity Seriously," 334.

47 Evans, "Subsidiarity and Federalism," 186.

48 Greg Taylor, "Germany: A Slow Death for Subsidiarity?" *International Journal of Constitutional Law* 7, no. 1 (2009): 139–54.

49 Eugenie Brouillet, "Canadian Federalism and the Principle of Subsidiarity: Should We Open Pandora's Box?" *Supreme Court Law Review* 54, no. 1 (2011): 601–32.

50 Bermann, "Taking Subsidiarity Seriously," 335.

51 Aroney, "Federalism and Subsidiarity."

52 Aroney, "Federalism and Subsidiarity." See also Nathalie Behnke "Towards a New Organization of Federal States? – Lessons from the Processes of Constitutional Reform in Germany, Austria, and Switzerland," *Polis Nr. 66/2009* (Institut für Politikwissenschaft, FernUniversität in Hagen, 2009); Jörg Broschek, "Pathways of Federal Reform: Australia, Canada, Germany, and Switzerland," *Publius* 45, no. 1 (2014): 51–76.

53 Commonwealth of Australia, *Parliamentary Debates*, Senate (27 April 2016) 30.

54 Aroney, "Federalism and Subsidiarity."

55 See, e.g., W.H. Riker, *Federalism: Origin, Operation, Significance* (Boston: Little Brown and Company, 1964).

56 Ian Gray and A.J. Brown, "The Political Viability of Federal Reform: Interpreting Public Attitudes," in *Federalism and Regionalism in Australia: New Approaches, New Institutions?* ed. A.J. Brown and Jennifer Bellamy (Canberra: Australian National University Press, 2007), 33–53, 33.

57 John Howard, "Prime Minister John Howard's Tasmanian Hospital Announcement," *YouTube*, 31 July 2007, https://www.youtube.com/watch?v=y1qU2nQ-1gY, accessed 15 March 2016.

58 Nicholas Jacobs "An Experimental Test of How Americans Think about Federalism," *Publius* 47, no. 4 (2017): 572–98.

59 Patrick Fafard, Francois Rocher, and Catherine Cote, "The Presence (or

Lack Thereof) of a Federal Culture in Canada: The Views of Canadians," *Regional and Federal Studies* 20, no. 1 (2010): 19–43.

60 Cited in Robert A. Rutland, *The Papers of James Madison*, vol. 14, (Charlottesville: University Press of Virginia, 1983), 170.

61 Jacob Deem, "Deliberating Federalism: Can Public Attitudes Help Solve Federalism's Triple Challenge?" in *A People's Federation*, ed. Mark Bruerton, Tracey Arkley, Robyn Hollander, and Ron Levy (NSW: Federation Press, 2017), 230–43.

62 Kevin Arceneaux, "Does Federalism Weaken Democratic Representation in the United States?" *Publius* 35 no. 1 (2005): 297–311, 311.

63 Goelzhauser and Konisky, "The State of American Federalism 2018–2019."

64 Rodney Smith, *Australian Political Culture* (NSW: Pearson Education Australia, 2001), 1.

65 William H. Riker, "Six Books in Search of a Subject or Does Federalism Exist and Does it Matter?" *Comparative Politics* 2, no. 1 (1969): 135–46, 142.

66 E.g., Brown, "Measuring the Mysteries."

67 Australian Constitution, Preamble. For a discussion of Western Australia's late joining of the federation, which resulted in it not being explicitly mentioned in the constitution itself, see Thomas Musgrave, "The Western Australian Secessionist Movement," *Macquarie Law Journal* 3, no. 1 (2003): 95.

68 George Williams, "Race and the Australian Constitution," *Australasian Parliamentary Review* 28, no. 1 (2013): 4–16, 5. Italics as per original.

69 Local government is not mentioned or provided for under the constitution despite two referenda in 1974 and 1988. Instead, local councils are creatures of state law.

70 S109, Australian Constitution.

71 *Amalgamated Society of Engineers v Adelaide Steamship Co Ltd* (1920) 28 CLR 129.

72 *South Australia v Commonwealth* (1942) 65 CLR 373; *Victoria v Commonwealth* (1957) 99 CLR 575.

73 See, e.g., Didier Caluwaerts and Min Reuchamps, "Combining Federalism with Consociationalism: Is Belgian Consociational Federalism Digging its Own Grave?" *Ethnopolotics* 14, no. 3 (2015): 277–95.

74 Peter Thijssen, Sarah Arras, and Dave Sinardet, "Federalism and Solidarity in Belgium: Insights from Public Opinion," in *Identities, Trust, and Cohesion in Federal Systems: Public Perspectives*, ed. Jack Jedwab and John Kincaid (Montreal and Kingston: McGill-Queen's University Press, 2019), 85–114.

75 Vandamme, "From Federated Federalism," 525.
76 David Bell and Lorne Tepperman, *The Roots of Disunity: A Look at Canadian Political Culture* (Toronto: McClelland and Stewart Publishers, 1979).
77 Renamed the Constitution Act in 1982.
78 Articles 55, 56, and 90. See also Garth Stevenson, *Unfulfilled Union. Canadian Federalism and National Unity* (Montreal and Kingston: McGill-Queen's University Press, 2009), 33; André Lecours, "Dynamic De/centralization in Canada, 1867–2010," *Publius* 49, no. 1 (2019): 57–83.
79 Lecours, "Dynamic De/Centralization in Canada," 75.
80 Ibid. See also Richard Simeon, "Considerations on centralization and decentralization," *Canadian Public Administration* 28, no. 1 (1986): 445–61; Grace Skogstad, *The Politics of Agricultural Policy-Making in Canada* (University of Toronto Press, 1987).
81 Lecours, "Dynamic De/Centralization in Canada."
82 Simeon, "Considerations on centralization and decentralization," 449.
83 Alistair Cole, Stuart Fox, Romain Pasquier, and Ian Stafford, "Political trust in France's multi-level government," *Journal of Trust Research* 8, no. 1 (2018): 45–67, 50.
84 Ibid.
85 Edward A. Freeman, *History of Federal Government in Greece and Italy* (Florida: Hardpress Publishing, originally published by Macmillan & Co, 1893), 5; Samuel von Pufendorf, cited in Solomon Rufus Davis, *The Federal Principle: A Journey Through Time in Quest of Meaning* (California: University of California Press, 1978), 55.
86 André Kaiser and Stephan Vogel "Dynamic De/Centralization in Germany, 1949–2010," *Publius* 49, no. 1 (2019): 84–111.
87 Paolo Dardanelli and Sean Müller "Dynamic De/Centralization in Switzerland, 1848–2010," *Publius* 49, no. 1 (2019): 138–65.
88 Ibid., 155.
89 See, e.g., Philip Booth, "Brexit: The Role of Subsidiarity," 29 June 2016, *The Tablet*, accessed 10 January 2018, http://www.thetablet.co.uk/features/2/8573/brexit-the-role-of-subsidiarity; Benjamin Wiker, "Brexit and the Principle of Subsidiarity" Blog Post in the National Catholic Register, accessed 7 June 2017, http://www.ncregister.com/blog/benjamin-wiker/brexit-and-the-principle-of-subsidiarity.
90 Paul H. Douglas "The Development of a System of Federal Grants-in-aid," *Political Science Quarterly* 35, no. 2 (1920): 255–71, 255.
91 Burgess, *In Search of the Federal Spirit*.

92 Davis, *The Federal Principle*.
93 Duchacek, *Comparative Federalism*, 344.

CHAPTER TWO

1 Ronald Reagan "Remarks at a Rally for Senator Malcolm Wallop of Wyoming in Cheyenne," speech delivered 2 March 1982, National Archives, https://www.reaganlibrary.gov/archives/speech/remarks-rally-senator-malcolm-wallop-wyoming-cheyenne, emphasis added.
2 David A. Smith, *Cowboy Presidents: The Frontier Myth and U.S. Politics since 1900* (Oxford: Oxford University Press, 2021).
3 Daniel J. Elazar, *Exploring Federalism* (Alabama: University of Alabama Press, 1987), 193.
4 Ibid.
5 Ibid.
6 John Kincaid and Richard Cole, "Citizen Attitudes Toward Issues of Federalism in Canada, Mexico, and the United States," *Publius* 41, no. 1 (2010): 53–75, 54.
7 Jan Erk, *Explaining Federalism: State, Society and Congruence in Austria, Belgium, Canada, Germany and Switzerland*, (New York: Routledge, 2008).
8 Gabriel Almond and Sidney Verba, *The Civic Culture, Political Attitudes and Democracy in Five Nations* (Boston: Little Brown, 1965). See also Dieter Fuchs, "The Political Culture Paradigm," in *The Oxford Handbook of Political Behavior*, ed. Russell J. Dalton and Hans-Dieter Klingemann (Oxford: Oxford University Press, 2007), 163.
9 E.g., Ivo D. Duchacek, *Comparative Federalism: The Territorial Dimension of Politics* (Maryland: University Press of America, 1987), 344; Daniel J. Elazar, *Exploring Federalism* (Alabama: University of Alabama Press, 1987).
10 Rod Hague, Martin Harrop, and John McCormick, *Comparative Government and Politics: An Introduction*, 10th ed. (London: Palgrave Macmillan, 2016), 201.
11 See also Fuchs, "The Political Culture Paradigm," 164.
12 Colin Hay, *Political Analysis: A Critical Introduction* (Palgrave, 2002), 14.
13 Ibid., 94.
14 See, e.g., Stuart McAnulla, "Making Hay with Actualism? The Need for a Realist Concept of Structure," *Politics* 25, no. 1 (2005): 31–8; Nigel Pleasants, "Structure, Agency and Ontological Confusion: A Response to Hay," *Political Studies* 57, no. 1 (2009): 885–91.

15 William S. Livingston, "A Note on the Nature of Federalism," *Political Science Quarterly* 67, no. 1 (1952): 81, 83–4.
16 See, e.g., Riker and Birch's early critiques – William H. Riker, *Federalism: Origin, Operation, Significance* (Boston: Little, Brown and Company, 1964); Anthony H. Birch, "Approaches to the Study of Federalism," *Political Studies* XIV, no. 1 (1966): 15–33.
17 Michael Stein, "Federal Political Systems and Federal Societies," *World Politics* 20 (1968): 721–47, 725–9.
18 Harry Eckstein, "Congruence Theory Explained," 1997 Centre for the Study of Democracy working paper, https://escholarship.org/uc/item/2wb616g6.
19 Erk, *Explaining Federalism*, 1–2.
20 Gabriel Almond and Sidney Verba, *The Civic Culture, Political Attitudes and Democracy in Five Nations* (Boston: Little Brown, 1965), 21.
21 Erk, *Explaining Federalism*, x.
22 Elazar, *Exploring Federalism*, 192.
23 Livingston, "A Note on the Nature of Federalism," 84.
24 Erk, *Explaining Federalism*, 87.
25 Livingston, "A Note on the Nature of Federalism," 95.
26 Michael Burgess, *In Search of the Federal Spirit: New Comparative Empirical and Theoretical Perspectives* (Oxford: Oxford University Press, 2012), 67.
27 Duchacek, *Comparative Federalism*, 344.
28 A.J. Brown, Jacob Deem, and John Kincaid, "Federal Constitutional Values and Citizen Attitudes to Government: Explaining Federal System Viability and Reform Preferences in Eight Countries," *Publius* 52, no. 1 (2022): 1–25. Emphasis added.
29 David McGrane and Loleen Berdahl, "Reconceptualizing Canadian Federal Political Culture: Examining Differences between Quebec and the Rest of Canada," *Publius* 50, no. 1 (2019): 109–34.
30 Preston King, *Federalism and Federation* (London: Croom and Helm, 1982).
31 Patrick Fafard, Francois Rocher, and Catherine Cote, "The Presence (or Lack Thereof) of a Federal Culture in Canada: The Views of Canadians," *Regional and Federal Studies* 20, no. 1 (2010): 19–43.
32 See, e.g., Jacob Deem, "Deliberating Federalism: Can Public Attitudes Help Solve Federalism's Triple Challenge?" in *A People's Federation*, ed. Mark Bruerton, Tracey Arklay, Robyn Hollander, and Ron Levy (NSW: Federation Press, 2017), 230–43.
33 E.g., Nicholas Jacobs, "An Experimental Test of How Americans Think

about Federalism," *Publius* 47, no. 4 (2017): 572–98; Jennifer M. Connolly, Casey Klofstad, Joseph Uscinski, and Jonathan West, "Public Preferences for Zika Policy and Responsibility in the Absence of Partisan Cues," *Journal of Public Policy* 40, no. 3 (2020): 402–27; Brad T. Gomez and J. Matthew Wilson, "Political Sophistication and Attributions of Blame in the Wake of Hurricane Katrina," *Publius* 38, no. 4 (2008): 633–50; Kevin Arceneaux, "The Federal Face of Voting: Are Elected Officials Held Accountable for the Functions Relevant to their Office," *Political Psychology* 27, no. 5 (2006): 731–54.

34 Elazar, *Exploring Federalism*, 192.

35 Ibid., 193.

36 See, e.g., "State of Origin," New South Wales Rugby League, accessed 13 March 2021, https://www.nswrl.com.au/origin/.

37 Thomas Fleiner, "The Current Situation of Federalism in Switzerland," *REAF* 9, no. 1 (2009): 51–90, 84.

38 See, e.g., A.J. Brown, "Measuring the Mysteries of Federal Political Culture in Australia," in *Tomorrow's Federation: Reforming Australian Government*, ed. Paul Kildea, Andrew Lynch, and George Williams (The Federation Press, 2012), 310–31; A.J. Brown, "From Intuition to Reality: Measuring Federal Political Culture in Australia," *Publius* 43, no. 2 (2013): 297–314; Richard Cole, John Kincaid, and Alejandro Rodriguez, "Public Opinion on Federalism and Federal Political Culture in Canada, Mexico, and the United States," *Publius* 34, no. 3 (2004): 201–21; Kincaid and Cole, "Citizen Attitudes Toward Issues of Federalism in Canada, Mexico, and the United States,"; Fafard, Rocher, and Cote, "The Presence (or Lack Thereof) of a Federal Culture in Canada."

39 Samuel Huntington, *The Clash of Civilizations and the Remaking of World Order* (New York: Simon and Schuster, 1996).

40 Hague, Harrop, and McCormick, *Comparative Government and Politics*, 201.

41 Nelson Wiseman, *In Search of Canadian Political Culture* (Vancouver: UBC Press, 2008), 1.

42 See, e.g., Karl Deutsch, *The Nerves of Government: Models of Political Communication and Control* (New York: Free Press, 1966); Ailsa Henderson, *Hierarchies of Belonging: National Identity and Political Culture in Scotland and Quebec* (Montreal: Queen's University Press, 2007); Sidney Verba, "Conclusion: Comparative Political Culture," in *Political Culture and Political Development*, ed. Lucian W. Pye and Sidney Verba (New Jersey: Princeton University Press, 2015; first published 1965).

43 Verba, "Conclusion."

44 Deutsch, *The Nerves of Government*.

45 Henderson uses this term to describe places such as Quebec and Scotland, rather than nation-states. For clarity, in this chapter, "country" refers to the broader political nation such as "Canada," while entities or areas such as Quebec, which Henderson calls nations and others have called "non-nations" (e.g., Erika Arban, "Beyond Sub-State Nationalism. Accommodating Strong, Distinct and Non-National Regions in Large Polities," Paper delivered at International Political Science Association World Congress, 23–8 July 2016) will follow Henderson's label of "nation."

46 Henderson, *Hierarchies of Belonging*.

47 See, e.g., Henderson, *Hierarchies of Belonging*, 8.

48 Fafard, Rocher, and Cote, "The Presence (or Lack Thereof) of a Federal Culture in Canada," 21. Italics as per original.

49 Livingston, "A Note on the Nature of Federalism," 90.

50 Ibid.

51 David Bell and Lorne Tepperman, *The Roots of Disunity: A Look at Canadian Political Culture* (Toronto: McClelland and Stewart Publishers, 1979), 84–6.

52 Ibid., 86.

53 Ibid. See also Allan Smith, "Metaphor and Nationality in North America," *Canadian Historical Review* 51, no. 3 (1970): 245.

54 Kincaid and Cole, "Citizen Attitudes Toward Issues of Federalism in Canada, Mexico, and the United States," 69.

55 Bell and Tepperman, *The Roots of Disunity*, 89.

56 Will Kymlicka, "The Current State of Multiculturalism in Canada and Research Themes on Canadian Multiculturalism 2008–2010," Report prepared for the Department of Immigration and Citizenship (2011), 15–6. See also Jeffrey Reitz and Rupa Banjeree, "Racial Inequality, Social Cohesion and Policy Issues in Canada," in *Belonging? Diversity, Recognition and Shared Citizenship in Canada*, ed. Keith Banting, Thomas J. Courchene, and F. Leslie Seidle (Montreal: Institute for Research on Public Policy, 2007).

57 See, e.g., John Hopkins "Trans-Tasman Governance: A Quiet Form of Federalism?" *Canterbury Law Review* 16 (2010): 23–30.

58 William S. Livingston *Federalism and Constitutional Change* (Oxford: Clarendon Press, 1956), 269–72.

59 Elazar, *Exploring Federalism*; Duchacek, *Comparative Federalism*.

60 Cole, Kincaid, and Rodriguez, "Public Opinion on Federalism and Federal Political Culture in Canada, Mexico, and the United States," 217.

61 Erk, *Explaining Federalism*.

62 Ibid., 10.

63 Brown, Deem, and Kincaid, "Federal Constitutional Values and Citizen Attitudes to Government."

64 See, e.g., John Curtice, "A Stronger or Weaker Union? Public Reactions to Asymmetric Devolution in the United Kingdom," *Publius* 36 no. 1 (2006): 95–113; Ailsa Henderson, Charlie Jeffrey, Daniel Wincott, and Richard Wyn Jones, "Reflections on the 'Devolution Paradox': A Comparative Examination of Multi-Level Citizenship," *Regional Studies* 47 no. 3 (2013): 303–22; Charlie Jeffrey, "Devolution and Divergence: Public Attitudes and Institutional Logistics," in *Devolution in Practice*, ed. John Adams and Katie Schmuecker (IPPR, 2005); Charlie Jeffrey, "Devolution and Social Citizenship: Which Society, Whose Citizenship?" in *Territory, Democracy and Justice*, ed. Scott Greer (London: Palgrave Macmillan, 2006); Carol S. Weissert and David Blake Jones, "Devolution Paradox and the US South," *Regional and Federal Studies* 25 no 3. (2015): 259–76.

65 Daniel Weinstock, "Cities and Federalism," in *Federalism and Subsidiarity*, ed. James Fleming and Jacob Levy (New York: New York University Press, 2014), 259–90, 261.

66 Eugenie Brouillet, "Canadian Federalism and the Principle of Subsidiarity: Should We Open Pandora's Box?" *Supreme Court Law Review* 54, no. 1 (2011): 601–32.

67 Jacob Deem, "Federal Reform: The Case for Supportive Subsidiarity in Australia," UNSW *Law Journal* 44, no. 2 (2021): 613–36.

68 Arthur Benz, "The Federal Constitutional Court of Germany: Guardian of Unitarism and Federalism," in *Courts in Federal Countries: Federalists or Unitarists?* ed. Nicholas Aroney and John Kincaid (Toronto: University of Toronto Press, 2017), 193–222.

CHAPTER THREE

1 Prime Minister's Office, "PM Speech on EU reform: 2 February 2016," speech delivered by David Cameron at Siemens Headquarters, Wiltshire, 2 February 2016, https://www.gov.uk/government/speeches/pm-speech-on-eu-reform-2-february-2016; grammar and punctuation corrected from original, emphasis added.

2 Andreas Føllesdal, "Competing Conceptions of Subsidiarity," in *Federalism and Subsidiarity*, ed. James Fleming and Jacob Levy (New York: New York University Press, 2014), 214–30, 215.

3 Russell Hittinger, "The Coherence of the Four Basic Principles of Catholic Social Doctrine: An Interpretation," in *Pursuing the Common Good: How Solidarity Can Work Together* (Vatican City: Pontifical Academy of Social Sciences, Acta 14, 2008), 109; Thomas C. Behr, "Luigi Taparelli D'Azeglio, S.J. (1793–1862) and the Development of Scholastic Natural-Law Thought As a Science of Society and Politics," *Journal of Markets & Morality* 6, no. 1 (2003): 99–115, 105.

4 See, e.g., Michelle Evans, "Subsidiarity and Federalism: A Case Study of the Australian Constitution and Its Interpretation," in *Global Perspectives on Subsidiarity*, ed. Michelle Evans and Augusto Zimmermann (London: Springer, 2014), 185–205.

5 See, e.g., Nicholas Aroney, "Subsidiarity in the Writings of Aristotle and Aquinas," in *Global Perspectives on Subsidiarity*, ed. Michelle Evans and Augusto Zimmermann (London: Springer, 2014), 9–27; Otfried Höffe, "Subsidiarity as a principle in the philosophy of government," *Regional and Federal Studies* 6, no. 3 (2007): 56–73; Chantal Millon-Delsol, "L'Etat subsidiaire: Ingérence et non-ingérence de l'etat: Le principe de subsidiarité aux fondements de l'historie Européenne," 15–27 (1992) cited in Paolo G. Carozza, "Subsidiarity as a Structural Principle of Human Rights Law," *The American Journal of International Law* 97, no. 1 (2003): 38–79, 40–1.

6 Aroney, "Subsidiarity in the Writings of Aristotle and Aquinas," 14.

7 Ibid., 21.

8 Solomon Rufus Davis, *The Federal Principle: A Journey Through Time in Quest of Meaning* (California: University of California Press, 1978), 12–16.

9 I use this term to avoid the controversy of distinguishing between confederal and federal arrangements, as such distinctions are not strictly relevant to this book. See Davis, *The Federal Principle*, 13–14.

10 Edward A. Freeman, *History of Federal Government in Greece and Italy* (Florida: Hardpress Publishing, originally published by Macmillan & Co, 1893), 4–5.

11 Davis, *The Federal Principle*, 3, 11.

12 Michelle Evans and Augusto Zimmermann, "The Global Relevance of Subsidiarity: An Overview," in *Global Perspectives on Subsidiarity*, ed. Michelle Evans and Augusto Zimmermann (London: Springer, 2014), 1–7, 1.

13 Hittinger, "The Coherence of the Four Basic Principles of Catholic Social Doctrine," 109.

14 Behr, "Luigi Taparelli D'Azeglio, S.J. (1793-1862) and the Development

of Scholastic Natural-Law Thought As a Science of Society and Politics," 105.

15 Ibid., 105.

16 See, e.g., Petru Ureche, "About the Tactics and Fighting Particularity of the Auxiliary Infantry in Roman Dacia," *Acta Musei Napocensis*, 43–4 (2008): 247–61, 247.

17 Ibid.

18 John F. Cox, cited in Edmund Aku, *Solidarity, Subsidiarity and Common Good: Fundamental Principles for Community and Social Cohesion* (Indiana: Xlibris Corporation, 2011).

19 Ibid.

20 Ronald A. Edwards, "Federalism and the Balance of Power: China's Han and Tang Dynasties and the Roman Empire," *Pacific Economic Review* 14, no. 1 (2009): 1–21, 1.

21 Ibid.

22 Ibid, 12.

23 Aroney, "Subsidiarity in the Writings of Aristotle and Aquinas."

24 Ibid., 21. See also also C.N.S. Woolf, *Bartolus of Sassoferrato: His Position in the Political Thought of his Time* (Cambridge University Press, 1913), cited in Aroney, "Subsidiarity in the Writings of Aristotle and Aquinas."

25 Aroney, "Subsidiarity in the Writings of Aristotle and Aquinas," 19.

26 Ibid., 20.

27 Ibid., 20. See also Nicholas Aroney, "Subsidiarity, federalism and the best constitution: Thomas Aquinas on city, province and empire," *Law and Philosophy* 26, no. 1 (2007): 161–228; John Finnis, *Aquinas: Moral, Political and Legal Theory* (Oxford: Oxford University Press, 1998); Edgar Scully, "The place of the state in society according to Thomas Aquinas," *The Thomist* 45, no. 3 (1981): 407–29.

28 Aroney, "Subsidiarity in the Writings of Aristotle and Aquinas," 21–2.

29 Ibid., 22.

30 Heinz H.F. Eulau, "Theories of Federalism under the Holy Roman Empire," *The American Political Science Review* 35, no. 4 (1941): 643–64, 655.

31 Ludolph Hugo, cited in Davis, *The Federal Principle*, 66.

32 Andreas Føllesdal "Survey Article: Subsidiarity," *The Journal of Political Philosophy* 6, no. 2 (1998): 190–218, 203.

33 Freeman, *History of Federal Government in Greece and Italy*, 5.

34 Ibid.

35 Samuel von Pufendorf, cited in Davis, *The Federal Principle*, 55.

36 See, e.g., Føllesdal, "Competing Conceptions of Subsidiarity," 216.

37 Ibid.
38 Johannes Althusius, *Politica: Politics Methodically Set Forth and Illustrated with Sacred and Profane Examples*, trans. Frederick S. Carney, Translator's Introduction (Indianapolis: Liberty Fund, 1995), xi.
39 Ibid. See also Føllesdal, "Competing Conceptions of Subsidiarity," 216.
40 Føllesdal, "Competing Conceptions of Subsidiarity," 216.
41 Ibid., 216–17.
42 Aristotle, *Politics*, trans. William Ellis (Darlington: JM Dent & Sons, first published 1912), 35.
43 Althusius, *Politica*, 191.
44 Ibid., 193.
45 Føllesdal "Survey Article: Subsidiarity," 202.
46 Ibid. Here, Føllesdal cites James Harrington, *The Commonwealth of Oceania* (Henry Morley, 1656) and James Madison *Federalist Paper #20* (1788) in *The Federalist*, ed. Jacob E. Cooke, (Connecticut: Wesleyan University Press, 1982).
47 Føllesdal "Survey Article: Subsidiarity," 202.
48 Ibid., 204.
49 Ibid.
50 See, e.g., N.W. Barber, "The Limited Modesty of Subsidiarity," *European Law Journal* 11, no. 3 (2005): 308–25, 310; Carozza, "Subsidiarity as a Structural Principle of Human Rights Law," 40–2; Christoph Henkel, "The Allocation of Powers in the European Union: A Closer Look at the Principle of Subsidiarity," *Berkley Journal of International* 20, no. 1 (2002): 359–86, 363.
51 Leo XIII, *Rerum Novarum: Encyclical on Capital and Labor* (1891) online, http://www.vatican.va/holy_father/leo_xiii/encyclicals/documents/hf_l-xiii_enc_15051891_rerum-novarum_en.html, 51–3.
52 Ibid., 53.
53 Behr, "Luigi Taparelli D'Azeglio, S.J. (1793-1862) and the Development of Scholastic Natural-Law Thought As a Science of Society and Politics," 22.
54 Leo XIII, *Rerum Novarum*, 51.
55 Ibid.
56 Pius XI, *Quadragesimo Anno: Encyclical on Reconstruction of the Social Order* (1931) online, http://www.vatican.va/holy_father/pius_xi/encyclicals/documents/hf_p-xi_enc_19310515_quadragesimo-anno_en.html.
57 Ibid., 79.
58 Føllesdal, "Competing Conceptions of Subsidiarity," 218.

59 Hittinger, "The Coherence of the Four Basic Principles of Catholic Social Doctrine," 22.
60 Joseph A. Komonchak "Subsidiarity in the Church: The State of the Question," *Jurist* 48, no. 1 (1988): 298–349, 302.
61 Føllesdal, *Subsidiarity and the Global Order*, 211.
62 Komonchak "Subsidiarity in the Church."
63 Ibid., 209.
64 Ibid.
65 Ibid., 205. See also Richard Musgrave, *The Theory of Public Finance: A Study in Political Economy* (McGraw Hill, 1959), 179–80.
66 However, Føllesdal identifies that, rather than preventing decision-making overload, fiscal federalism may in fact cause it, as "it requires comparative assessments of sub-unit and central unit action". Føllesdal, "Survey Article: Subsidiarity," 207.
67 See, e.g., Colin Clark, "Australia's Economic and Population Capacity," *Australian Journal of Politics and History* 1, no. 1 (1955): 49–58; Colin Clark, *Population growth and land use* (New York: St Martin's Press, 1977); Colin Clark, "Welfare Taxation: Opting Out to Shrink the State," *Economic Affairs* 7, no. 3 (1987): 38–9.
68 Føllesdal, "Survey Article: Subsidiarity."
69 Thomas M. Scanlon "Rights, Goals and Fairness," in *Public and Private Morality*, ed. Stuart Hampshire (Cambridge: Cambridge University Press, 1978) 102, cited in Føllesdal "Survey Article: Subsidiarity," 210.
70 Føllesdal, "Survey Article: Subsidiarity," 211.
71 Ibid., 210.
72 Paragraph 13, Preamble of the Treaty on European Union.
73 Article 5(3), Treaty on European Union.
74 See, e.g., *United Kingdom v Council* (C-84/94) [1996] ECR I-5793 ("Working Time case"); *Germany v Parliament and Council* (C-233/94) [1997] ECR I-2405 ("Deposit Guarantee case"); and *Germany v Commission* (Case T-374/04) [2007] ECR II-4431.
75 See, e.g., Philip Booth, "Brexit: The Role of Subsidiarity," 29 June 2016, *The Tablet*, accessed 10 January 2018, http://www.thetablet.co.uk/features/2/8573/brexit-the-role-of-subsidiarity; Benjamin Wiker, "Brexit and the Principle of Subsidiarity," blog post, National Catholic Register, accessed 7 June 2017, http://www.ncregister.com/blog/benjamin-wiker/brexit-and-the-principle-of-subsidiarity.
76 Patrick McKinley Brennan, "Subsidiarity in the Tradition of Catholic Social Doctrine," in *Global Perspectives on Subsidiarity*, ed. Michelle Evans and Augusto Zimmermann (London: Springer, 2014), 29–47, 29.

77 See, e.g., Eugenie Brouillet, "Canadian Federalism and the Principle of Subsidiarity: Should We Open Pandora's Box?" *Supreme Court Law Review* 54, no. 1 (2011): 601–32, 605; Arthur Utz, "The Principle of Subsidiarity and Contemporary Natural Law," *Natural Law Forum*, paper 33 (1958): 170–83, 181.

78 Steven Gosepath, "The Principle of Subsidiarity," in *Real World Justice*, ed. Andreas Føllesdal and Thomas Pogge (London: Springer, 2005), 162.

79 Ibid.

80 Ibid.

81 Ibid.

82 Benjamen F. Gussen, "Subsidiarity as a Constitutional Principle in New Zealand," *New Zealand Journal of Public and International Law* 12, no. 1 (2014): 123–44, 129.

83 Jenna Bednar, "Subsidiarity and Robustness: Building the Adaptive Efficiency of Federal Systems," in *Federalism and Subsidiarity*, ed. James Fleming and Jacob Levy (New York: New York University Press, 2014), 231–56, 231; A.J. Brown, "Measuring the Mysteries of Federal Political Culture in Australia" in *Tomorrow's Federation: Reforming Australian Government*, ed. Paul Kildea, Andrew Lynch, and George Williams (The Federation Press, 2012), 310–31, 317; John F. Kenney, "The Principle of Subsidiarity," *The American Catholic Sociological Review* 16, no. 1 (1955): 31–6, 31; Loren King, "Cities, Subsidiarity, and Federalism," in *Federalism and Subsidiarity*, ed. James Fleming and Jacob Levy (New York: New York University Press, 2014), 291–331, 291; Robert A. Sirico, "Subsidiarity and the Reform of the Welfare of the Nation State," in *Global Perspectives on Subsidiarity*, ed. Michelle Evans and Augusto Zimmermann (London: Springer, 2014), 107–27, 109; Patrice Ranjault, "On the Principle of Subsidiarity," *Journal of European Social Policy* 2, no. 1 (1992): 49–52, 49; Anne Twomey and Glenn Withers, *Federalist Paper 1 – Australia's Federal Future: Delivering Growth and Prosperity* (Council for the Australian Federation, 2007) 4, 28; Daniel Weinstock, "Cities and Federalism," in *Federalism and Subsidiarity*, ed. James Fleming and Jacob Levy (New York: New York University Press, 2014), 259–90, 261; Augusto Zimmermann, "Subsidiarity, Democracy and Individual Liberty in Brazil," in *Global Perspectives on Subsidiarity*, ed. Michelle Evans and Augusto Zimmermann (London: Springer, 2014), 85–106, 85.

84 John W. Bridge, "Constitutions, Powers and the Doctrine of Subsidiarity," *The Bracton Law Journal* 31, no. 1 (1999): 49–57.

85 Bednar, "Subsidiarity and Robustness," 231.

86 Pius XI, *Quadragesimo Anno*, 79.

87 See, e.g., Sean Mueller, *Theorising (De)Centralisation: Comparative Evidence from Sub-National Switzerland* (Colchester: ECPR Press, 2015).

88 See, e.g., ongoing if sporadic debates about the Constitutional recognition of local governments in Australia – A.J. Brown, "Subsidiarity or Subterfuge? Resolving the Future of Local Government in the Australian Federal System," *Australian Journal of Public Administration* 61, no. 4 (2002): 24–42.

89 See, e.g., Benjamen F. Gussen, "A Comparative Analysis of Constitutional Recognition of Aboriginal Peoples," *Melbourne University Law Review* 40, no. 3 (2017): 867–904; Janet Hunt, "Engaging with Indigenous Australia – Exploring the Conditions for Effective Relationships with Aboriginal and Torres Strait Islander Communities," Closing the Gap Clearing House, Issues Paper No. 5, 10; Mark Moran and Ruth Elvin, "Coping with Complexity: Adaptive Governance in Desert Australia," *GeoJournal* 74, no. 5 (2009): 415; Patrick Sullivan, "Indigenous Governance: The Harvard Project, Australian Aboriginal Organisations and Cultural Subsidiarity," in *Against the Grain: Advances in Postcolonial Studies*, ed. Anshuman Prasad (Copenhagen: Copenhagen Business School Press, 2012).

90 Jonathan Chaplin, "Subsidiarity and Social Pluralism," in *Global Perspectives on Subsidiarity*, ed. Michelle Evans and Augusto Zimmermann (London: Springer, 2014), 65–83, 72, emphasis in original.

91 Hittinger, "The Coherence of the Four Basic Principles of Catholic Social Doctrine," 16. See also Kenneth L. Grasso, "The Subsidiarity State," in *Christianity and Civil Society: Catholic and Neo-Calvinist Perspectives*, ed. Jeanne Heffernan Schindler (Lexington, 2008).

92 Chaplin, "Subsidiarity and Social Pluralism," 72.

93 Weinstock, "Cities and Federalism," 261.

94 See, e.g., Andreas Føllesdal, "Subsidiarity and the Global Order," in *Global Perspectives on Subsidiarity*, ed. Michelle Evans and Augusto Zimmermann (London: Springer, 2014), 207–20, 209.

95 Daniel Halberstam, "Federal powers and the principle of subsidiarity," in *Global Perspectives on Constitutional Law*, ed. V.D. Amar and M.V. Tushnet (Oxford: Oxford University Press 2009), 34.

96 Komonchak, "Subsidiarity in the Church," 302. Emphasis in original.

97 See, e.g., Charlie Jeffrey, "German Federalism from Cooperation to Competition," in *German Federalism*, ed. Maiken Umbach (London: Palgrave Macmillan, 2002), 172.

98 Føllesdal, "Survey Article: Subsidiarity," 207.

99 Brennan, "Subsidiarity in the Tradition of Catholic Social Doctrine," 35.

100 Ibid.
101 Føllesdal, "Survey Article: Subsidiarity," 215.
102 Komonchak, "Subsidiarity in the Church," 302.
103 R.R. McCrae and P.T. Costa, "Validation of the five factor model of personality across instruments and observers," *Journal of Personality and Social Psychology*, 52 no. 1 (1987): 81–90.
104 Føllesdal, "Survey Article: Subsidiarity," 202.

CHAPTER FOUR

1 Justin Trudeau, "Letter to the Premier of Quebec from Liberal Party of Canada Leader Justin Trudeau," 22 August 2015, https://liberal.ca/letter-to-the-premier-of-quebec-from-liberal-party-of-canada-leader-justin-trudeau/, emphasis added.
2 Sonia Gandhi, cited in PTI "Centre has No Exit Strategy for Lockdown, Says Sonia Gandhi at Opposition Mee," *The New Indian Express*, 22 May 2020, https://www.newindianexpress.com/nation/2020/may/22/spirit-of-federalism-forgotten-govt-has-abandoned-any-pretence-of-being-democratic-sonia-gandhi-2146710.html.
3 Michael Burgess, *In Search of the Federal Spirit: New Comparative Empirical and Theoretical Perspectives* (Oxford: Oxford University Press, 2012), 3.
4 Ivo D. Duchacek, *Comparative Federalism: The Territorial Dimension of Politics* (Maryland: University Press of America 1987), 344; see also Burgess, *In Search of the Federal Spirit*, 254.
5 Richard Cole, John Kincaid, and Alejandro Rodriguez, "Public Opinion on Federalism and Federal Political Culture in Canada, Mexico, and the United States," *Publius* 34 no. 3 (2004): 201–21.
6 Ibid.
7 A.J. Brown, "Measuring the Mysteries of Federal Political Culture in Australia" in *Tomorrow's Federation: Reforming Australian Government*, ed. Paul Kildea, Andrew Lynch, and George Williams (The Federation Press, 2012), 310–31; A.J. Brown, "From Intuition to Reality: Measuring Federal Political Culture in Australia" *Publius* 43 no. 2 (2013): 297–314.
8 The project was greatly assisted by an expert workshop of members of the International Political Science Association's Research Committee 28, in Montreal, on 22 July 2014. For their involvement the project thanks Sonja Walti (American University; RC28 Convenor), Michael Stein (University of Toronto), Paolo Dardanelli (University of Kent), Arjan Schakel (Maastricht University), Wilfried Swenden (University of Edinburgh), Sean Muller (University of Berne), Philipp Trein (Universi-

ty of Lausanne), Soeren Keil (Canterbury Christ Church University), Mike Medeiros (University of Montreal), Andre Le Cours (University of Ottawa), Tom Lancaster (Emory University), Sumitrra Kumar Jain (University of Delhi), Doug Brown (St Francis Xavier University), Elodie Fabre, Sandrina Antunes (University of Minho), Chris Chhim (McGill University), and Blanka Richova (Charles University), along with project colleague Robyn Hollander (Griffith University). Notes of the workshop are available on request. The project also thanks Professors Guy Lachapelle (Concordia University), Pat Weller (Griffith University), Russell Trood (formerly Chair, Australian Senate Select Committee on Reform of the Australian Federation) and Kath Gelber (University of Queensland) for their participation in an earlier workshop at Griffith University, 31 March 2014.

9 A.J. Brown, John Kincaid, Jacob Deem, and Richard Cole, "Measuring Citizen Attachment to Federal Principles: Results from Australia, Canada, the United States, Germany and Great Britain," International Political Science Association, World Congress of Political Science, Poznan, Poland, July 2016.

10 Brown, "Measuring the Mysteries"; Brown, "From Intuition to Reality."

11 Brown et al., "Measuring Citizen Attachment to Federal Principles."

12 See, e.g., Rudolf Hrbek, "Germany," in *Handbook of Federal Countries*, ed. Anne Griffiths (Montreal: Forum of Federations/McGill-Queen's University Press, 2005), 156; Greg Taylor, "The Division of Power in Federal Systems," in *The Future of Australian Federalism: Comparative and Interdisciplinary Perspectives*, ed. Gabrielle Appleby, Nicholas Aroney, and Thomas John (Cambridge: Cambridge University Press, 2012), 107.

13 Patrick Fafard, Francois Rocher, and Catherine Cote, "The Presence (or Lack Thereof) of a Federal Culture in Canada: The Views of Canadians," *Regional and Federal Studies* 20, no. 1 (2010): 19–43, 21.

14 See Michael Burgess, *Comparative Federalism* (London: Routledge, 2006).

15 John Kincaid, "Values and Value Tradeoffs in Federalism," *Publius* 25 no. 2 (1995): 29–44, 30.

16 Fafard, Rocher, and Cote, "The Presence (or Lack Thereof) of a Federal Culture in Canada," 28. See also Charles Sancy Herrera, and Guy Lachapelle "Politicians, Public Opinion, and Reasonable Accommodation in Quebec," *Quebec Studies* 49 no. 1 (2010): 87–106, 87.

17 David McGrane and Loleen Berdahl, "Reconceptualizing Canadian Federal Political Culture: Examining Differences between Quebec and the Rest of Canada," *Publius* 50 no. 1 (2019): 109–34, 124.

18 Brown, "Measuring the Mysteries."

19 Ibid., 317; A.J. Brown and Jacob Deem, "Challenging the Irrevocable Decline: Democratic Satisfaction, National Cohesion, and Federal Political Culture in Australia (2008–2014)," in *Identities, Trust and Cohesion in Federal Countries: Perspectives from Public Opinion*, ed. Jack Jedwab and John Kincaid (Montreal and Kingston: Queen's University Press, 2019), 223–54; Jacob Deem, Robyn Hollander, and A.J. Brown, "Subsidiarity in the Australian Public Sector: Finding Pragmatism in the Principle," *Australian Journal of Public Administration* 74, no. 4 (2015): 419–34.

20 Russell Hittinger, "The Coherence of the Four Basic Principles of Catholic Social Doctrine: An Interpretation," in *Pursuing the Common Good: How Solidarity Can Work Together* (Vatican City: Pontifical Academy of Social Sciences, Acta 14, 2008), 16.

21 Jonathan Chaplin, "Subsidiarity and Social Pluralism," in *Global Perspectives on Subsidiarity*, ed. Michelle Evans and Augusto Zimmermann (London: Springer, 2014), 65–83, 65.

22 Andreas Føllesdal, "Subsidiarity and the Global Order," in *Global Perspectives on Subsidiarity*, ed. Michelle Evans and Augusto Zimmermann (London: Springer, 2014), 207–20.

23 Føllesdal, "Subsidiarity and the Global Order," 209.

24 Ibid.

25 Michelle Evans and Augusto Zimmermann, "The Global Relevance of Subsidiarity: An Overview," in *Global Perspectives on Subsidiarity*, ed. Michelle Evans and Augusto Zimmermann (London: Springer, 2014), 1–7, 1.

26 Joseph A. Komonchak "Subsidiarity in the Church: The State of the Question," *Jurist* 48, no. 1 (1988): 298–349, 302.

27 E.g., Shelley Metzenbaum, "From Oversight to Insight: federal agencies as learning leaders in the information age," in *Intergovernmental Relations in the 21st Century*, ed. T.J. Conlan and P. Posner (Washington, DC: The Brookings Institution, 2008), 210.

28 A.J. Brown and Jennifer Bellamy, eds, *Federalism and Regionalism in Australia: New Approaches, New Institutions?* (ANU Press, 2007).

29 Brown, "Measuring the Mysteries"; Brown, "From Intuition to Reality"; A.J. Brown "Mapping Federal Political Culture and Support for Political Reform in the World's First 'Top Down' Federation: The Strange Case of Australia," Panel for Triennial Meeting, International Political Science Association, Madrid, Spain: *Panel: Implications of Public Attitudes for Boundaries of National, Regional and Local Power in Federal and Nonfederal Systems*, 8–11 July 2012; A.J. Brown and Jacob Deem, "A Tale of Two

Regionalisms: Improving the measurement of Regionalism in Australia and Beyond," *Regional Studies* 50, no. 7 (2014): 1154–69.

30 Cole, Kincaid, and Rodriguez, "Public Opinion on Federalism and Federal Political Culture in Canada, Mexico, and the United States"; John Kincaid and Richard Cole, "Citizen Attitudes Toward Issues of Federalism in Canada, Mexico, and the United States" *Publius* 41, no. 1 (2010): 53–75.

31 See, e.g., Stephen Ansolabehere and Brian Schaffner, "Does Survey Mode Still Matter? Findings From a 2010 Multi-mode Comparison," *Political Analysis* 22, no. 3 (2014): 285–303; Charles Breton, Fred Cutler, Sarah Lachance, and Alex Mierke-Zatwarnicki, "Telephone versus Online Survey Modes for Election Studies: Comparing Canadian Public Opinion and Vote Choice in the 2015 Federal Election," *Canadian Journal of Political Science* 50, no. 4 (2017): 1005–36, 1005; Josh Pasek, "When will Nonprobability Surveys Mirror Probability Surveys? Considering Types of Inference and Weighting Strategies as Criteria for Correspondence," *International Journal of Public Opinion Research* 28, no. 2 (2016): 269–91, 269.

32 See, e.g., Ansolabehere and Schaffner, "Does Survey Mode Still Matter?".

33 Paul Furlong and David Marsh, "A Skin Not a Sweater: Ontology and Epistemology in Political Science" in *Theory and Methods in Political Science*, 3rd ed., ed. David Marsh and Gerry Stoker (Palgrave Macmillan, 2010), 204.

34 Don't Know responses to the "decentralist" subsidiarity item: ACVS 2008: 6.7 per cent; 2010: 6.7 per cent; 2012: 11.6 per cent; 2014: 8.6 per cent; 2016: 18.7 per cent.

35 The Confronting the Devolution Paradox project was greatly supported by Sean Müller (University of Lausanne), Jean-Philippe Gauvin (Queen's University), Mike Medeiros (University of Amsterdam), and Arjan Schakel (University of Bergen), who assisted with the translations.

36 See A.J. Brown, Jacob Deem and John Kincaid, "Federal Constitutional Values and Citizen Support: Explaining the Viability of Federalism and Federalist Reforms in Eight Countries," *Publius* 52, no. 1 (2022): 1–25.

37 Komonchak, "Subsidiarity in the Church," 302.

38 Decentralism: F (7, 6442) = 15.892, $p < .001$; nonabsorption: F (7, 6740) = 18.257, $p < .001$; support: F (7, 7291) = 15.417, $p < .001$.

39 Michelle Evans, "Subsidiarity and Federalism: A Case Study of the Australian Constitution and Its Interpretation," in *Global Perspectives on Subsidiarity*, ed. Michelle Evans and Augusto Zimmermann (London: Springer, 2014), 185–205.

40 Thomas Vandamme, "From Federated Federalism to Converging Federalism? The Case of EU Subsidiarity Scrutiny in Spain and Belgium" *Regional and Federal Studies* 22, no. 5: (2012) 515–31, 525.
41 Paolo Dardanelli and Sean Müller "Dynamic De/Centralization in Switzerland, 1848–2010," *Publius* 49, no. 1 (2019): 138–65.
42 William S. Livingston *Federalism and Constitutional Change* (Oxford: Clarendon Press, 1956), 269–72.
43 Chaplin, "Subsidiarity and Social Pluralism," 72, emphasis in original.
44 Patrick McKinley Brennan "Subsidiarity in the Tradition of Catholic Social Doctrine," in *Global Perspectives on Subsidiarity*, ed. Michelle Evans and Augusto Zimmermann (London: Springer, 2014), 29–47, 29.
45 https://jacobdeem.com/rethinking-decentralization.
46 Duchacek, *Comparative Federalism*, 344.
47 Daniel Weinstock, "Cities and Federalism," in *Federalism and Subsidiarity*, ed. James Fleming and Jacob Levy (New York: New York University Press, 2014), 259–90, 261.
48 Andreas Føllesdal, "Competing Conceptions of Subsidiarity," in *Federalism and Subsidiarity*, ed. James Fleming and Jacob Levy (New York: New York University Press, 2014), 214–30, 217.

CHAPTER FIVE

1 Daniel J. Elazar, *Exploring Federalism* (Alabama: University of Alabama Press, 1987).
2 Pew Research Centre, "Political Polarization in the American Public" (Washington, DC: Pew), http://www.people-press.org/2014/06/12/political-polarization-in-the-american-public/.
3 John Kincaid and Richard Cole "Attachments to Multiple Communities, Trust in Governments, Political Polarization, and Public Attitudes Toward Immigration in the United States," in *Identities, Trust and Cohesion in Federal Countries: Perspectives from Public Opinion*, ed. Jack Jedwab and John Kincaid (Montreal and Kingston: McGill-Queen's University Press, 2019), 147–80.
4 A.J. Brown, Jacob Deem, and John Kincaid, "Federal Constitutional Values and Citizen Support: Explaining the Viability of Federalism and Federalist Reforms in Eight Countries," *Publius* 52, no. 1 (2022): 1–25.
5 Notably, this interpretation emphasizes the importance of presidential power and minimizes Congress's role.
6 See, e.g., Sheila Grigsby, Alicia Hernàndez, Sara John, Désirée Jones-Smith, Katie Kaufmann, Cordaryl Patrick, Christopher Prener, Mark

Tranel and Adriano Udani, "Resistance to Racial Equality in U.S. Federalism and Its Impact on Fragmented Regions," *American Review of Public Administration* 50, no. 6–7 (2020): 658–67.

7 In a separate analysis, the region in which a respondent lived was also not a significant predictor of attitudes toward subsidiarity.

8 Andreas Føllesdal, "Survey Article: Subsidiarity," *The Journal of Political Philosophy* 6, no. 2 (1998): 190–218.

9 Ibid., 204.

10 I use this term in the sense described by Davis as a form of federation with a loose fit or weak centre, which is distinct from "confederacy" as used in relation to the Civil War – Solomon Rufus Davis, *The Federal Principle: A Journey Through Time in Quest of Meaning* (California: University of California Press, 1978), 13–14.

11 *United States v Sprague* (1931) 282 US 716, 733–4.

12 Steven G. Calabresi and Lucy D. Bickford, "Federalism and Subsidiarity: Perspectives from U.S. Constitutional Law," in *Federalism and Subsidiarity*, ed. James Fleming and Jacob Levy (New York: New York University Press, 2014), 123–89, 148–9.

13 Ibid., 125.

14 Joe Biden, "Inaugural Address by President Joseph R. Biden Jnr," 20 January 2021, https://www.whitehouse.gov/briefing-room/speeches-remarks/2021/01/20/inaugural-address-by-president-joseph-r-biden-jr/.

15 Jürgen Bröhmer, "Subsidiarity and the German Constitution," in *Global Perspectives on Subsidiarity*, ed. Michelle Evans and Augusto Zimmermann (London: Springer, 2014), 129–56, 129–30.

16 Greg Taylor, "Germany: A slow death for subsidiarity?" *International Journal of Constitutional Law* 7, no. 1 (2009): 139–54.

17 Ibid.

18 See, for example, its styling as *Freistaat Bayern* (the "Free State of Bavaria").

19 Russell J. Dalton and Steven Weldon, "Germans Divided? Political Culture in a United Germany," *German Politics* 19, no. 1 (2010): 9–23.

20 André Kaiser and Stephan Vogel, "Dynamic De/Centralization in Germany, 1949–2010," *Publius* 49, no. 1 (2019): 84–111, 2.

21 See, e.g., John Curtice, "A Stronger or Weaker Union? Public Reactions to Asymmetric Devolution in the United Kingdom," *Publius* 36, no. 1 (2006): 95–113; Ailsa Henderson, Charlie Jeffrey, Daniel Wincott, and Richard Wyn Jones, "Reflections on the 'Devolution Paradox': A Comparative Examination of Multi-Level Citizenship," *Regional Studies* 47 no. 3 (2013): 303–22; Charlie Jeffrey, "Devolution and Divergence: Pub-

lic Attitudes and Institutional Logistics," in *Devolution in Practice*, ed. John Adams and Katie Schmuecker (IPPR, 2005); Charlie Jeffrey, "Devolution and Social Citizenship: Which Society, Whose Citizenship?" in *Territory, Democracy and Justice*, ed. Scott Greer (London: Palgrave Macmillan, 2006); Carol S. Weissert and David Blake Jones, "Devolution Paradox and the US South," *Regional and Federal Studies* 25, no 3. (2015): 259–76.

22 Henry Schneller, "German Federalism: On the Way to a 'Cooperative Centralism,'" in *Identities, Trust and Cohesion in Federal Countries: Perspectives from Public Opinion*, ed. Jack Jedwab and John Kincaid (Montreal and Kingston: McGill-Queen's University Press, 2019), 255–79, 255–6.

23 Celia Applegate, *A Nation of Provincials: The German Idea of Heimat* (California: University of California Press, 1990), 4.

24 See, e.g., Applegate's critique of the Nazi corruption of Heimat – Applegate, *A Nation of Provincials*. See also Peter Blickle, *Heimat, A Critical Theory of the German Idea of Homeland* (New York: Camden House, 2002), x.

25 Ibid; Beate M.W. Ratter and Kira Gee, "*Heimat* – A German concept of regional perception and identity as a basis for coastal management in the Wadden Sea," *Ocean and Coastal Management* 68, no. 1 (2012): 127–37.

26 Schneller "German Federalism," 255–6.

27 Applegate, *A Nation of Provincials*, 19. Italics as per original.

28 Ratter and Gee, "*Heimat*," 129. Italics as per original.

29 Blickle, *Heimat*.

30 Ibid., ix.

31 Applegate, *A Nation of Provincials*, 19.

32 Ratter and Gee, "*Heimat*."

33 Blickle, *Heimat*, 4. Italics as per original.

34 Ibid., 1.

35 Ratter and Gee, "*Heimat*," 128.

36 Table 5.5n Paired samples t-test

	M	SD	*t*	*p*	*d*
Decentralism/nonabsorption	–.390	.706	–14.650	<.001	0.552
Decentralism/support	.119	.714	4.504	<.001	0.167
Nonabsorption/support	.500	.597	23.791	<.001	0.838

37 Blickle, *Heimat*, 1.

38 See, e.g., Paolo Dardanelli and Sean Müller, "Dynamic De/Centralization in Switzerland, 1848–2010," *Publius* 49, no. 1 (2019): 138–65.

CHAPTER SIX

1 John Paul II, *Centesimus Annus* (1991), accessed 16 March 2021, http://www.vatican.va/content/john-paul-ii/en/encyclicals/documents/hf_jp-ii_enc_01051991_centesimus-annus.html, emphasis added.
2 Patrick McKinley Brennan, "Subsidiarity in the Tradition of Catholic Social Doctrine," in *Global Perspectives on Subsidiarity*, ed. Michelle Evans and Augusto Zimmermann (London: Springer, 2014), 29–47, 35.
3 See especially McGrane and Berdahl's meta-analysis as well as their own survey – David McGrane and Loleen Berdahl, "Reconceptualizing Canadian Federal Political Culture: Examining Differences between Quebec and the Rest of Canada," *Publius* 50 no. 1 (2019): 109–34.
4 See, e.g., Michelle Evans, "Subsidiarity and Federalism: A Case Study of the Australian Constitution and Its Interpretation," in *Global Perspectives on Subsidiarity*, ed. Michelle Evans and Augusto Zimmermann (London: Springer, 2014), 185–205; Mark Bruerton, Tracey Arkley, Robyn Hollander, and Ron Levy, eds, *A People's Federation* (New South Wales: Federation Press, 2017).
5 See, e.g., Eugenie Brouillet, "Canadian Federalism and the Principle of Subsidiarity: Should We Open Pandora's Box?" *Supreme Court Law Review* 54, no. 1 (2011): 601–32; Hugo Cyr, "Autonomy, Subsidiarity, Solidarity: Foundations of Cooperative Federalism," *Constitutional Forum constitutionnel* 23 no. 1 (2014): 20; Dwight Newman, "Changing Division of Powers Doctrine and the Emergent Principle of Subsidiarity," *Saskatchewan Law Review* 74 no. 1 (2011): 21.
6 André Lecours, "Dynamic De/centralization in Canada, 1867–2010," *Publius* 49, no. 1 (2019): 57–83, 76.
7 Garth Stevenson, *Unfulfilled Union. Canadian Federalism and National Unity* (Montreal and Kingston: McGill-Queen's University Press, 2009), 72.
8 Lecours, "Dynamic De/Centralization in Canada."
9 Renamed the Constitution Act in 1982.
10 Articles 55, 56, and 90.
11 Stevenson, *Unfulfilled Union*, 33.
12 Lecours, "Dynamic De/Centralization in Canada."
13 Peter B. Waite, *The Life and Times of Confederation, 1864–1867: Politics, Newspapers, and the Union of British North America* (Toronto: University of Toronto Press, 1962), 37–8.
14 Lecours, "Dynamic De/Centralization in Canada." See also Richard

Simeon, "Considerations on centralization and decentralization," *Canadian Public Administration* 28, no. 1 (1986): 445–61; Grace Skogstad, *The Politics of Agricultural Policy-Making in Canada* (Toronto: University of Toronto Press, 1987).

15 Ibid.

16 Simeon, "Considerations on centralization and decentralization," 449.

17 Brouillet, "Canadian Federalism and the Principle of Subsidiarity."

18 $p < .001$, $d = 0.56$; 2018: $p < .001$, $d = 0.39$.

19 Brouillet, "Canadian Federalism and the Principle of Subsidiarity."

20 McGrane and Berdahl, "Reconceptualising Canadian Federal Political Culture," 118.

21 Ibid., 117.

22 Jack Jedwab, "Federalist Governance, Provincial Grievances, and Attachment to Canada," in *Identities, Trust and Cohesion in Federal Countries: Perspectives from Public Opinion*, ed. Jack Jedwab and John Kincaid (Montreal and Kingston: McGill-Queen's University Press, 2019), 25–56, 34.

23 Nelson Wiseman, *In Search of Canadian Political Culture* (Vancouver: UBC Press, 2008), 1.

24 McGrane and Berdahl, "Reconceptualising Canadian Federal Political Culture," 121.

25 See, e.g., Jan Erk, *Explaining Federalism: State, Society and Congruence in Austria, Belgium, Canada, Germany and Switzerland* (New York: Routledge, 2008).

26 See, e.g., Patrick Fafard, Francois Rocher, and Catherine Cote, "The Presence (or Lack Thereof) of a Federal Culture in Canada: The Views of Canadians," *Regional and Federal Studies* 20, no. 1 (2010): 19–43, 28.

27 Wiseman, *In Search of Canadian Political Culture*, 2, 3.

28 Eric Nicol and Peter Whalley, *One Hundred Years of What?* (Toronto: Ryerson Press, 1966), vii–viii.

29 Richard Simeon and David Elkins, "Regional Political Cultures in Canada," *Canadian Journal of Political Science* 7, no. 3 (1974): 397–437; Richard Simeon and David Elkins, "Provincial Political Cultures in Canada," in *Small Worlds: Provinces and Parties in Canadian Political Life*, ed. David Elkins and Richard Simeon (London: Methuen, 1980).

30 J. Murray Beck, "Nova Scotia, Tradition and Conservatism," in *Canadian Provincial Politics*, ed. Martin Robin (Prentice-Hall, 1978).

31 Wiseman, *In Search of Canadian Political Culture*.

32 Jared J. Wesley, *Code Politics: Campaigns and Cultures on the Canadian Prairies* (Vancouver: UBC Press, 2011).

33 Harold D. Clarke, Jane Jenson, Lawrence LeDuc, Jon H. Pammett, *Political Choice in Canada* (McGraw Hill, 1979).
34 Michael D. Ornstein and Michael Stevenson, *Politics and Ideology in Canada, Elite and Public Opinion in the Transformation of a Welfare State* (Montreal and Kingston: McGill-Queen's University Press, 1999); Michael D. Ornstein, H. Michael Stevenson, and A. Paul Williams, "Region, Class and Political Culture in Canada," *Canadian Journal of Political Science* 13, no. 2, (1980): 227–71.
35 Ailsa Henderson, "Regional Political Cultures in Canada," *Canadian Journal of Political Science* 37, no. 3 (2004): 595–615; Ailsa Henderson, "Greater than the Sum of its Parts: Political Cultures and Regions in Canada," in *Election*, ed. Heather Ivor (Emond Montgomery, 2010).
36 David McGrane and Loleen Berdahl, "'Small Worlds' No More: Reconsidering Provincial Political Cultures in Canada," *Regional and Federal Studies* 23, no. 4 (2013): 479–93.
37 David Bell and Lorne Tepperman, *The Roots of Disunity: A Look at Canadian Political Culture* (Toronto: McClelland and Stewart Publishers, 1979), 85.
38 Ibid., 84–6.
39 Will Kymlicka, "The Current State of Multiculturalism in Canada and Research Themes on Canadian Multiculturalism 2008–2010," Report prepared for the Department of Immigration and Citizenship (2011), 15–16. See also Jeffrey Reitz and Rupa Banjeree, "Racial Inequality, Social Cohesion and Policy Issues in Canada," in *Belonging? Diversity, Recognition and Shared Citizenship in Canada*, ed. Keith Banting, Thomas J. Courchene, and F. Leslie Seidle (Montreal: Institute for Research on Public Policy, 2007).
40 William H. Riker, *Federalism: Origin, Operation, Significance* (Boston: Little, Brown and Company, 1964), 113.
41 William Livingston, "Canada, Australia and the United States: Variations on a Theme," in *Federalism: Infinite Variety in Theory and Practice*, ed. Valerie Earle (Itasca: Peacock 1968), 140.
42 A.J. Brown and Jacob Deem, "Challenging the Irrevocable Decline: Democratic Satisfaction, National Cohesion, and Federal Political Culture in Australia (2008–2014)," in *Identities, Trust and Cohesion in Federal Countries: Perspectives from Public Opinion*, ed. Jack Jedwab and John Kincaid (Montreal and Kingston: Queen's University Press, 2019), 223–54.
43 A.J. Brown, "Subsidiarity or Subterfuge? Resolving the Future of Local Government in the Australian Federal System," *Australian Journal of Public Administration* 61, no. 4 (2002): 24–42, 39.

44 See, e.g., Colin Clark, "Australia's Economic and Population Capacity," *Australian Journal of Politics and History* 1, no. 1 (1955): 49–58; Colin Clark, *Population Growth and Land Use* (New York: St Martin's Press, 1977); Colin Clark, "Welfare Taxation: Opting Out to Shrink the State," *Economic Affairs* 7, no. 3 (1987): 38–9.
45 Brian Galligan, *A Federal Republic: Australia's Constitutional System of Government* (Cambridge: Cambridge University Press, 1995), 205.
46 Commonwealth of Australia, "Reform of the Federation Issues Paper 1: A Federation for Our Future," (2015), v.
47 Ibid., 18.
48 Bronwyn Hinz, *Schooling Federalism: Evaluating the Options for Reform* (University of Melbourne School of Governance, 2015), 6. See also Bronwyn Hinz "Policy Coherence Across the Education Continuum in Australia: Understanding and Improving Service Delivery," in *A People's Federation*, ed. Mark Bruerton, Tracey Arklay, Robyn Hollander, and Ron Levy (Federation Press, 2017).
49 Christopher Ritzer, Marc Rutloff, and Karin Linhart, "How to sharpen a dull sword – The principle of subsidiarity and its control," *German Law Journal* 7, no. 9 (2006): 733–60.
50 Evans, "Subsidiarity and Federalism," 195.
51 Ibid.
52 Paul Kildea, Andrew Lynch, and George Williams, "Introduction" in *Tomorrow's Federation: Reforming Australian Government*, ed. Paul Kildea, Andrew Lynch, and George Williams (Federation Press, 2012), 1.
53 Excluding Belgium, see chapter 4 of this volume.
54 Jacob Deem, Robyn Hollander, and A.J. Brown, "Subsidiarity in the Australian Public Sector: Finding Pragmatism in the Principle," *Australian Journal of Public Administration* 74, no. 4 (2015): 419–34, 423.
55 Jacob Deem, "Federal Reform: The Case for Supportive Subsidiarity in Australia," *UNSW Law Journal* 44, no. 2 (2021): 613–36.
56 Martin Painter, *Collaborative Federalism: Economic Reform in Australia in the 1990s* (Cambridge: Cambridge University Press, 1998); Tracey Arklay, Mark Bruerton, and Robyn Hollander, "Working Together: Policy Makers' Opinions on Improving Intergovernmental Collaboration in Australia," in *A People's Federation*, ed. Mark Bruerton, Tracey Arklay, Robyn Hollander, and Ron Levy (New South Wales: Federation Press, 2017).
57 Queensland is notable as the only mainland Australian state where more residents live outside the capital city than within it.
58 Jacob Deem and Anne Tiernan, "Beyond the Canberra Bubble: Rebuild-

ing Trust in Federal Australia," in *From Turnbull to Morrison*, ed. Mark Evans, Michelle Grattan, and Brendan McCaffrie (Melbourne: Melbourne University Press, 2019), 93–108.

59 Nicholas Aroney, Scott Prasser, and Alison Taylor, "Federal Diversity in Australia – A Counter Narrative," in *The Future of Australian Federalism: Comparative and Interdisciplinary Perspectives*, ed. Gabriella Appleby, Nicholas Aroney, and Thomas John (Cambridge University Press, 2012).

60 David Denemark and Campbell Sharman, "Political Efficacy, Involvement and Trust: Testing for Regional Political Culture in Australia," *Australian Journal of Political Science* 29, no. 1. (1994): 81–102, 82.

61 A.J. Brown and Jacob Deem, "A Tale of Two Regionalisms: Improving the Measurement of Regionalism in Australia and Beyond," *Regional Studies* 50, no. 7 (2014): 1154–69.

62 Rodney Smith, *Australian Political Culture* (NSW: Pearson Education Australia, 2001), 305.

63 Thomas Musgrave, "The Western Australian Secessionist Movement," *Macquarie Law Journal* 3, no. 1 (2003): 95.

64 Smith, *Australian Political Culture*, 95.

65 Ibid., 96.

66 Elaine Thompson, *Fair Enough* (University of New South Wales Press, 1994), 240.

67 For instance, poverty levels, gender disparities, and treatment of immigrants and Indigenous Australians – Smith, *Australian Political Culture*, 96.

68 Francis Castles, *The Working Class and Welfare* (Allen and Unwin, 1985).

69 Ibid.

70 Andreas Føllesdal "Survey Article: Subsidiarity," *The Journal of Political Philosophy* 6, no. 2 (1998): 190–218, 207.

71 Smith, *Australian Political Culture*, 88, referring to Charles Bean, *The Story of Anzac* (University of Queensland Press, 1981), 550.

72 Bruce Kapferer, *Legends of People, Myths of State* (Smithsonian Institute Press, 1988), 168–71 cited in Smith, *Australian Political Culture*, 89.

73 Smith, *Australian Political Culture*, 89.

74 See, e.g., Kenneth Wiltshire, "Reforming Australian Governance: Old States, No States or New States?" in *Federalism and Regionalism in Australia: New Approaches, New Institutions?* ed. A.J. Brown and Jennifer Bellamy (Australian National University Press, 2007), 193.

75 Nick Dyrenfurth, "John Howard's Hegemony of Values: The Politics of 'Mateship' in the Howard Decade," *Australian Journal of Political Science* 42, no. 2 (2007): 211–30.

76 See, e.g., Stephanie Convery, "Morrison's Government on the Bushfires: From Attacking Climate 'Lunatics' to Calling in the Troops," *Guardian* (online), 4 January 2020, https://www.theguardian.com/australia-news/2020/jan/04/morrisons-government-on-the-bushfires-from-attacking-climate-lunatics-to-calling-in-the-troops.

77 Deem, Hollander, and Brown, "Subsidiarity in the Australian Public Sector."

78 Hugh Collins, "Political Ideology in Australia: The Distinctiveness of a Benthamite Society," *Daedalus* 114, no. 1 (1985): 147–69.

79 Smith, *Australian Political Culture*, 113, 114.

80 Robyn Hollander and Haig Patapan, "Pragmatic Federalism: Australian Federalism from Hawke to Howard," *Australian Journal of Public Administration* 66, no. 3 (2007): 280–97. See also Amanda Smullen, "Conceptualising Australia's Tradition of Pragmatic Federalism," *Australian Journal of Political Science* 49, no. 4 (2014): 677–93.

81 Hollander and Patapan, "Pragmatic Federalism," 281.

82 Patrick Keane, "In Celebration of the Constitution," address to the National Archives Commission, 12 June 2008, 1.

83 Smullen, "Conceptualising Australia's Tradition of Pragmatic Federalism," 108.

84 Deem, Hollander, and Brown, "Subsidiarity in the Australian Public Sector."

85 Smith, *Australian Political Culture*, 88, referring to Charles Bean, *The Story of Anzac* (University of Queensland Press, 1981), 550.

86 Ibid., 88.

87 Ibid., 90.

88 See, e.g., Charles Grant, *Inside the House that Jacques Built* (Nicholas Brealey Publishing, 1994), 218.

89 Cited in John Peterson, "Subsidiarity: A Definition to Suit Any Vision?" *Parliamentary Affairs* 47, no. 1 (1994): 116–32.

90 Philip Booth, "Brexit: The Role of Subsidiarity," *The Tablet*, 29 June 2016, accessed 10 January 2018, http://www.thetablet.co.uk/features/2/8573/brexit-the-role-of-subsidiarity; Benjamin Wiker, "Brexit and the Principle of Subsidiarity," blog post in the National Catholic Register, accessed 7 June 2017, http://www.ncregister.com/blog/benjamin-wiker/brexit-and-the-principle-of-subsidiarity.

91 Tony Blair, *Leading the Way – A New Vision for Local Government*, Institute for Public Policy Research, London, cited in Mike Raco, "Governmentality, Subject-Building, and the Discourses and Practices of Devolu-

tion in the UK," *Transactions of the Institute of British Geographers* 28, no. 1 (2003): 75–95, 75.

92 Paul Cairney, "The Scottish Independence Referendum: What are the Implications of a No Vote?" *The Political Quarterly* 86, no. 2 (2015): 186–91, 187.

93 Ibid., 189. See also Joanna Sharp, Andy Cumbers, Joe Painter, and Nichola Wood, "Deciding Whose Future? Challenges and Opportunities of the Scottish Independence Referendum 2014 for Scotland and Beyond," *Political Geography* 41 (2014): 32–42.

94 Paolo Dardanelli and John Kincaid, "A New Union? Federalism and the UK," *Political Insight* 7, no. 3 (2016): 12–15.

95 William S. Livingston, "A Note on the Nature of Federalism," *Political Science Quarterly* 67, no. 1 (1952): 81.

96 Michael Kenny, *The Politics of English Nationhood* (Oxford: Oxford University Press, 2014), 38. See also Jeremy Paxman, *The English: A Portrait of a People* (Penguin, 2007); Andrew Marr, *History of Modern Britain* (Pan Macmillan, 2009); Cole Moreton, *Is God Still and Englishman? How Britain Lost its Faith (But Found New Soul)* (Abacus, 2011).

97 Krishan Kumar, *The Making of English National Identity* (Cambridge University Press, 2003).

98 Kenny, *The Politics of English Nationhood.*

99 Richard Wyn Jones, Guy Lodge, Charlie Jeffery, Glenn Gottfried, Roger Scully, Ailsa Henderson, and Daniel Wincott, *England and Its Two Unions: The Anatomy of a Nation and Its Discontents – The 2012 Future of England Survey* (Institute for Public Policy Research, 2013).

100 Michael Kenny, "The Return of 'Englishness' in British Political Culture – The End of the Unions?" *Journal of Common Market Studies* 53, no. 1 (2015): 35–51, 43.

101 David Golemboski, "Federalism and the Catholic Principle of Subsidiarity," *Publius* 45, no. 4 (2015): 526–51.

102 83.4 per cent and 85.7 per cent of Northern Irish respondents were attached to decentralism and nonabsorption, respectively, compared to: decentralism: 69.2 per cent (England), 73.2 per cent (Scotland) and 69.5 per cent (Wales); and nonabsorption: 73.3 per cent (England), 79.7 per cent (Scotland) and 70.2 per cent (Wales). Further details in online appendix, available at the author's website, https://jacobdeem.com/rethinking-decentralization.

103 Ailsa Henderson, Charlie Jeffery, Dan Wincott, and Richard Wyn Jones, "How Brexit was made in England," *British Journal of Politics and International Relations* 19, no. 4 (2017): 631–46, 633.

104 A Gabriel post hoc analysis of variance was used as it is robust against variations in sample size between groups. ANOVA: Decentralism: $F (3, 770) = 1.876$, $p = .132$; Nonabsorption: $F (3, 813) = 1.495$, $p = .215$; Support: $F (3, 853) = 2.526$, $p = .056$.

CHAPTER SEVEN

1 Michael Burgess, "Success and Failure in Federation: Comparative Perspectives," paper presented at the *Festschrift* for Ronald L. Watts, October 2007, Queen's University, 1–21.
2 Burgess, "Success and Failure in Federation," 8.
3 Philip G. Roeder "Ethnofederalism and the Mismanagement of Conflicting Nationalisms," *Regional and Federal Studies* 19 no. 2, (2009): 203–19.
4 Thomas Vandamme, "From Federated Federalism to Converging Federalism? The Case of EU Subsidiarity Scrutiny in Spain and Belgium," *Regional and Federal Studies* 22, no. 5 (2012): 515–31.
5 Peter Thijssen, Sarah Arras, and Dave Sinardet, "Federalism and Solidarity in Belgium: Insights from Public Opinion' in *Identities, Trust, and Cohesion in Federal Systems: Public Perspectives*, ed. Jack Jedwab and John Kincaid (Montreal and Kingston: McGill-Queen's University Press, 2019), 85–114.
6 Ibid.
7 Ibid.
8 Ibid.
9 Ibid.
10 35.9%; ibid., 98.
11 37.4%; ibid., 98.
12 16.8% of respondents wanted regional autonomy in all seven policy domains as per the study by Thijssen and colleagues; ibid., 98.
13 Matthew Taub (14 February 2019) "Inside the Belgian Library that Tore Itself Apart," accessed 29 January 2021, https://www.atlasobscura.com/articles/when-was-the-leuven-library-divided.
14 Cited in Taub, "Inside the Belgian Library that Tore Itself Apart."
15 Ivo D. Duchacek, *Comparative Federalism: The Territorial Dimension of Politics* (Maryland: University Press of America, 1987), 344; Daniel J. Elazar, *Exploring Federalism* (Alabama: University of Alabama Press, 1987).
16 Cited in Taub, "Inside the Belgian Library that Tore Itself Apart."

17 Jaak Billiet, Bart Maddens and Andre-Paul Frognier, "Does Belgium (Still) Exist? Differences in Political Culture between Flemings and Walloons," *West European Politics* 29 no. 5 (2006): 912–32.
18 Thijssen, Arras, and Sinardet, "Federalism and Solidarity in Belgium," 110.
19 Ibid.
20 χ^2 (60, n= 691) = 116.861, $p < .001$.
21 Alistair Cole, Stuart Fox, Romain Pasquier, and Ian Stafford, "Political trust in France's multi-level government," *Journal of Trust Research* 8, no. 1 (2018): 45–67.
22 Ibid.
23 Elazar, *Exploring Federalism*, 154.
24 Ibid.
25 Eric Nicol and Peter Whalley, *One Hundred Years of What?* (Toronto: Ryerson Press, 1966), vii–viii.
26 Ajay Kumar Singh "Dynamic De/Centralization in India, 1950–2010," *Publius* 49 no. 1 (2019): 112–37.

CHAPTER EIGHT

1 See, e.g., Jenna Bednar, "Subsidiarity and Robustness: Building the Adaptive Efficiency of Federal Systems," in *Federalism and Subsidiarity*, ed. James Fleming and Jacob Levy (New York: New York University Press, 2014), 231–56, 231; A.J. Brown, "Measuring the Mysteries of Federal Political Culture in Australia," in *Tomorrow's Federation: Reforming Australian Government*, ed. Paul Kildea, Andrew Lynch, and George Williams (The Federation Press, 2012), 310–31, 317; John F. Kenney, "The Principle of Subsidiarity," *The American Catholic Sociological Review* 16, no. 1 (1955): 31–6, 31; Loren King, "Cities, Subsidiarity, and Federalism," in *Federalism and Subsidiarity*, ed. James Fleming and Jacob Levy (New York: New York University Press, 2014), 291–331, 291; Robert A. Sirico, "Subsidiarity and the Reform of the Welfare of the Nation State," in *Global Perspectives on Subsidiarity*, ed. Michelle Evans and Augusto Zimmermann (London: Springer, 2014), 107–27, 109; Patrice Ranjault, "On the Principle of Subsidiarity" *Journal of European Social Policy* 2, no. 1 (1992): 49; Anne Twomey and Glenn Withers, *Federalist Paper 1 – Australia's Federal Future: Delivering Growth and Prosperity* (Council for the Australian Federation, 2007) 4, 28; Daniel Weinstock, "Cities and Federalism," in *Federalism and Subsidiarity*, ed. James Fleming and Jacob Levy (New York: New York University Press, 2014), 259–90, 261; Augusto Zimmermann, "Subsidiarity, Democracy and Individ-

ual Liberty in Brazil," in *Global Perspectives on Subsidiarity*, ed. Michelle Evans and Augusto Zimmermann (London: Springer, 2014), 85–106, 85.

2 Daniel J. Elazar, *Exploring Federalism* (Alabama: University of Alabama Press, 1987), others.

3 Michael Burgess, "Success and Failure in Federation: Comparative Perspectives' paper presented at the *Festschrift* for Ronald L. Watts, October 2007, Queen's University, 1–21, 15.

4 Pius XI, *Quadragesimo Anno: Encyclical on Reconstruction of the Social Order* (1931), online, http://www.vatican.va/holy_father/pius_xi/encyclicals/documents/hf_p-xi_enc_19310515_quadragesimo-anno_en.html, 79.

5 Alistair Cole, Stuart Fox, Romain Pasquier, and Ian Stafford, "Political Trust in France's Multi-level Government," *Journal of Trust Research* 8, no. 1 (2018): 45–67.

6 Robyn Hollander and Haig Patapan, "Pragmatic Federalism: Australian Federalism from Hawke to Howard," *Australian Journal of Public Administration* 66, no. 3 (2007): 280–97; Rodney Smith, *Australian Political Culture* (NSW: Pearson Education Australia, 2001).

7 A.J. Brown and Jacob Deem, "Challenging the Irrevocable Decline: Democratic Satisfaction, National Cohesion, and Federal Political Culture in Australia (2008–2014)," in *Identities, Trust and Cohesion in Federal Countries: Perspectives from Public Opinion*, ed. Jack Jedwab and John Kincaid (Montreal and Kingston: McGill-Queen's University Press, 2019), 223–54.

8 André Lecours, "Dynamic De/centralization in Canada, 1867–2010," *Publius* 49, no. 1 (2019): 57–83.

9 Alan Fenna, "The Centralization of Australian Federalism 1901–2010: Measurement and Interpretation," *Publius* 49, no. 1 (2019): 30–56.

10 Nathalie Behnke, "Towards a New Organization of Federal States? – Lessons from the Processes of Constitutional Reform in Germany, Austria, and Switzerland," *Polis Nr. 66/2009* (Institut für Politikwissenschaft, FernUniversität in Hagen, 2009); Jörg Broschek, "Pathways of Federal Reform: Australia, Canada, Germany, and Switzerland," *Publius* 45, no. 1 (2014): 51–76.

11 A.J. Brown, Jacob Deem, and John Kincaid, "Federal Constitutional Values and Citizen Attitudes to Government: Explaining Federal System Viability and Reform Preferences in Eight Countries," *Publius* 52, no. 1 (2022): 1–25.

12 Jack Jedwab, "Federalist Governance, Provincial Grievances, and Attachment to Canada," in *Identities, Trust and Cohesion in Federal Countries:*

Perspectives from Public Opinion, ed. Jack Jedwab and John Kincaid (Montreal and Kingston: McGill-Queen's University Press, 2019), 25–56.

13 David Golemboski, "Federalism and the Catholic Principle of Subsidiarity," *Publius* 45, no. 4 (2015): 526–51.

14 See, e.g., Narisong Huhe, Daniel Naurin, and Robert Thomson, "Decision-making and Networks in the Council of the European Union after Brexit," Paper presented at Australian Political Studies Association Annual Conference, 24–27 September 2017, Melbourne, Australia.

15 Arthur Benz, "The Federal Constitutional Court of Germany: Guardian of Unitarism and Federalism," in *Courts in Federal Countries: Federalists or Unitarists?* ed. Nicholas Aroney and John Kincaid (Toronto: University of Toronto Press, 2017), 193–222, 215.

16 Paolo Dardanelli and Sean Müller, "Dynamic De/Centralization in Switzerland, 1848–2010," *Publius* 49, no. 1 (2019): 138–65.

17 Chris Varcoe, "Welcome to the oilsands prime minister. Now, about that pipeline," *National Post*, 5 April 2018, accessed 6 April 2018, http://nationalpost.com/business/energy/varcoe-welcome-to-the-oilsands-prime-minister-now-about-that-pipeline/wcm/0047d4fd-61c7-4ac8-a9de-46ca8971480d.

18 Don Braid, "The NDP Tries to Fight Off Ottawa's Bloated Bill C-69," *National Post*, 5 April 2018, accessed 6 April 2018, http://nationalpost.com/news/politics/braid-the-ndp-tries-to-fight-off-ottawas-bloated-bill-c-69/wcm/42a3488f-fb04-42e3-9077-134bc22cf211.

19 Jedwab, "Federalist Governance, Provincial Grievances, and Attachment to Canada."

20 Michelle Evans, "Subsidiarity and Federalism: A Case Study of the Australian Constitution and Its Interpretation," in *Global Perspectives on Subsidiarity*, ed. Michelle Evans and Augusto Zimmermann, 185–205 (London: Springer, 2014), 195.

21 See, e.g., Commonwealth of Australia, "Reform of the Federation Issues Paper 1: A Federation for Our Future" (2014), Department of Prime Minister and Cabinet, accessed 22 November 2022, https://apo.org.au/node/41596.

22 See, e.g., Nicholas Aroney, "Federalism and Subsidiarity: Principles and Processes in the Reform of the Australian Federation," *Federal Law Review* 44, no. 1 (2016): 1–24.

23 Jacob Deem, "Federal Reform: The Case for Supportive Subsidiarity in Australia," *UNSW Law Journal* 44, no. 2 (2021): 613–36.

CHAPTER NINE

1 Solomon Rufus Davis, *The Federal Principle: A Journey Through Time in Quest of Meaning* (California: University of California Press, 1978), 1.

2 Greg Taylor, "Germany: A Slow Death for Subsidiarity?" *International Journal of Constitutional Law* 7, no. 1 (2009): 139–54; R.A.B. Leaper, "Subsidiarity and the Welfare State," *Social and Economic Administration* 9, no. 2 (1975): 82–97, 82.

3 Gabriel A. Moens and John Trone, "The Principle of Subsidiarity in EU Judicial and Legislative Practice: Panacea or Placebo?" *Journal of Legislation* 41, no. 1 (2015): 65–102, 65.

4 Jack Jedwab, "Federalist Governance, Provincial Grievances, and Attachment to Canada," in *Identities, Trust and Cohesion in Federal Countries: Perspectives from Public Opinion*, ed. Jack Jedwab and John Kincaid, 25–56 (Montreal and Kingston: Queen's University Press, 2019).

5 Michael Burgess, "Success and Failure in Federation: Comparative Perspectives," paper presented at the *Festschrift* for Ronald L. Watts, October 2007, Queen's University, 1–21.

6 Michelle Evans, "Subsidiarity and Federalism: A Case Study of the Australian Constitution and Its Interpretation," in *Global Perspectives on Subsidiarity*, ed. Michelle Evans and Augusto Zimmermann (London: Springer, 2014), 185–205.

7 Jacob Deem, "Federal Reform: The Case for Supportive Subsidiarity in Australia," *UNSW Law Journal* 44, no. 2 (2021): 613–36.

8 Burgess, "Success and Failure in Federation."

9 Nicholas Jacobs, "An Experimental Test of How Americans Think About Federalism," *Publius: The Journal of Federalism* 47, no. 4 (2017): 572–98.

10 Michael Burgess, *In Search of the Federal Spirit: New Comparative Empirical and Theoretical Perspectives* (Oxford: Oxford University Press, 2012).

11 Jedwab, "Federalist Governance, Provincial Grievances, and Attachment to Canada."

12 Daniel J. Elazar, *Exploring Federalism* (Alabama: University of Alabama Press, 1987).

13 Jenna Bednar, "Subsidiarity and Robustness: Building the Adaptive Efficiency of Federal Systems," in *Federalism and Subsidiarity*, ed. James Fleming and Jacob Levy, 231–56 (New York: New York University Press, 2014), 231.

14 See, e.g., John Curtice, "A Stronger or Weaker Union? Public Reactions to Asymmetric Devolution in the United Kingdom," *Publius* 36 no. 1

(2006): 95–113; Ailsa Henderson, Charlie Jeffrey, Daniel Wincott, and Richard Wyn Jones, "Reflections on the 'Devolution Paradox': A Comparative Examination of Multi-Level Citizenship," *Regional Studies* 47, no. 3 (2013): 303–22; Charlie Jeffrey, "Devolution and Divergence: Public Attitudes and Institutional Logistics," in *Devolution in Practice*, ed. John Adams and Katie Schmuecker (IPPR, 2005); Charlie Jeffrey, "Devolution and Social Citizenship: Which Society, Whose Citizenship?" in *Territory, Democracy and Justice*, ed. Scott Greer (London: Palgrave Macmillan, 2006); Carol S. Weissert and David Blake Jones, "Devolution Paradox and the US South," *Regional and Federal Studies* 25, no. 3 (2015): 259–76.

15 Augusto Zimmermann, "Subsidiarity, Democracy and Individual Liberty in Brazil," in *Global Perspectives on Subsidiarity*, ed. Michelle Evans and Augusto Zimmermann (London: Springer, 2014), 85–106, 85.

16 Thomas M. Franck, *Why Federations Fail: An Inquiry into the Requisites for Successful Federalism* (London: University of London Press, 1968), 197.

17 Christopher Ritzer, Marc Rutloff, and Karin Linhart, "How to Sharpen a Dull Sword – The Principle of Subsidiarity and Its Control," *German Law Journal* 7, no. 9 (2006): 733–60.

18 George Bermann, "Taking Subsidiarity Seriously: Federalism in the European Community and the United States," *Columbia Law Review* 94, no. 2 (1994): 332–456, 334.

Index

www.ingramcontent.com/pod-product-compliance
Lightning Source LLC
LaVergne TN
LVHW100913220826
846271LV00024B/147